HISTORICAL
ATLAS
OF THE
HOLY
LANDS

They come from a distant land,
from the end of the heavens,
the Lord and the weapons of his indignation,
to destroy the whole land.
Isaiah 13:5
(The Judgement of Babylon)

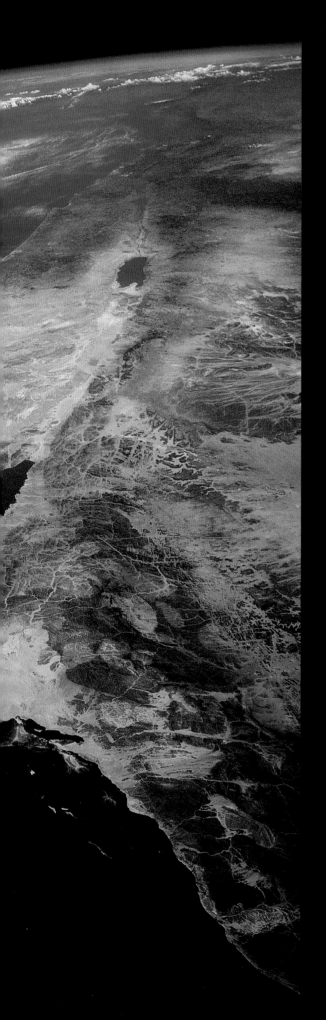

HISTORICAL
ATLAS
OF THE
HOLY
LANDS

KAREN FARRINGTON

The Lord spoke to Moses in the
wilderness of Sinai, in the tent of
meeting, in the second year after they
had come out of Egypt, saying, "Take a
census of all the congregation of the
people of Israel, by clans, by fathers'
houses, according to the number of
names, every male, head by head."
Numbers 1:1–2

MERCURY BOOKS
LONDON

HISTORICAL ATLAS OF THE HOLY LANDS

Published in 2005 by Mercury Books London
20 Bloomsbury Street, London WC1B 3JH

For Thalamus Publishing
Project editor: Neil Williams
Maps and design: Roger Kean
Illustrations: Oliver Frey
Four-color separation: Proskanz, Ludlow, England

ISBN: 1-904668-14-3

Printed in China by Sun Fung Offset Binding Co., Ltd.

PICTURE CREDITS

Paul Almasy/CORBIS: 23, 89, 93, 96, 156; Archivo Iconografico, S.A./CORBIS: 46–7, 57 (both), 64, 124 (bottom), 132, 137 (bottom), 145, 149 (top), 155, 159 (bottom), 164, 178; Yann Arthus-Bertrand/CORBIS: 10, 165; Dave Bartruff/CORBIS: 48, 49 (bottom), 76, 106, 154, 186–7; Bettman/CORBIS: 42, 62; Tibor Bognar/CORBIS: 120–1; Christie's Images/CORBIS: 13 (top), 26–7, 49 (top); Dean Conger/CORBIS: 12, 18, 20 108, 139 (bottom); CORBIS: 144; Gianni Dagli Orti/CORBIS: 1, 25, 34 (bottom), 56, 63, 123, 134, 135 (bottom), 142, 173; Araldo de Luca/CORBIS: 172, 177, 179; Shai Ginott/CORBIS: 71 (top); Annie Griffiths/CORBIS: 129; Dallas and John Heaton/CORBIS: 171; Chris Hellier/CORBIS: 157, 167; Historical Picture Archive/CORBIS:103, 119; AngeloHornak/CORBIS: 21; Hulton-Deutsch Collection/CORBIS: 66, 183; Hanan Isachar/CORBIS: 52, 71 (bottom), 73, 80–1, 86–7, 111; Mimmo Jodice/CORBIS: 170; Steve Kaufman/CORBIS: 84–5; David Lees/CORBIS: 28, 53, 60–1, 126; Danny Lehman/CORBIS: 116–117; Charles Lenars/CORBIS: 11, 40, 65, 128; Charles & Josette Lenars/CORBIS: 107 (top), 124 (top), 127 (both); Massimo Listri/CORBIS: 176; Francis G. Mayer/CORBIS: 22, 35; Ali Meyer/CORBIS: 59; Michael Maslan Historic Photographs/CORBIS: 54; NASA/ CORBIS: 2–3; Richard T. Nowitz/CORBIS: 15, 36, 38, 47, 74, 75, 77, 79, 82, 83, 104–5, 107 (bottom), 110, 114, 115, 158; Jose Fusta Raga/CORBIS: 118; Carmen Redondo/CORBIS: 55, 58, 94–5, 95; REZA/CORBIS/SIGMA/CORBIS: 133; Reza/Webistan/CORBIS: 160–1; Ricki Rosen/CORBIS: 67; David Rubinger/CORBIS: 30–1, 34 (top), 72, 86, 184–5; SETBOUN/CORBIS: 15; George Shelley/CORBIS: 6–7; Paul A. Souders/CORBIS: 13 (bottom); Ted Spiegel/CORBIS: 14, 78, 88; Thalamus Publishing: 28–9; Tim Thompson/CORBIS: 159 (top); Peter Turnley/CORBIS: 50, 102; Gian Berto Vanni/CORBIS: 166; West Semitic Research/Dead Sea Scrolls Foundation/CORBIS: 43; K.M. Westerman/CORBIS: 24–5, 122; Nik Wheeler/CORBIS: 70–1, 137 (top), 143; Werner Forman Archive: 39 (British Museum, London), 146 (Iraq Museum, Bagdhad), 147 (British Museum, London), 148 (British Museum, London), 149 (bottom, British Museum, London); Roger Wood/CORBIS: 92, 97, 99, 135 (top), 138, 139 (top), 168–9; Adam Woolfitt/CORBIS: 41

First page: Many invasions were to be inflicted on the tribes of Israel, most from the lands of Mesopotamia to the east. From the earliest times, these peoples practiced war, as this panel from the Stele of Vultures (2525 BC) shows.

Previous page: The Nile delta, Sinai peninsula, Israel, and parts of Jordan and Saudi Arabia seen from the space shuttle *Columbia*.

Contents

Introduction

In the beginning, God created the heavens and the
earth. The earth was without form and void, and
darkness was over the face of the deep. And the spirit
of God was hovering over the face of the waters.
Genesis 1:1–2

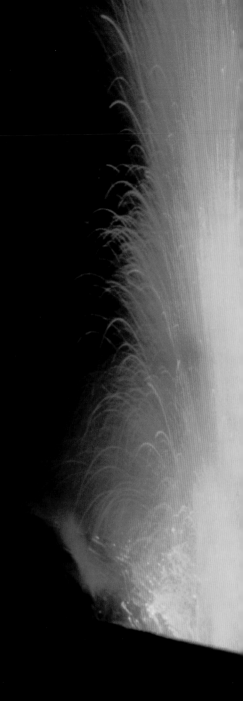

The Bible leads us to believe that the above
happened in the Holy Land. The term
"Holy Land" may mean something different to
each person: purely the part of Palestine that
witnessed the birth and mission of Christ or as
widely encompassing as the countries mentioned
in the Old Testament—the collected books of
the Jewish faith and history. And what of that
newer faith, Islam? While it grew first in
Arabia, its bastions became the Mesopotamian
cities that had once oppressed the Israelites, and
its prophets were largely those who had also
inspired the Hebrews to worship the One True
God. All these elements, and the "peripheral"
players, such as the Egyptians, Canaanites,
Phoenicians, and Philistines, contributed to
what three religions (and several related
offshoots) consider to be the Holy Lands—not
only a place, but a mental space.

Understanding the history of the Holy Lands
is a far from simple process. In this region, we
see the first human attempts to record history.
Yet these are histories written to provide specific
human responses to very particular social
conditions and events—and, as has ever been the
case, it is the victors who record the history.
There have been plenty of arguments stating
that, like Greek mythology, the Bible is a
collection of myths, a means of explaining the
almost inexplicable in easily understood human
terms. While this may be a useful moral guide, it
is extremely fallible when it comes to history.

For countless millions of Christians, the Bible
is a comfort and a guide, cushioning life's blows
and illuminating its mysteries. In it there is wit,
wisdom, drama, disaster, dread fear, doom,
glory, infamy, heroism, and hope. For many it

Unfortunately, it has also suffered the effects of
many translations, not least the first from
Hebrew and Aramaic into Greek. While the
gist of the fine sentiments may remain much as
they were when first written, the sense of many
finer points has become distorted. This is
another reason why many claim that while the
Bible may be the Good Book, it is not a good
table of real events.

Some of its accounts are seemingly out of
place or suspect, and some of its characters are
inconsistent. Even the true identities of the
authors of some of the biblical books is in
doubt. Perhaps most important, since the
Renaissance the development of science has
done much to undermine the Bible and all it

Sifting fact from fiction

However, in recent years, there has been a re-evaluation of the Bible's—especially the Old Testament's—reliability. Given that the Bible *is* a collection of books written by very different people for very different purposes, it follows that some, maybe a lot, is accurate to history, while some may be purely mythically or ideologically motivated.

The archaeologist is no longer restricted to the trowel to recover artifacts that tell a story about the past. Tools at his disposal include the best, most reliable scientific techniques available. Using them he can scrape away at the hallowed facts laid out in the Bible to expose mythology. But more excitingly he can substantiate Biblical stories with hard evidence that gives the Bible

fresh authority, bringing voices that previously seemed distant very much closer. Visitors to the Holy Lands can trip over remnants of antiquity, which are thrown up like daisies in a field.

The purpose of this book is to explore life in the Holy Lands in Biblical times. It is temptingly easy to underestimate the Bible in our secular, scientific age because it has been in existence for so many millennia. Here is a new investigation into an old, influential book to find out what information it yields on our forbears and how society has evolved from it. Through the study of 45 major Biblical centers, as well as some key social aspects of the various periods, and by superimposing today's atlas onto a region that is steeped in history, we can discover what the modern world can learn from the ancient.

CHAPTER ONE
The Bible Explored

So Israel lived in safety, Jacob lived alone in a land of grain and wine, whose heavens drop down dew.

Deuteronomy 33:28

The Bible's intricate plot is played out in an area known as Palestine. Then, as now, Palestine was a region rather than a fully-fledged country, the land bridge between Europe, Asia, and Africa bordering the Mediterranean Sea. Also known as the Holy Land and even the Fertile Crescent, the area sounds idyllically serene. Alas, Palestine was the backdrop for turbulent events in Biblical times and remains so today.

It is impossible to exactly define the geographical limits of ancient Palestine, since it was an area rather than a nation-state. It approximately translates to what we know as Israel and the occupied territories of the West Bank and Gaza Strip. To the north, in modern terms, lie Lebanon and Syria, to the east is Jordan, and in the south is the Sinai peninsula, belonging to Egypt. In ancient times, of course, those national boundaries did not exist. The borders between tribes, kingdoms, and empires shifted as the centuries went by.

The region is dissected by the River Jordan, flowing between Lake Galilee and the Dead Sea. The deepest part of the Dead Sea is more than 2,600 feet below sea level—the lowest point on the earth. Its extreme salinity means there is no life in its waters or on its shores. Surrounding the Dead Sea wind erosion has carved out a lunar landscape, lending an unearthly eeriness to this still, silent place.

Not many miles away to the south and east is the stark contrast of the Transjordan, a mountainous area rising to over 6,500 feet, keeping the nearby Arabian Desert at bay. Lower in height but nonetheless spectacular are the central highlands, hill country that incorporates Mount Carmel. Further there is the coastal plain, the plain of Megiddo and Galilee, a fruit basket until the fertile land wanes among some climbing peaks.

The climate in these cultivated areas, largely speaking, is both warm and wet, encouraging bountiful crops. Items cultivated include figs, dates, olives, grapes, almonds, oranges, and pomegranates.

Wildlife of the region

Although much of the flora and fauna of the region still resembles that of the Biblical era, the profile of mammals there has changed. Lions and leopards would have been familiar sights to anyone inhabiting the Holy Land

The wealth of the Fertile Crescent at the dawn of the Biblical Era.

ITALY

GREECE

Sicily

Rhodes

Crete

MEDITERRANEAN SEA

LIBYA

EGYPT

Fertile Crescent and Egypt
modern border
ISRAEL modern state
gold trading goods

during Old Testament times, roaming in forests and thickets around the Jordan valley. Lions were, of course, kept captive in some of the Biblical empires and dissidents were fed to them. But even before the death of Jesus the big cat population was in decline.

There were wolves, jackals, and foxes in the area, and the Bible assigned them characters that have endured to this day. The wolf is a menace to be feared, hence the quote "a wolf in sheep's clothing." Jackals, of course, are nature's scavengers and there are mentions of Jerusalem being "a lair of jackals." Jesus acknowledged the cunning of the fox when he described King Herod as one. The Syrian brown bear was a shy but feared animal living in seclusion in wooded hills. God's capacity for punishment is succinctly illustrated with the comment: "I will fall upon them like a bear robbed of her cubs."

The dangerous Palestinian viper was considered all the more loathsome after it was cursed in *Genesis* "above all cattle and above all wild animals." Other animals featuring in the Bible include camels, cattle, sheep, goats, donkeys and asses, quails, ibex, ravens, storks, doves, and pigeons. The Asiatic elephant was used as a vehicle of war against the populations of the Holy Land by the eastern empires. Horses are also mentioned but were not kept in Israel until the time of King David. Given its flexibility and speed on the battlefield, the horse was for many years a symbol of power.

Remains of the early Bronze Age temple of Canaanite construction, with its round altar, at the archaeological site of Megiddo (*see pages 74–5*).

BLACK SEA

obsidian

Lake Van

Lake Urmia

silver
tin

TURKEY

ANATOLIA

copper

IRAN

ZAGROS MOUNTAINS

TAURUS MOUNTAINS

silver

• Nineveh

MESOPOTAMIA

Tigris
grain

timber • Ebla

Mari •

ELAM

Ugarit •

Euphrates

• Hamath

• Nippur

grain

SYRIA

IRAQ

Cyprus

LEBANON

Syrian Desert

• Uruk

timber

Eridu • • Ur

PERSIA

modern coastline

ISRAEL

Jericho

JORDAN

Ancient Phoenician sculpture of a man's head. Occupying the Mediterranean coastal strip of what is now Syria and Lebanon, the Phoenicians were the Mediterranean's most successful early traders. Their financial and building skills were in widespread use by both the newly founded Israelite state and by the older Mesopotamian kingdoms.

Jerusalem •
Dead Sea

alabaster gold

• Petra

PERSIAN GULF

copper

SINAI

Memphis •

KINGDOM OF EGYPT
C.3000 BC

SAUDI ARABIA

Nile

RED SEA

Peoples of the Holy Lands

"Come, let us go down and there confuse their language, so that they may not understand one another's speech."

Genesis 11:7

Below: Aerial view of the Hittite ruins of Hattusas in northern Anatolia. The city became the Hittite capital in about 1650 BC, and was destroyed by invading Phrygians in about 1200.

The Bible had numerous authors during many centuries, but throughout, its focus audience stayed the same, the Jewish people of the Holy Land. The Jewish people were not always known by that name. First they were called Hebrews, then they were Israelites, and finally they were identified as Jewish. Whatever name they were known by, here was a people inspired by divine guidance and possessing a social and spiritual thread that could be traced back through time.

They were not alone in peopling the Holy Lands. Other peoples who did not share the faith frequently became the enemies of the Israelites. Most were followers of pagan religions such as the worship of Baal, but these tended to be cults and sects that flourished and then faded. No native pagan religion from the era has endured to the present day, with the possible exception of a very small following of Horus, the ancient Egyptian god.

Christianity began as a Jewish sect and at the time the Gospels were written it had not yet evolved as a separate faith. There were no Muslims in the early centuries AD since the religion did not come into being until the advent of Mohammed, who was born in about AD 570 and died in 632. Like Christianity, Islam is also based on the Jewish faith. The Islamic religion spread through Palestine rapidly in the seventh and eighth centuries.

So to understand the people of the Bible it is essential to understand the relevance of Judaism. Over and above that, there are peoples and cultures that wielded an effect on the Jews. Traditionally, the Jewish faith has absorbed and assimilated aspects of other civilizations for its own enhancement.

The earliest ancestor of the Jewish faith is Abraham who came from Ur, a city in Sumer, in southern Mesopotamia, between the Tigris and the Euphrates rivers. It is in Sumer, historians concur, that the earliest urban civilization evolved during the fourth millennium BC. Ur was one of maybe a dozen walled city-states, each worshipping a chosen deity. Ultimately the cities joined forces but even their combined strength was not sufficient to ward off attacks from predatory empires.

Abraham moved to Canaan, an area that also defies the cartographers' best efforts for categorization. Sometimes Canaan is construed as Palestine and Syria in their entirety. Otherwise it is believed to be the land between the Jordan and the Mediterranean Sea or perhaps even a smaller strip of land still, north of Acre. According to *Genesis*, the Canaanites were descended from Canaan, a son of Ham and a grandson

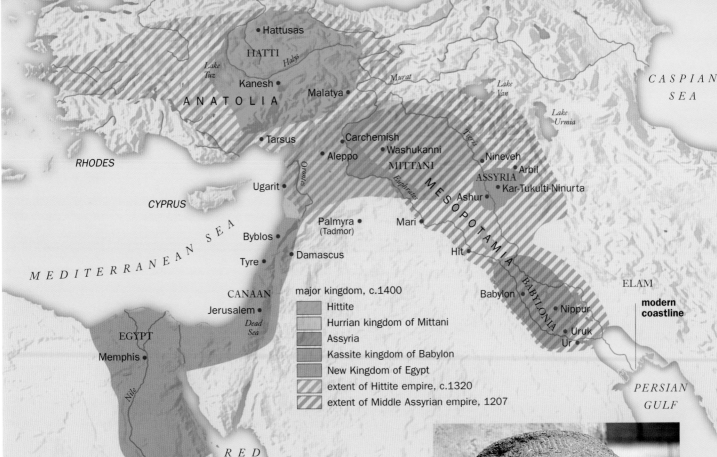

major kingdom, c.1400

- Hittite
- Hurrian kingdom of Mittani
- Assyria
- Kassite kingdom of Babylon
- New Kingdom of Egypt
- extent of Hittite empire, c.1320
- extent of Middle Assyrian empire, 1207

modern coastline

of Noah. Archaeology has proved that there was human habitation of Canaan since the dawn of humankind.

Frequent invaders

Prominent in the history of Canaan were the Egyptians who frequently surged into the region from the south. In the north the area was vulnerable to invasion by the Hyksos, a nomadic Asian tribe periodically at war with the Egyptians. It is thought they were driven out of the region in about 1570 BC.

Succeeding the Hyksos came the Hittites of Anatolia and the Hurrians from eastern Anatolia and northern Mesopotamia. The kingdom of Mittani, an ally of ancient Egypt, was swallowed up in the Hittite expansion of the 13th century BC. The coastal enclaves were devastated by the arrival of the Sea Peoples, violent invaders from places unknown—but who are sometime associated with the Dorian invaders of Greece—who swept into the Holy Land with a scorched earth policy.

After that there were waves of aggression from empire builders. There were the Syrians who were soon themselves overwhelmed by the mighty Assyrians. Their campaigns of conquest were known for bloody destruction and mass deportation.

The Babylonians were likewise fierce and barbaric. When they captured Jerusalem, exiled its population, and burned down the Temple, they inflicted a scar on the Jewish psyche that took centuries to heal. It wasn't long before the Babylonians were in turn ousted by the Persians, cultured by comparison but nevertheless capable of terrible atrocities. They reserved the worst for their clashes for the ancient Greeks.

Alexander the Great enjoyed a short spell of dominance in the region, although the inheritors of his empire failed to maintain the realm he created. When the Romans arrived they brought with them the longest spell of peace the region had ever known. *Pax Romana* came at a price, however, and that was the subjugation of the indigenous people to Roman rule. The Romans still held sway when the last pages of the New Testament were penned.

Above: Hittite sphinx sculpture, 8th–9th centuries BC, from the palace of Tell Alaf, which is situated in northern Syria, almost on the Turkish border.

11

Communicating the Word

That the collection of texts we know as the Bible exists at all is remarkable. When the events it relates in the distant past were occurring there were of course no computers, typewriters, pens, or even quills. In the earliest days, accounts were passed from father to son, mother to daughter, and so traversed the generations until those times that events could be recorded in writing. Oral traditions were much stronger then.

Revered Bible stories were kept alive by word of mouth until finally they were gathered by religiously motivated writers and bound together into what we now know as the Bible.

Certainly, written records were kept long ago on clay tablet in cuneiform script or hieroglyphics. Stores of tablets uncovered at Mari in Syria dating from the 18th century BC testify to that. But there's no single, ancient source for the Bible as yet uncovered in the dusty vaults of some forgotten temple. Its evolution was a lengthy one—although it seems the core writings of the Old Testament have varied little since the third century BC.

But the Bible should not be considered an accurate or verifiable diary. Scholars have long warned of the perils of perceiving the early Old Testament books as a version of written history. It seems likely that nothing was set down in writing until the sixth century BC. Even then compilers were presumably faced with differing stories on the same subject emanating from various tribes and had to mesh them together. One result may be that the tales are akin to folk legends. Many have surely been embellished beyond recognition. The mystery of Bible authorship will run and run.

Origins lost in time

For instance, take the authorship of the first five books of the Bible, collectively known as the *Pentateuch* or the *Torah*. For years it was supposed that Moses was the author. This occurred even though the books related his own death. In reality a collection of different writing styles indicates that there were numerous contributors. Likewise, doubt has arisen over the date and the scale of the Exodus, which clearly affects our view of the books of *Genesis*, *Exodus*, and so forth. Further discrepancies created by translations and modifications down the centuries have further diluted the Bible's historical accuracy.

Although there are many anomalies in the

Bible, many scholars accept that the Bible at least partially backs up the data being gained from archaeological digs. This cannot have been the work of some band of priests—as one theory would have it—writing without historical reference, merely to keep a dwindling faith alive.

The limitations of written resources mean that archaeology—the recovery and interpretation of items from the past—is vital in the analysis of ancient events in the Holy Lands.

The Old Testament

Also known as the Hebrew Bible, it comprises 39 separate books grouped together in four different sections: the *Pentateuch* (*see picture, right*), historical books, wisdom literature, and the prophets. The New Testament is made up of four gospels, one book of Acts and a further 22 epistles. There is also the *Apocrypha* for the Old and New Testaments, apparently written to fill in some historical gaps, but not usually embraced by the term "Bible." Jews and Christians approach the Old Testament from different viewpoints.

Biblical Archaeology: Faith or Fact?

U p until the 1970s, many Biblical archaeologists thought the whole point of fieldwork, excavation, and interpretation was to prove the historical validity of the Bible. This was the received wisdom championed by respected figures like the American academic William Foxwell Albright, who in the 1930s declared that "discovery after discovery has established the accuracy of innumerable details and has brought increased recognition of the Bible as a source of history."

Albright's best-known student, G. Ernest Wright, went further. He claimed that Biblical archaeology's chief concern "is not with strata, or pots, or methodology" and that "its central and absorbing interest is the understanding and exposition of the scriptures." Even as late as 1982 the distinguished Israeli expert Yigael Yadin, commenting on the Israelite "conquest" of the Promised Land, insisted: "The fact is that excavation results from the last 50 years or so support in a most amazing way, except in some cases, the basic historicity of the Biblical account."

So what has changed? Why do all but the most conservative scholars now dispute the notion that the Bible is an accurate history book? Before considering this it is worth looking at areas of consensus—not least the groundbreaking work of the pioneers of archaeology.

True archaeology—as opposed to treasure hunting—probably began in 1853 with the discovery of the Assyrian king Ashurbanipal's palace library. The find by Hormuzd Rassam, a Chaldean Christian working with the British explorer Henry Layard (*see page 150*), included cuneiform texts later translated by the British Museum cataloger George Smith. Smith's work caused a sensation because it showed that a Noah-like story (complete with ship grounding on mountains and the release of a dove) existed in non-Biblical sources.

Now the race was on to find additional material substantiating Old Testament accounts. Layard went on to make crucial finds at Nineveh while the geographer Edward Robinson and his student Eli Smith identified more than 100 major Palestinian sites—an exercise that crucially saved time and expense for the archaeological community. Most important, the British Egyptologist Sir Flinders Petrie established the key disciplines of stratification and pottery typology.

Petrie's work at Tel el-Hesi in Israel was based on his discovery that tells (large mounds created by re-building settlements on the same site) were composed of differing layers or strata of occupation. He used an analysis of pottery styles to sequence-date these layers and then applied his findings to all objects found. While this was an over-simplification, there is no doubt that his pioneering studies drove archaeology from the realms of romantic adventuring into hard science.

Improved techniques

The early to mid-20th century was the golden age of Biblical excavation. In 1907 two German archaeologists, Carl Watzinger and Ernest Sellin, began the first assessment of Jericho's old city; William Albright made further breakthroughs in the dating of pottery, architecture, and artifacts; there were the momentous Valley of Kings finds in Egypt by Howard Carter; and there were major digs at Beth Shan (modern Beit Shean) and Megiddo. The outstanding work of Dame Kathleen Kenyon at Jericho (1952–58) and Jerusalem (1961–67) established new parameters for excavation and stratigraphy, the essence of which remains standard practice today.

Yet despite this wealth of new information on the nuts and bolts of Old Testament life, archaeologists still struggle with interpretation. How do our fragments of knowledge fit into the big picture? And in the bearpit of Middle

Above: Israeli archaeologist Yigael Yadin, seen here working on the Temple scroll, believes that excavation results support the historicity of Biblical accounts. Yadin's team also discovered scrolls found at Masada, one of which proved to be the 33rd chapter of the book of *Deuteronomy*.

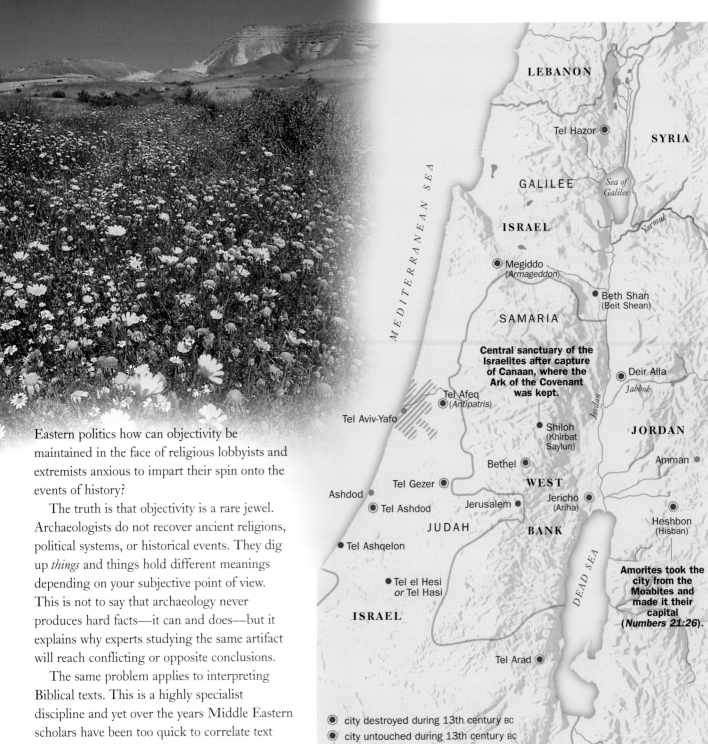

Eastern politics how can objectivity be maintained in the face of religious lobbyists and extremists anxious to impart their spin onto the events of history?

The truth is that objectivity is a rare jewel. Archaeologists do not recover ancient religions, political systems, or historical events. They dig up *things* and things hold different meanings depending on your subjective point of view. This is not to say that archaeology never produces hard facts—it can and does—but it explains why experts studying the same artifact will reach conflicting or opposite conclusions.

The same problem applies to interpreting Biblical texts. This is a highly specialist discipline and yet over the years Middle Eastern scholars have been too quick to correlate text with excavation results before, as N.P. Lemche put it, "either…has had an opportunity to speak for itself." Since the 1970s there has been a growing appreciation that Biblical accounts cannot be taken uncritically. There's no space here to re-visit all the academic squabbles but one of the most controversial revisionist theories concerns the Israelite conquest of Canaan.

Most scholars believe the archaeological arguments for this event no longer stack up. There should be a pattern that shows the razing of cities across a very specific timespan. Yet while there was destruction in the 13th century at Megiddo, Hazor, Ashdod, Afeq, Bethel, Gezer, and Deir Alla (*see map*), nothing similar has turned up at Arad, Heshbon or, crucially,

Jericho. Great civil unrest in Canaan is not the same as a conquering army seizing the land.

Given that much of the Bible was written long after the events it describes, there is a need to get inside the minds of the writers, understand their perception of Israel's culture and history and, most importantly, its religion. Archaeology is the key to this. By properly interpreting the data we can start to see how and why the Bible's authors grappled with the great issues of the day. This will not, ultimately, make archaeology an enemy of religion. On the contrary, it will give many believers a clearer path to faith.

Above: Spring flowers carpet the desert at the site of ancient Tel Arad. Scholars argue that if the references in the Bible are factually correct, most Canaanite cities should have suffered similar destruction in the 13th century BC, yet Arad—like others—was left untouched.

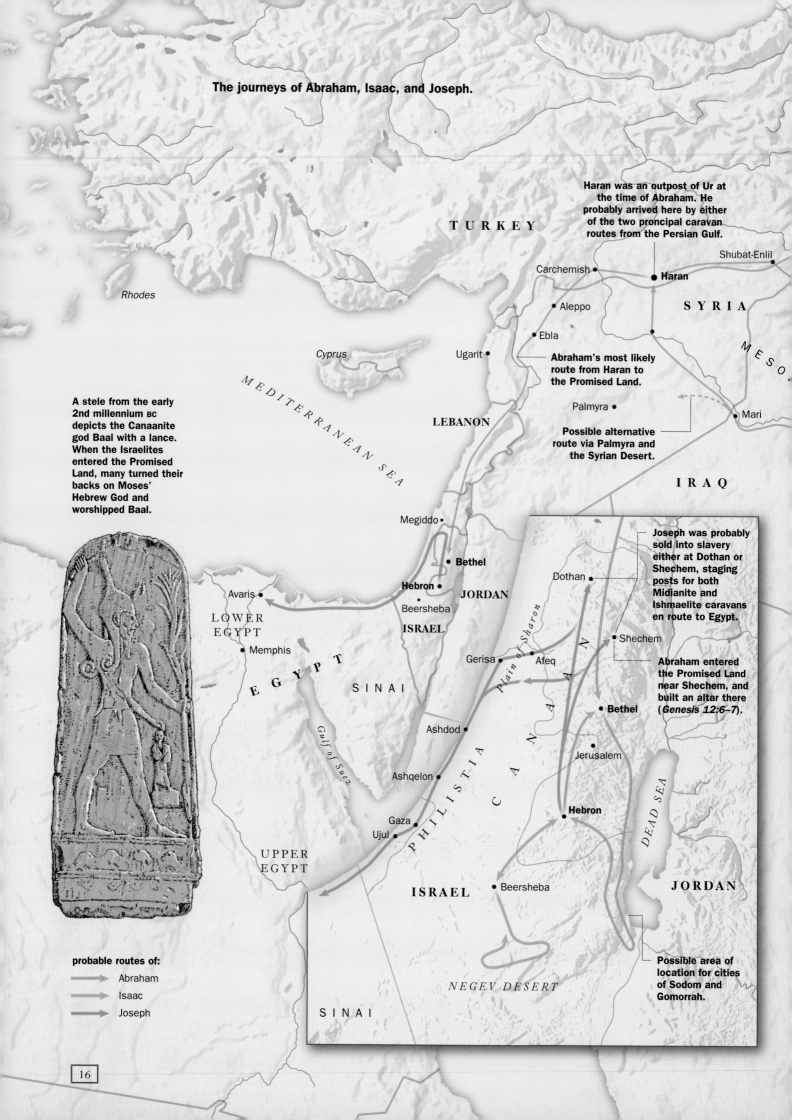

The journeys of Abraham, Isaac, and Joseph.

TURKEY

Haran was an outpost of Ur at the time of Abraham. He probably arrived here by either of the two proncipal caravan routes from the Persian Gulf.

Shubat-Enlil

Carchemish

Haran

SYRIA

Aleppo

Ebla

M E S O

Rhodes

Ugarit

Abraham's most likely route from Haran to the Promised Land.

LEBANON

Palmyra

Mari

M E D I T E R R A N E A N   S E A

Possible alternative route via Palmyra and the Syrian Desert.

IRAQ

A stele from the early 2nd millennium BC depicts the Canaanite god Baal with a lance. When the Israelites entered the Promised Land, many turned their backs on Moses' Hebrew God and worshipped Baal.

Megiddo

Joseph was probably sold into slavery either at Dothan or Shechem, staging posts for both Midianite and Ishmaelite caravans en route to Egypt.

Dothan

Bethel

Hebron

JORDAN

Beersheba

ISRAEL

Shechem

Avaris

Gerisa

Afeq

Abraham entered the Promised Land near Shechem, and built an altar there (*Genesis 12:6–7*).

LOWER EGYPT

Plain of Sharon

C A N A A N

Memphis

Bethel

EGYPT

Jerusalem

SINAI

Ashdod

Gulf of Suez

PHILISTIA

DEAD SEA

Ashqelon

Hebron

Gaza

Ujul

ISRAEL

Beersheba

JORDAN

UPPER EGYPT

Possible area of location for cities of Sodom and Gomorrah.

probable routes of:

Abraham

Isaac

Joseph

N E G E V   D E S E R T

S I N A I

CHAPTER TWO

Epic Bible Journeys

The Lord said to Moses, "Depart; go up from here, you and the people whom you have brought up out of the land of Egypt, to the land which I swore to Abraham, Isaac, and Jacob, saying, 'Unto your offspring will I give it.'"

Exodus 33:1

Nineveh

Ashur

major Mesopotamian trading routes.

M I A

I R A N

Sippar

Babylon

Borsippa

Nippur

Isin

Uruk

Ur

modern coastline

P E R S I A N   G U L F

An unusually intimate portrait of Ramesses II (r.1279–13 BC). Is this the pharaoh who let the Hebrews go? The debate has never been satisfactorily settled.

Many classical civilizations had richly woven myths that sustained their populations in turbulent times. In Egypt favorite tales were of the murdered Osiris, while in Mesopotamia it was the adventures of the Sumerian king Gilgamesh that seized the imagination.

The Bible is different because its legends are rooted on earth, among humans rather than semi-divine characters. Readers can identify with where the Israelite heroes were born, the sights they saw, and sometimes even their burial places.

In the pages of *Genesis* we hear about the trek undertaken by Abraham and we can still track his route today. There is sufficient evidence to show that Abraham was probably a composite figure and his journey was at least possible to undertake. Even though some of the Biblical settlements have names that appear obscure, many have been positively identified in archaeological fieldwork in the last few decades. This gives Bible readers a wonderful insight into how people lived and worked more than 3,000 years ago. Also, the Bible goes beyond the hero worship that is the hallmark of other classical epics. It offers a very human approach to history that helps endear it to the reader.

Biblical excavation is far from complete, but our knowledge increased many-fold in the last two decades of the 20th century. There's no reason to doubt that in this perpetually evolving field similar leaps forward will take place in the next 20 years, changing once again the accepted beliefs about the Bible and the Holy Land.

Abraham, Father of Faith

Now the Lord said to Abram, "Go from your country and from your kindred and your father's house, to the land that I will show you."

Genesis 12:1

To Jews, Christians, and Muslims, he is the father of their faith, a noble figure known for hospitality, compassion, loyalty and faith while still vulnerable to human frailties. Inevitably, much of his existence—if he existed at all—is cloaked in mystery.

In Europe's Age of Enlightenment scholars put forward the notion that Abraham was not a real figure but a composite one, a kind of folk hero created to communicate a religious message. Yet, after the First World War, archaeologists turned up cuneiform tablets in a number of places that complemented information in *Genesis*. Perhaps stories of Abraham that traveled down the generations before being recorded in the Bible had remained faithful to the truth after all?

However, it remains difficult to state anything with certainty. Even his birthplace is in doubt. The Bible suggests it was Ur in present day Iraq, which was indeed a thriving city even in those early times (*see pages 60–63*) But this may not be the correct Ur. Two other towns with similar names (Ura and Urfa) are to be found within the modern Turkish borders and both are within a short distance of Haran, the first place

visited by Abraham, lying more than 1,000 miles distant from Ur. Did he join a merchant's caravan on that immense journey? Cuneiform sources have confirmed such journeys were made by traders. As the image of Abraham setting off on a bold adventure is central to his saga, the Ur of Iraq remains the favored choice.

At Haran, his father Terah died and Abraham became the chief of his clan. And here God directed him to Canaan, some 400 miles distant, to found a great nation. Haran was without doubt an important trading post at the time. As if to endorse the fact, it was not only the initial destination for Abraham but also for his son Isaac, who met his wife Rebekah near there. Isaac's son Jacob spent 20 years near Haran working as a shepherd in return for the hand of Rachel in marriage. But for all its

patriarchal associations, it was a pagan place, worshipping the moon god Sin. Much later, under Roman occupation, Haran became known as Carrhae and was twice the scene of disastrous defeats of Roman forces. The first in 53 BC saw Crassus humbled by the Parthians. Then, in AD 297, the emperor Galerius was roundly beaten by King Narses of Persia. Today the place is little more than a village, distinguished only by its beehive-shaped houses.

Vengeful God

Abraham allegedly also visited Sodom and Gomorrah, two cities tainted by their occupants' evil behavior. When God was poised to wreak vengeance on the two communities Abraham pleaded that the righteous be spared. His nephew Lot and family lived there and were saved by angels as "fire and brimstone" rained down. Famously, Lot's wife could not contain her curiosity and turned to look back, against divine orders. She was turned into a pillar of salt.

For years the tale of Sodom and Gomorrah appeared metaphorical, a dire warning about the consequences of immorality. Now it seems the cities probably did exist and were swallowed up by an earthquake in about 1900 BC, although some experts date the seismic eruptions at some four centuries prior. Oil and gases occurring naturally in the region would have ignited, causing colossal explosions and perhaps a firestorm like that related in *Genesis*. Afterward, the waters of the Dead Sea closed over the sites.

It is likely that this notoriously barren area was once fertile, with fresh water running through it supporting a thriving settlement. The historian Josephus claimed it was possible to see the ruins of ancient cities south of the Dead Sea. Archaeologists have since discovered cemeteries in the vicinity of the Dead Sea containing the remains of thousands of people and dating from as early as 3200 BC.

Abraham also visited Hebron when it occupied Tel Rumeida, a mound that stands near the existing city. Archaeologists have discovered a fortified tower and a nine-foot-thick city wall dating from the middle Bronze Age period (about 1700 BC). Valuable artifacts have been found at the site. Jews in Hebron, believing it to be the one-time home of Abraham, have seized on the news, believing it proves that they have rights of possession.

Facing: The city of Haran was founded c.2000 BC, probably as a trading outpost of Ur. If Abraham had been born in Ur, it would have been a likely city for him to have visited at the other end of Mesopotamia. The name comes from the Sumerian and Akkadian *Haran-U*, meaning "journey," "caravan," or "crossroad." Before the beginning of the Christian era, the moon god, Sin, was the supreme deity (making Harrians the original sinners). Today, modern Haran is no more than a small village of curiously beehive-shaped houses.

Isaac, Jacob, and the Founding of Bethel

Abraham called the name of his son who was born to him, whom Sarah bore him, Isaac.

Genesis 21:3

Then he said, "Your name shall no longer be called Jacob, but Israel, for you have striven with God and with men, and have prevailed."

Genesis 32:28

By contrast with his much-traveled father, Isaac was something of a home-loving man, never traveling more than 50 miles from his birthplace near Beersheba. He lived in the Negev Desert with his flocks. His son Jacob, however, had an adventurous nature although he is strongly associated with Bethel. Inspired by a dream of a ladder linking earth and sky, Jacob established an altar at Bethel before traveling onward to his uncle, Laban, and to marriage

with Leah and Rachel. At this time Bethel was located near the main highway running north from Jerusalem. Jacob was tracking the footsteps of Abraham who had pitched his tent at Bethel on several occasions. Abraham may have even pre-empted Jacob in bringing holy associations to this place for he, too, built an altar here. But it is Jacob and his potent vision that is most strongly linked to Bethel, which, translated from Hebrew, means "House of God"

For the visitor there is of course no marker or plaque to mark the spot where Jacob slept and saw the ladder although, the Bible relates that he took the stone he had used as a pillow and anointed it with oil. Nor will any amount of archaeological investigation reveal the site. However, excavations have helped to pinpoint some important facts. They have revealed that the site was inhabited in the early Bronze Age, about 3000 BC, and that communities thrived there until the Arab conquest of the seventh century AD. Bethel was soundly constructed and fortified in its early years.

Earliest holy city

According to *Genesis*, God identifies himself specifically with the settlement by saying "I am the God of Bethel." This indicates at the very least that Bible writers believed it to be an important site. Following the Exodus it became an important religious center and was for a while the home of the Ark of the Covenant. But its elevated status was not sufficient to protect it from further attack. Although it is not mentioned in the Bible, it is believed that Bethel was sacked not once but twice during this period, probably by Philistines.

For political purposes King Solomon decided to make Jerusalem rather than Bethel the key religious center and ultimately its importance was deliberately diminished. Conflict over the siting of the real "house of God" was one of the crucial conflicts between Judah and Israel when they were separate nations.

In this time of conflict, Bethel and its sacred status was altered by King Jeroboam who established his own cult there to divert the attention of his people from Jerusalem. Jeroboam established a new temple, altar, and golden calf especially for his cult. This is related in the first book of *Kings* and there is speculation that the calf was linked to the worship of Baal. There is condemnation of the cult at Bethel in the Bible, and ultimately an initiative by Josiah to eradicate every religious base outside Jerusalem succeeded. According to the Second Book of *Kings*, Josiah brought ashes of all the burnt idols in his realm to Bethel after they were incinerated outside the walls of Jerusalem.

Facing: In a landscape almost unchanged since Abraham grazed his flocks here and Jacob dreamed of a ladder to heaven, a farmer plows his rocky field near Bethel.

Have kings sat where Jacob slumbered?

While evidence for the legend is sadly lacking, it is said that the stone upon which Jacob rested his head as he dreamed later became known as the Stone of Tara, and arrived in Ireland in 700 BC via Egypt, Sicily, and Spain. In AD 840, it was taken to Scotland by victorious Celts where, as the Stone of Scone, it was used in the coronation of the Scottish kings. Edward I (r.1272–1307) took the stone in 1296 to Westminster Abbey in London and it was eventually placed under the coronation throne of British royalty (*pictured above*). In 1996 it was returned to Scotland by Prime Minister John Major's government. Another title for this rectangular block of yellow sandstone weighing some 336 pounds is the Stone of Destiny.

Joseph, the Dream Prophet...

Then the Midianite traders passed by. And they drew Joseph up and lifted him out of the pit, and sold him to the Ishmaelites for twenty shekels of silver. They took Joseph to Egypt.

Genesis 37:28

Below: *Potiphar's Wife Shows her Husband Joseph's Garment*, by Lucas Van der Leyden, c.1510. Joseph's travels in Egypt have given rise to numerous works of art, but whether he was there at the time of Potiphar in the 19th century BC, or two hundred years later is hotly debated.

The story in *Genesis* about Joseph places him as one of Jacob's twelve sons, the patriarchs of the twelve tribes of Israel. Joseph is his father's favorite and is given a "coat of many colors." Consumed by jealousy, his brothers abduct him from Canaan and sell him into slavery with the Egyptians where his interpretation of dreams finds favor with Pharaoh. Joseph is promoted to become a high official and saves his family from famine by re-settling them in Egypt.

Joseph's long, exhausting march into slavery is described on the following pages. The Bible offers few clues to the route taken and in truth

there is little to substantiate the Joseph story among other sources. The best we can do is to apply archaeological tests that indicate whether it *could* be true. These center on attempting to pinpoint the time Joseph lived and the feasibility of a slave attaining one of the highest ranks in the Egyptian government.

The task is complicated because no reference to Joseph has ever been found in Egyptian sources. This is unsurprising since little information exists about officials before the New Kingdom (c.1539–1075 BC) and, depending on a number of historical factors, Joseph may belong in either the 17th or 19th centuries BC. However, given that there is not even a consensus about his Egyptian name, written records are unlikely to help.

Servant of invaders?

Supporters of a 17th century BC Joseph say their theory fits perfectly with the chronology of a "Late Date" Jewish Exodus during the 13th-century BC reign of Ramesses II (*see pages 138–39*). They point out that in c.1700 BC Canaanite invaders known as Hyksos had seized control of northern Egypt and, since Joseph was also a Canaanite, he would have found favor with the new pharaoh. Yet, given the bitter inter-tribal rivalries in Canaan at the time, this is questionable.

Those who place Joseph in the 19th century BC point out that he was sold as a slave to Potiphar, described in *Genesis* (39:1) as an Egyptian and commander of the king's guard. It would have been nonsensical, they argue, for a Hyksos pharaoh to appoint a native Egyptian as his chief bodyguard. Furthermore, Joseph is described several times in *Genesis* as a high official responsible for all Egypt, not just the Delta region controlled by the Hyksos. If Joseph lived in the 19th century BC he would have served under the 12th dynasty pharaohs Sesostris II and Sesostris III.

Further support for an "early" Joseph comes from a papyrus held in the Brooklyn Museum, translated by William C Hayes in 1955. This is a complex document but it sheds light on the debate by revealing information about Asiatic (i.e. Canaanite) slaves in 19th century BC Egypt. The papyrus tells how they were usually assigned jobs as household servants—precisely the role demanded of Joseph when Potiphar appointed him "overseer of his house."

Joseph's predictions to Pharaoh of seven years of plenty followed by seven years of famine may also have been based on actual events. Nile levels during the mid 12th dynasty were erratic according to a study of Nubian records and statuary published by Barbara Bell in 1975. An unusually high Nile, says Bell, would have delayed planting due to floods. Food shortages would have caused the kind of social disruption described in a contemporary literary document titled "The Complaint of Khahkeperre-Seneb."

None of the above approaches provide proof of Joseph's life story, or even of his existence. They simply show that Biblical accounts can—at least in part—be reconciled with archaeological research and other contemporary sources. However, a discovery in an ancient garden near Ramesses II's capital Pi-Ramesse has taken the debate into a new dimension (*see next page*). Controversially, some archaeologists are convinced that the tomb of Joseph has been discovered here.

Below: Photographed in 1950, the annual innundation of the Nile has become a thing of the past since the building of the High Dam at Aswan. Joseph's predictions of years of plenty and years of famine may have coincided with historical fact and uncertain Nile flooding.

...and Figure of Legend

The Joseph made the sons of Israel swear, saying, "God will surely visit you, and you shall carry up my bones from here." So Joseph died, being 110 years old. They embalmed him and he was put in a coffin in Egypt.

(*Genesis* 50:25–26)

The significance of a tomb discovered in a villa garden at Tell el-Daba, on the eastern Nile delta, should not be understated. It provides strong evidence of a Joseph-type official whose grave was entered and whose body was removed. There were many tomb-robbers in Egypt during the third and second

millennia BC but it was very unusual for the body itself to be taken. Supporters argue that the body was Joseph's and that the robbers were fulfilling the oath recorded in *Genesis* requiring the return of his bones to Canaan. This duty is said to have been performed by Moses about 500 years later.

Discovered by archaeologist Manfred Bietak in the mid-1980s the grave is the largest and most impressive of a dozen found in the small cemetery. Dating to the early 12th dynasty it contained an inscribed limestone statue of a seated official, one-and-a-half times life size. The skin was yellow and the hair painted red in mushroom-shaped style—all traditional features of Canaanites and other Asiatics in Egyptian art. A throwstick—the hieroglyph for a foreigner—was held against the right shoulder.

The statue had been dragged into the robbers' tunnel and the facial features intentionally smashed. A limestone sarcophagus was found, indicating that while this man was a foreigner he was buried according to Egyptian custom. Bietak suggested that the villa was the headquarters of an official who supervised trade

Below: Workers digging exploratory trenches at the archaeological site of Tell el-Daba, Egypt.

and mining expeditions across Egypt's northeast border.

This is some way from Joseph's supposed role in charge of the entire country but it does show that, as early as the Middle Kingdom, Asiatics could rise to a position of prominence. This man was important enough to have lived in a substantial dwelling and sufficiently wealthy to commission a respectable tomb and a statue of some quality.

The destruction of the statue is intriguing and impossible to explain. Was it shattered at the time of the robbery? If so, this suggests a hatred of the deceased that goes beyond motive for personal gain. An alternative theory is that it was attacked soon after the Hyksos came to power (c.1663 BC), a period when Israelites in Egypt were under intense levels of oppression. In this event, local Israelites may have decided that the body of the official had to be removed for safekeeping.

Left: Is this the head of a pharaoh who knew Joseph? Some scholars place Joseph in Egypt during the 19th century BC, while others prefer a later date in the 17th century. If the earlier date is correct, it would have put Joseph in Egypt while Sesostris II or Sesostris III (*pictured*) was on the throne. This head of the pharaoh was created c.1870s BC.

Journey Into Slavery

Joseph and his brothers are said to be the grandchildren of Abraham and are regarded as founders of the twelve tribes of Israel. The Bible says they were Isaac's offspring by four different mothers. Six were born to Leah (Issachar, Judah, Levi, Reuben, Simeon, and Zebulun), two to Rachel (Joseph and Benjamin), two to Zilpah (Gad and Asher), and two to Bilhah (Dan and Naphtali). As in any extended family, sibling rivalry must have been constantly simmering.

When the brothers abduct Joseph from the family home at Hebron their first inclination is to kill him. Then Judah persuades them that they could make money selling him into slavery. We are told how they strike a deal with a band of Arabian Midianite or Ishmaelite nomads (both groups are mentioned in the *Genesis* passage), who drag Joseph out of the pit where he is held prisoner and take him to Egypt, a journey of some 400 miles. The price they pay is 20 pieces of silver.

It seems likely that Joseph's brothers traveled north to the Canaanite towns of Shechem and Dothan to conduct their deceitful business. Afterward, the Ishmaelite caravan, which originated in Gilead, east of the Jordan, would have headed south to the Plain of Sharon, traveling on down the main coastal route—the Biblical "Way of the Land of the Philistines." From here it would have passed into Egypt and the Nile delta, bound for the slave markets of Avaris.

Moses, The Early Years

Then Moses stretched out his hand over the sea, and the Lord drove the sea back by a strong east wind all night and made the sea dry land, and the waters were divided.

Exodus 14:21

According to *Exodus*, Hebrew boys were once sentenced to death by royal command in a bid to curb a population explosion. One mother, desperately wishing to sidestep the wholesale infanticide, cast her baby into the Nile in a bulrush basket. Soon baby and basket were hooked to the shore by no lesser person than the pharaoh's daughter. Delighted by her find, she reared the child as her own.

This is the story of Moses, one of the best loved Bible tales which, in modern terms, begins in Egypt, dips into Saudi Arabia, returns to Egypt and then meanders around the (Egyptian) Sinai peninsula before breaching the borders of Israel. The story continues with Moses slaying an Egyptian, fleeing to Midian and marrying a priest's daughter. As a humble shepherd, Moses heard the voice of God coming from a burning bush. Empowered by a profound religious conviction and assisted by his brother Aaron, Moses returned to his former home, challenged the pharaoh to "let my people go," and induced a series of plagues through God.

Pharaoh permitted the Hebrews to leave,

then belatedly ordered pursuit. The waters of the Sea of Reeds parted (*see also page 30*) until the fleeing population had reached safety, then came together to engulf their foe. Moses and his people were in the wilderness for 40 years before achieving the Promised Land.

Miracles leave no archaeological footprints. None of the mythical story related so often about Moses' life can be rooted in fact by modern scientific methods. There is sparse evidence to say that it might have occurred and much that leads one to believe it simply did not happen. What about the case for the Exodus? For a century Egypt, or parts of it, was ruled by the Hyksos, nomads from Palestine who wrought a Canaanite influence in the realm. Their dynasty was markedly different from those that came before and apparently ended when they were forcibly expelled from the region. Following the eviction of the Hyksos in 1570 BC, Egypt's

rulers despised the Hebrews living and working in the Nile Delta region, branding them "wretched Asiatics" and "sand dwellers."

Texts give no clues

History also proves that the new breed of pharaoh had large-scale building programs and thus pressed Hebrew laborers into service to carry out the construction. So it is quite feasible that the Hebrew people were oppressed and sorely in need of a freedom fighter. But the chronology of the 15th century BC implied to us in the Bible is suspect, leading most scholars to believe a possible ruling pharaoh at the time of Moses was Ramesses II (r.1279–13 BC).

Yet there is no mention in Egyptian texts of an exodus of any sort. Given that the Egyptians constructed a string of defensive forts along the borders, it now seems inconceivable that a group the size of that being led by Moses could have slipped through. The Biblical estimate given for those under the care of Moses is some 600,000 men, women, and children. This is an astonishing number to water, feed, and maneuver at the best of times.

Neither is there visible evidence of a mass migration through Sinai, not even the slimmest pottery fragment. In fact, archaeology says that the entire region was largely unoccupied, in contrast to Biblical accounts of kingdoms and cities. Perhaps the Exodus occurred much later? If so, it probably drags the tale of Joseph and his brothers further forward in time. The debate over whether Moses was a true or false figure is unlikely to be resolved in the foreseeable future. Given the nature of saga and legend, it seems likely that the story reflects a momentous confrontation between an Israelite leader, who may not have been Moses, and a pharaoh whose identity remains unknown.

Left: An Egyptian woman harvests Nile bulrushes in a painting by Frank Dillon (c.1845–1909) titled *The Pyramids from the Island of Roda.* The Nile is the river of life for Egypt, as it was in the time of Moses. In the story of an anguished mother setting her infant son loose on the waters in a bulrush basket, there is also the symbolic gesture of the river offering life.

Origins of the Passover

Moses' last plague was the death of all firstborn male Egyptians, including the pharaoh's own son. Hebrew families evaded the curse by eating unleavened bread for a week, eating a ritual meal, and marking their doorposts with lambs' blood. The event is the basis of the Jewish Passover festival, still prominent in the faith today.

Mount Sinai

And Moses said to the Lord, "The people cannot come up to Mount Sinai: for you yourself warned us, saying, 'Set bounds around the mountain and consecrate it.'"

Exodus 19:23

Right: In the care of a dozen Greek Orthodox monks, ancient St. Catherine's Monastery sits in a dry valley below the sacred Mount Sinai, or Gebel Mûsa (Mount Moses). The monastery claims to still have the original burning bush.

Below: A Biblical scene—the sun sets over Mount Sinai, Egypt. According to the Old Testament, it was on this mountain that Moses received laws to govern the tribes of Israel: the Ten Commandments.

It was at Mount Sinai (Gebel Mûsa, Mount of Moses) that God made an agreement or covenant with the Hebrews Moses led from captivity in Egypt. They were to become God's chosen people and, in return, were to live by the laws He prescribed. Moses was presented with the Ten Commandments, famously engraved upon tablets of stone. These were the rules distilled from a broad array of laws covering every aspect of daily life, imparted during the 40 days that Moses spent on the peak.

Even while Moses was in conversation with God, his followers at the foot of the mountain were indulging themselves with wild behavior. The site of their camp is believed to be Gebel Harun (Aaron), lying to the northeast of Mount Sinai. When he witnessed this behavior, Moses dropped the stone tablets, which shattered. He instigated terrible punishments before renewing the covenant with God and returning with a second set of tablets.

According to the Bible and other sources, the tablets were stored in a specially built chest, or ark, made of acacia wood and decorated with gold, and carried with the Hebrew people on their travels. David brought it to Jerusalem when he was made king of the Israelites. His son Solomon built a temple to house it during his reign in the tenth century BC.

Despite its significance, the Ark of the Covenant disappeared some five centuries later, probably when the temple was destroyed and the exile into Babylon began. It remains one of today's most highly sought archaeological prizes. Theories concerning its whereabouts abound—Ethiopia is a strong contender—and numerous expeditions have been mounted to search for it, without any success. Moses is thought to have lived within a century of Tutankhamun; since his burial goods were

found in 1922 in excellent condition, it is entirely feasible that the Ark similarly survived and remains intact.

Sacred summit

Mount Sinai rises to some 7,500 feet and there are 2,700 rocky steps leading to the summit. On top of the mountain is a chapel founded in Byzantine times and a mosque incorporating a niche in which Moses is said to have hidden on his initial encounter with God.

There is another Muslim structure at Gebel Harun (*see map, right*), which protects an ancient tomb. Christians and Muslims hold that this is the burial site of Aaron, brother of Moses and the man who wrought the Golden Calf. Intriguingly, local Bedouin—who are Islamic by faith and traditional by nature—do not concur.

When Christian hermits sought seclusion from the fifth century onward, they came to Sinai. A magnificent tribute to the monastic tradition is St. Catherine's, which rises squarely out of the desert floor in sun-baked granite. Roman Emperor Justinian ordered the monastery be built to replace a fortified church, apparently the work of St. Helena during her pilgrimage to the Holy Land in 326. This is said to be the spot where, as a lowly herdsman, Moses saw the burning bush and heard the voice of God telling him to deliver the Hebrews from Egypt into "a land flowing with milk and honey." Within its walls are a Byzantine basilica, ten chapels, monks' cells, and a mosque built behind the church in

1106. Externally the monastery is austere but inside it is abundant with icons and precious art. The library has some 3,000 manuscripts and once housed the *Codex Sinaiticus*, a fourth-century version of the *Septuagint* (Biblical translation). The isolated location of the monastery has kept it secure over the centuries.

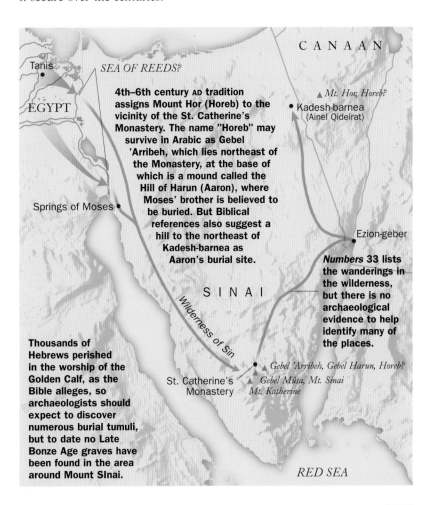

CANAAN

Tanis

SEA OF REEDS?

EGYPT

4th–6th century AD tradition assigns Mount Hor (Horeb) to the vicinity of the St. Catherine's Monastery. The name "Horeb" may survive in Arabic as Gebel 'Arribeh, which lies northeast of the Monastery, at the base of which is a mound called the Hill of Harun (Aaron), where Moses' brother is believed to be buried. But Biblical references also suggest a hill to the northeast of Kadesh-barnea as Aaron's burial site.

▲ *Mt. Hor, Horeb?*
• Kadesh-barnea
(Ain el Qideirat)

Springs of Moses •

Ezion-geber

Numbers **33 lists the wanderings in the wilderness, but there is no archaeological evidence to help identify many of the places.**

S I N A I

Wilderness of Sin

Thousands of Hebrews perished in the worship of the Golden Calf, as the Bible alleges, so archaeologists should expect to discover numerous burial tumuli, but to date no Late Bonze Age graves have been found in the area around Mount Sinai.

St. Catherine's ▲ *Gebel 'Arribeh, Gebel Harun, Horeb?*
Monastery ▲ *Gebel Musa, Mt. Sinai*
Mt. Katherine

RED SEA

Joshua and the Promised Land

Now therefore arise, go over this Jordan, you and all this people, into the land I am giving to them, to the people of Israel. Every place that the sole of your foot will tread upon I have given to you, just as I promised to Moses.

Joshua 1:2

Below: An Israeli truck crosses the Jordan during the Six-Day War of 1967, in a reverse echo of the arrival in the Promised Land.

Moses was not to see the Promised Land. According to the last verses of *Deuteronomy*, he climbed Mount Nebo, there to behold all that God had promised the Israelites on the other side of the nearby Jordan before he died. Before they arrived at this point, the Israelites had wandered in the wilderness for 40 years since leaving Egypt. *Numbers* chapter 33 cites no less than 42 placenames where they had pitched their tents before arriving at the foot of Mount Nebo. With the exception of a few names—Wilderness of Sin, Ezion-geber, Kadesh— not many are recognizable today.

The obvious route for the fleeing Israelites to have taken—the coastal road—was denied them because Egypt kept a string of strong forts along the road. This would have forced them to turn south into Sinai (the warterless diagonal route to the tip of the Gulf of Aqaba would not have supported a large migration). Then there is the parting of the waters of the Red Sea. It makes good reading, and a spectacular scene in a movie, but it never happened. The early Greek translations of the Old Testament mistranslated the Hewbrew *yam suph* as "Red Sea," when it actually means "Reed Sea."

This is a more easily understandable miracle. On leaving the region of Per-Rameses and Tanis, they Israelites would have encountered the many swamps, marshes and lagoons that line the route of the modern Suez Canal. While a mass of nomads on foot would face little difficulty negotiating these, the fast-moving chariots and mounted soldiers of the pharaoh would have quickly become bogged down.

Unwelcome visitors

After the events at Mount Sinai, the tribes moved north to Ezion-geber, and may well have

continued on toward the southern end of the Dead Sea. However, the presence of hostile Edomites probably dicated a turn to the north again, toward Kadesh-barnea, and what was felt to be the soft under-belly of Canaan. It turned out differently.

From Kadesh-barnea, Moses had sent out spies into Canaan, and a rash military expedition headed for Hormah and Hebron, only to be defeated and turned back. The Israelites appear then to have turned east. Confusingly, two accounts in *Numbers* differ on the route (*see map, right*), but whichever is correct, the Israelites arrived in Moab, and from there went north to Mount Nebo. With the death of Moses, Joshua became their leader.

The book of *Joshua* tells us that after crossing the Jordan they immediately set about reducing Jericho, the first large city encountered, before moving across the length and breadth of Canaan conquering every center in their path. However, the Old Testament also contains conflicting accounts of this "conquest," and archaeology has discovered little to prove Joshua's story (*see page 65*). By maintaining their covenant with Yaweh (God), the Israelites were given Canaan, and all in it, but the book of the Old Testament that follows, *Judges*, is a story of lost faith among the

Moses sends out spies from Israelite desert camp at Kadesh-barnea (**1**). They reach Hebron (**2**), although another verse (*Numbers 13:22*) claims as far as Rehob (**3**). Moses tells Israelites that only Joshua and Caleb will enter the Promised Land; disaffected Israelites attempt direct assault on Canaan, but are defeated at Hormah (**4**). After Moses' brother Aaron dies at Mount Hor (**5**), Israelites move eastward (**6**). According to *Numbers 20* and *21* via Sea of Suph (Red Sea) to avoid crossing Edom, then north to Iye-Abarim. They go around hostile Moab (**7**) and capture Amorite kingdom at Heshbon (**8**), before settling on Plains of Moab. A strike at Bashan secures Edrei from King Og (**9**). *Numbers 23* gives a different route across top of Edom, skirting Dibon (**10**). After giving final instructions, Moses climbs Mount Nebo (**11**) to be gathered to God. Joshua and Caleb cross the Jordan (**12**).

LEBANON

SYRIA

3 • Rehob
(Yunin)

Sea of Galilee

BASHAN

9 • Edrei
(Dar'a)

Jordan

WEST BANK

Plains of Moab

AMON

Ekron •
Ashdod •

12   8 •
           Heshbon

11
—— MT. NEBO

Ashqelon •

PHILISTIA

Gaza •   • Gath   2 • Hebron

GAZA

Dibon
(Dhiban)

Dead Sea

7

MOAB

• Hormah
4

• Iye-Abarim

1
Kadesh-
barnea
(Ainel
Qideirat)

5

Mt. Hor?

Negev Desert 10

JORDAN

• Zalmonah

ISRAEL

6

EDOM

EGYPT

SINAI

RED SEA ——
(*Gulf of Aqaba*)

Israelites' routes to the "land of milk and honey"

Promised Land of Canaan as defined in the Bible

Israelite spies

Israelite route according to *Numbers 20* and *21*

Israelite route according to *Numbers 23*

major Philistine city-state

"conquerors," and resulting disasters. *Judges* paints a picture of a very different kind of "conquest," and one that is more believable: a slow infiltration of squabbling Hebrew tribes among an indigenous population that did not always accommodate them, but did not also immediately throw them out.

CHAPTER THREE

Israel: Glory and Disaster

Then the children of Israel cried out to the Lord for help, for he had 900 chariots of iron and he oppressed the people of Israel cruelly for twenty years.

Judges 4:3

The image of Moses at a great age looking through tearful eyes at the Promised Land, knowing that although he would never set foot in it his people would prosper, signaled a new beginning for the Jewish people.

A clutch of family and tribal dramas had already passed. The Israelites had erred but returned to the path of righteousness. They had been oppressed but were free and their abiding dream was at last being realized. The code that would guide them for generations had been received and understood. Their arrival in the Promised Land was a new beginning.

But there was much more to come. Bible writers had further tales to impart in an illuminating history of the Hebrew people. There were additional triumphs and a considerable number of catastrophes—usually occurring when the Israelites strayed from God.

The saga is rich and at times both intricate and astounding. The early writings of the Bible were used as propaganda tools, of that there is little doubt. But there are certainly Biblical accounts based on historical facts. The books of *Kings* and *Chronicles* cover at least part of the era, both regarded as quite sound sources. And occasionally there is proof for Biblical claims from other sources, although no amount of archaeology or excavation will testify for the prophets and the miracles they performed. Yet the Old Testament conveys the story of monotheism and how it triumphed in adversity.

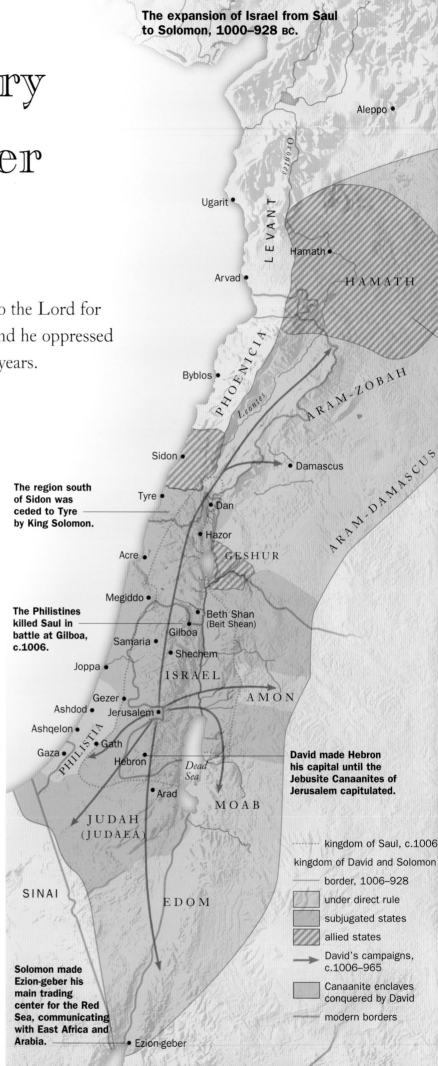

The region south of Sidon was ceded to Tyre by King Solomon.

The Philistines killed Saul in battle at Gilboa, c.1006.

David made Hebron his capital until the Jebusite Canaanites of Jerusalem capitulated.

Solomon made Ezion-geber his main trading center for the Red Sea, communicating with East Africa and Arabia.

kingdom of Saul, c.1006
kingdom of David and Solomon
border, 1006–928
under direct rule
subjugated states
allied states
David's campaigns, c.1006–965
Canaanite enclaves conquered by David
modern borders

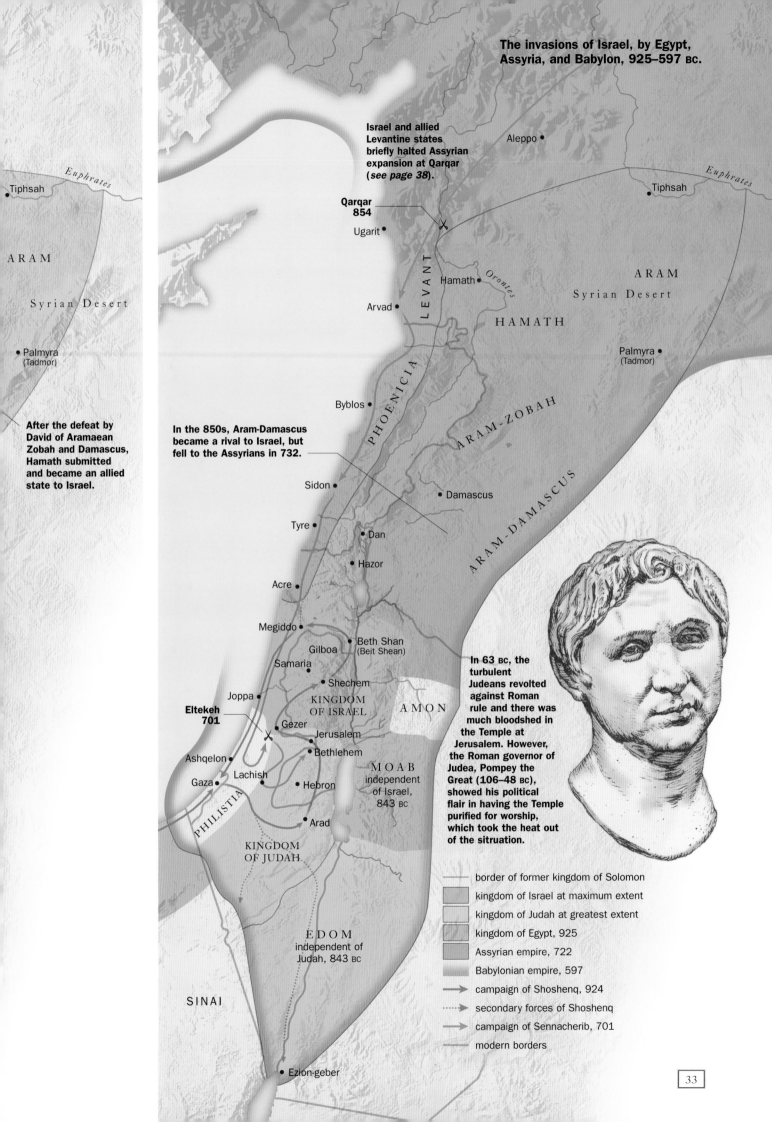

The invasions of Israel, by Egypt, Assyria, and Babylon, 925–597 BC.

Euphrates

Tiphsah

ARAM

Syrian Desert

Palmyra (Tadmor)

After the defeat by David of Aramaean Zobah and Damascus, Hamath submitted and became an allied state to Israel.

Israel and allied Levantine states briefly halted Assyrian expansion at Qarqar (*see page 38*).

Aleppo

Euphrates

Tiphsah

Qarqar 854

Ugarit

Hamath

Orontes

ARAM

Syrian Desert

Arvad

LEVANT

HAMATH

Palmyra (Tadmor)

Byblos

PHOENICIA

ARAM-ZOBAH

In the 850s, Aram-Damascus became a rival to Israel, but fell to the Assyrians in 732.

Sidon

Damascus

Tyre

Dan

ARAM-DAMASCUS

Acre

Hazor

Megiddo

Beth Shan (Beit Shean)

Gilboa

Samaria

Shechem

Joppa

KINGDOM OF ISRAEL

AMON

Eltekeh 701

Gezer

Jerusalem

Ashqelon

Bethlehem

Lachish

MOAB independent of Israel, 843 BC

Gaza

Hebron

PHILISTIA

Arad

KINGDOM OF JUDAH

EDOM independent of Judah, 843 BC

SINAI

In 63 BC, the turbulent Judeans revolted against Roman rule and there was much bloodshed in the Temple at Jerusalem. However, the Roman governor of Judea, Pompey the Great (106–48 BC), showed his political flair in having the Temple purified for worship, which took the heat out of the sitruation.

border of former kingdom of Solomon

kingdom of Israel at maximum extent

kingdom of Judah at greatest extent

kingdom of Egypt, 925

Assyrian empire, 722

Babylonian empire, 597

campaign of Shoshenq, 924

secondary forces of Shoshenq

campaign of Sennacherib, 701

modern borders

Ezion-geber

Saul and David

There was a long war between the house of Saul and the house of David. And David grew stronger and stronger, while the house of Saul became weaker and weaker.

2 Samuel 3:1

Right: Photographed in 1988, this Philistine dagger was found during a dig at Ekron.

Below: A relief sculpture from the walls of Ramesses III at Luxor, Egypt, depicts Philistine prisoners before their settlement in Palestine, as recorded in the Bible.

According to the Bible, David's achievements were many, but he is best remembered in our time as the diminutive youth who killed the giant Goliath with a single sling shot, thus proving that might is not always right or will necessarily prevail.

Goliath was from a people called the Philistines, who constantly competed with the Israelites for control of the same territories.

Although allegedly ten feet tall (perhaps in reality rather less than seve), the lumbering fellow was quickly outwitted in combat by David. The term *philistine* has endured to describe someone who is hostile or indifferent to culture. Despite their negative reputation, the Philistines were in fact a technologically advanced people renowned for their seafaring abilities, and played an important part in the development of the Holy Lands. From Egyptian texts of the 13th and 12th centuries BC we learn about attack by "peoples of the sea." Among those would-be invaders were the Philistines, who were initially repelled by the Egyptians and set their sights further north, to Canaan. The name Palestine is derived from them.

It is thought they originally came from Crete and the Aegean, since Philistine pottery discovered in Palestine is similar in constitution to that found in parts of Greece. They established five centers in Canaan: Ashdod, Ashqelon, Ekron, Gath, and Gaza. Soldiers in plumed headdresses and kilts armed with triangular daggers patrolled the coast road that linked the

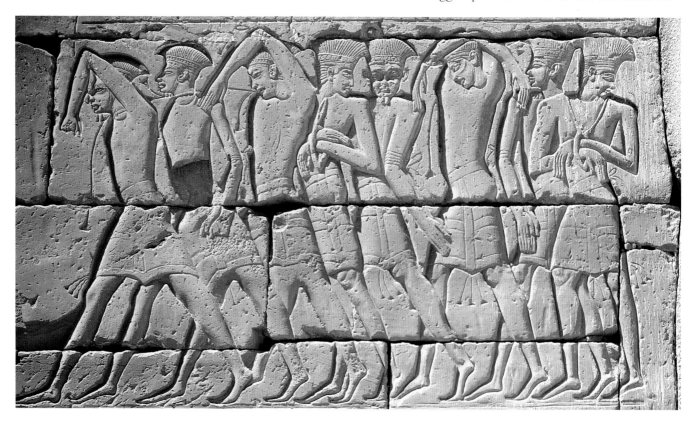

settlements, proving a fearsome obstacle. It is thought the wanderings of the Israelites following the Exodus from Egypt were considerably lengthened by these Philistine defenses.

Due to the threat posed by the pagan Philistines the Hebrew tribes finally coalesced under one man. Saul, the first king of Israel, was an able military leader but incurred the wrath of the prophet Samuel. The young David was anointed king in his place. After Saul grew jealous of David, the daring youngster—seen by artists until the present day as a model of manhood— became an outlaw in the manner of Robin Hood. Saul's story has all the ingredients of a Shakespearean tragedy, with him as the flawed hero. Saul was either slain in battle with the Philistines at Mount Gilboa or, according to a different version, threw himself on his sword after hearing that his sons had been killed by Philistines.

Saul never defeated the Philistines. During David's 40-year reign, which ended c.962 BC, they were slowly driven to the south where they continued to live until the late eighth century BC brought wholesale conquest in the region by Sargon, king of Assyria. When the Babylonians massed in the Holy Land in the early sixth century BC Philistine power was ended forever.

Unification of Israel

David finished the job that Joshua started, bringing all the settlements of the Promised Land into the Israelite fold. In reality the villages that he incorporated into his empire were scattered and rural, but he came to be regarded as a semi-divine figure. The cult he encouraged of the Israelite God, Yahweh, was potent and strengthened by the veneration of the Ark of the Covenant. Significantly, the Bible relates that David paid a purchase fee for the site of Jerusalem to Araunah the Jebusite. This is proof for some Orthodox Jews that Jerusalem rightfully belongs to the Jews.

The full extent of David's empire has not yet been revealed by archaeology. For generations it was thought the history of David was recorded soon after his demise, so detailed did it appear. Now scholars and historians wrestle with the knowledge that a man with an awesome Biblical

standing is barely noted elsewhere. Further, there are astonishingly few tenth-century BC artifacts coming out of Jerusalem. There is speculation that either the City of David was far less important than the Bible says or that building work in subsequent generations has entirely obliterated Davidian strata. King David was a man, not a myth, but the empire he forged may have been a lot less grand and glorious than the Bible writers would have us believe.

Left: Viewed by artists such as Michelangelo throughout the ages as a model of manhood, David's chroniclers were working within a tradition that painted the king as the founder of Israel's eternal dynasty in Jerusalem. In this respect, he is made to look glorious, faithful, and courageous, while Saul, his enemy, is portrayed as a failure. Yet there is evidence in the Bible of a darker, meaner streak in David—a clever politician and ruthless statesman.

David's deadly weapon

Sling shots were one of the most widely used weapons in an ancient arsenal. The stones used varied between the size of a modern golf ball to a tennis ball, many having been smoothed by tools. Slings measured up to about three feet in length and the weapons could match the distance of an archer's arrows. According to the Bible, there was an elite corps of slingers associated with the tribe of Benjamin.

Solomon

Thus King Solomon excelled all the kings of the earth in riches and in wisdom.

1 Kings 10:23

Below: Six miles north of Jerusalem and southwest of Ai (*see inset map*), the remains of Biblical Gibeon, now Al Jib can still be seen. Gibeon (meaning "hill-city") was an important Canaanite center at the time of Joshua, who feared it "because it was greater than Ai, and because all its men were warriors" (*Joshua 10:2*). The tabernacle was set up here, where it remained until Solomon built the Temple in Jerusalem. This occurred, as *Kings* tells us, when Solomon paid a state visit to offer sacrifices soon after he came to the throne, While there, the Lord appeared to him in a dream and told the king to build a new temple. When the temple was built all Israel assembled before Solomon, and the king took from Gibeon the tabernacle and all the holy vessels in the tabernacle to Jerusalem.

olomon, son of David, is a mysterious figure. According to the Bible, he came up with a unique, though seemingly cruel, solution over two bickering women claiming rights over the same baby. He knew that if he suggested the infant be cut in two, and half given to each woman, the real mother would become obvious through her agonized shrieks of protest. Yet, despite his renowned wisdom and ability to communicate with God, he began to worship idols and thus risked being regarded as a heretic. One of his most important legacies, however, was the "first temple."

No one is certain just how, where, or even if the first temple was constructed, although plenty of educated guesses have been made. Early archaeologists placed great faith on the accounts that appear in the Bible. In the First Book of *Kings* there is an elaborate description of the temple. Measuring about 99 feet in length and 33 feet in width, it was about 49 feet tall. Its central focus was the Holy of Holies, an inner sanctuary containing the Ark of the Covenant. Biblical descriptions tell us it was richly decorated. The Bible text also says construction of the temple began in the fourth year of Solomon's reign and was completed in seven years, figures that may well be accurate.

The construction of Solomon's temple is regarded by the Jewish people as a culmination of the covenant Abraham made with God many years earlier. The quest to discover the site of Solomon's temple was one of the earliest challenges of Biblical archaeology. When the evidence did not present itself, the critics became skeptical. Surely the Hebrew tribes of the era were not up to building something so sophisticated? The relevant Biblical passages were debunked as historic hyperbole.

Today, although there is no absolute proof, the overwhelming feeling among scholars is that the temple did indeed exist. There are other contemporary examples of architecture that indicate the temple was well within the capabilities of the Phoenicians, who were largely responsible for building it. There is also talk of Solomon's palace being in Jerusalem in the vicinity of the temple, but nothing has emerged to prove definitively the existence of either building. The remains may well lie below Jerusalem's more modern buildings.

Solomon's wealth was as legendary as his temple. The hunt for King Solomon's Mines, where gold and gems to finance his kingdom were reputedly extracted, has taken treasure hunters to numerous parts of Africa as well as more local sites around the Red Sea and Arabia. So far no definitive location has been identified.

Enigmatic queen

Solomon probably acquired a large amount of his income through a sophisticated system of taxation. His wealth and knowledge attracted the attentions of the Queen of Sheba, who brought him a caravan of exotic gifts from her realm in the south, which may have lain within the modern borders of Saudi Arabia, Ethiopia, or (most likely) Yemen. The tale of their liaison is romantic and there are hints in the scriptures that the two were lovers. This is a man who, according to the Bible, already had 700 wives and 300 concubines and whose "Song of Solomon" later in the Bible is seductively suggestive.

According to Ethiopian legend, he fathered a child with the Queen of Sheba who became the first king of Ethiopia. The royal line concluded

in the reign of 20th-century Rastafarian icon Haile Selassie. When Sheba departed Solomon, it says in the Bible, the king gave her "all her desire." Perhaps it was a child, or possibly the Ark of the Covenant, which some people believe remains intact in Ethiopia. Other theories maintain that it is buried beneath the Temple Mount in Jerusalem or hidden away in caves near the Dead Sea.

Archaeologists are scouring Marib in Yemen, where there are significant temple remains, for clues that would identify the site with the Queen of Sheba. Further, inscriptions linking her name to Solomon would give the Bible's account of Solomon further credibility. Although many artifacts have been sifted from the sands of the Marib region, the definitive piece of this puzzle has yet to be discovered.

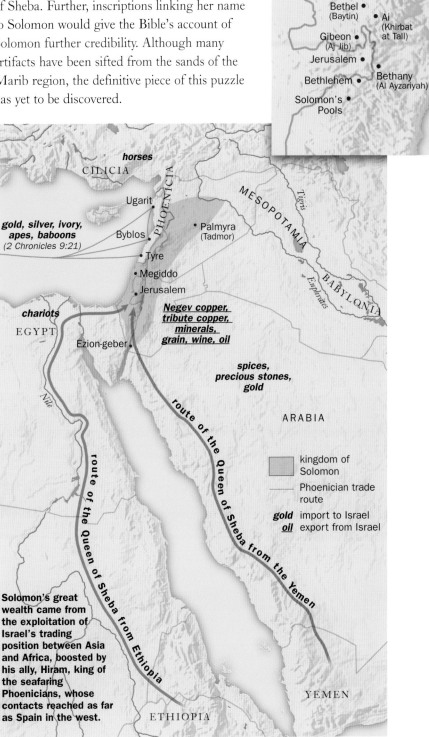

Did Solomon really exist?

Those who claim that he is one of history's "King Arthur" figures, an amalgam of several characters fused together through time, point to the exaggeration of the Bible. The Biblical accounts were, they say, written by sentimental scribes harking back to a mythical golden age. There was, and remains, a paucity of references to Solomon and David in sources outside the Bible. However, he has loomed so large in Biblical texts that his existence has to be considered likely.

Two Kingdoms

When Rehoboam came to Jerusalem, he assembled the house of Judah and Benjamin, 180,000 chosen warriors, to fight against Israel to restore the kingdom to Rehoboam.

2 Chronicles 11:1

Below: Columns of the Amri Ahab palace stand on the archaeological site of Sabastiya, once the ancient Samaria and at one time the capital of Israel.

King David had some success in binding the 12 tribes of Israel to a common purpose. Solomon tried to maintain unity by dividing the kingdom into a dozen districts, appointing one tribe to each. But when the tribes refused to ally with Solomon's son Rehoboam a fissure opened up in the kingdom that could not be healed. David's kingdom split in two, with neither nation capable of greatness.

Rehoboam retained Jerusalem and from there ruled the southern kingdom of Judah. The rebel Jeroboam took charge of Israel, taking Shechem as his capital. Other areas sheered away in favor of self-rule, including Damascus and the regions of Amon and Moab.

In general terms it seems the northern state of Israel was populous, with permanent settlements, while Judah had fewer people, who were probably more nomadic by nature. Consequently the archaeological finds from the south have been comparatively sparse.

Israel was militarily the stronger but that failed to prevent a succession of conflicts between the two. However, external enemies rather than internal strife proved pivotal. The first, in Rehoboam's fifth year, was the Biblical Shishak, generally believed to be the pharaoh Shoshenq I (*see page 139*). Mentioned only briefly in the Bible, the Egyptian exploits are fully described in accounts discovered in the Temple of Amon at Karnak, and there is evidence of conflagration that supports the Egyptian king's claims of capturing and destroying 150 settlements in Judah and Israel. He scooped numerous prisoners in the process. A fragment of stele was recovered at Megiddo, marking the Egyptian triumph. According to *1 Kings 14:26* Shishak "took away the treasures of the house of the Lord and the treasures of the king's house." Indeed the pharaoh's subsequent projects were on a grander scale than before, indicating that he benefited from looting treasures in Judah and Israel. Shoshenq III, for example, was buried in a coffin of pure silver. Shoshenq called off his campaign in Palestine when domestic troubles arose. However, his invasion ensured that neither Israel nor Judah would be a threat to his borders for some time.

Surrounded by enemies

Although the Bible does not mention a battle fought between Assyria and Israel along with their allies on the Orontes (Qarqar, 854 BC), this is communicated through records kept by the enemy, in this case, the Assyrian king Shalmaneser III. "They rose against me for a decisive battle," says Shalmaneser, who tells how

Left: Detail from Assyrian relief of the siege of Lachish, c.681 BC, shows Jewish slaves being forced to build a ramp for Sennacherib's soldiers to attack the heavily fortified city (*also see picture on page 147*).

King Ahab fielded 2,000 chariots. The battlefield was covered with corpses and the victory claimed by the Assyrians sounds hollow. Ahab is reviled in the Bible, as is his Phoenician wife Jezebel, who ordered that all the prophets of YHWH (God) in Israel be killed. Nevertheless, Ahab should be given credit for building up an effective military fighting force and for courage on the battlefield. Neither kingdom was consistently faithful to God, the notable exception being Judah under King Josiah (639–609 BC), who centralized worship at the Temple and abolished pagan cults.

The tragic end to the Davidian dynasty can be seen in the fragments of a monument discovered at Tel Dan in northern Israel. Describing the attack of Hazael, king of Damascus, on Israel in about 835, it reads: "[I killed Jeho]ram son of

[Ahab] king of Israel, and [I] killed [Ahaz]iahu son of [Jehoram, king of] the House of David. And I set [their towns into ruins and turned] their land into [desolation].

In fact the Davidian line in Judah was restored. In Israel there was a succession of weak kings until 721 BC when the capital, by that time Samaria, fell to the Assyrians. When the great Assyrian king Sargon died 20 years later, Judah under the rule of Hezekiah rebelled. Sargon's successor, Sennacherib, invaded in 701. After a lightning campaign, he besieged and captured Lachish. Thus Judah survived as a vassal state.

When the Assyrian star had faded in the region, Judah shone alone for a brief spell. The kingdom expanded, and damaged cities were rebuilt.

Into Exile

He carried away all Jerusalem and all the officials and all the mighty men of valor, 10,000 captives, and all the craftsmen and the smiths. None remained, except the poorest people of the land.

2 Kings 24:14

Below: Ruins of the ancient palace of Nebuchadnezzar at Babylon, Iraq. The plunder of Israel and Judah, and the slaves they provided, contributed to the splendor of the Akkadian king's buildings.

The story of Judah and Jerusalem's destruction at the hands of the Babylonians is one of catastrophe. Jerusalem survived a sacking in 597 BC when Nebuchadnezzar, king of Babylon, first surrounded the city with his horde. King Jehoiachin surrendered himself and was taken, with his people, back to Babylon. Nebuchadnezzar took for himself all the treasures of the temple, but although he stripped it bare he left it standing. The Babylonian king appointed a replacement for Jehoiachin, an uncle named Zedekiah, whom he intended to be a puppet ruler.

The *Babylonian Chronicle* records the event: "In the seventh year, the month of Kislev, the king of Akkad mustered his soldiers, marched to the Hatti-land, and encamped against the City of Judah and on the second day of the month of Adar he seized the city and captured the king. He appointed there a king of his own choice and taking heavy tribute brought it back into Babylon."

However, Zedekiah had ambitions of his own and within a few years he was plotting with neighboring kings to win back true independence for Judah. In doing so he provoked venomous rage in his former sponsor. Nebuchadnezzar sought wholesale retribution.

Babylonian forces swept through Judah during 587 BC, destroying everything in their path. Under siege for a period, Jerusalem's population began to starve and Zedekiah fled through a secret tunnel, heading for Jericho. He was overtaken and captured, however, and taken to face Nebuchadnezzar's wrath. According to the Bible he was forced to watch his sons being killed, then his eyes were gouged out and he was taken in chains to Babylon.

Destruction of Jerusalem

A month later, a captain of the Babylonian guard returned to Jerusalem and torched the city including the houses and the Temple.

Left: A 12th-century sculpture of the prophet Jeremiah stands on the central pillar of the south porch of Moissac Abbey, France. Synonymous with gloom and doom, the words of Jeremiah were spoken during the tragic 40 years between 627–587 BC, when the Temple was destroyed. As an educated man from a priestly family, he was well aware of the political forces at work against Judah, but explained them as divine retribution for the people's failure to adhere to their covenant with God. Although his views were often unpopular, his teachings in large part contributed to the survival of the Jews' faith during the Exile.

The remaining population was rounded up and taken into exile. Modern historical records rely primarily on the account in the Bible when describing the fall of Judah. However, soil samples taken from Jerusalem prove that there was an intense blaze in the city at this time.

This episode was undoubtedly a great catastrophe. Jerusalem was left as smoking rubble and those few who escaped exile probably fled to Egypt during an attempted uprising against the local Babylonian-approved ruler. Despite these events, Jewish culture and faith continued. Elders continued to define the religion for young people and so it survived.

Against expectations, the Neo-Babylonian empire fell to the Persians in 539 BC, barely a generation after the exile. The Persian king, Cyrus the Great, was perceived by many Jews as a prophet, or at least an instrument of God. This view was endorsed when the faithful realized that the ascendant ruler had followed the same path into the Promised Land as Abraham. Cyrus went further by permitting the Jews to repopulate Jerusalem and to build another Temple.

Jews in exile

When Judah's population was shipped out of their homeland by the Babylonians there began a history of Jews living abroad. It is called *diaspora*, a Greek word meaning dispersal. At first the term applied only to the Exile but later it was broadly used to describe Jews living outside Palestine. When Cyrus paved a return route to Jerusalem for the Jews not all seized the opportunity to go. Consequently, the Jewish population outside the homeland continued to grow. By the first century AD an estimated five million Jews lived outside Palestine, although they still looked toward the Promised Land for religious inspiration and culture. A debate over whether it is necessary to return to be truly Jewish has continued ever since.

The Hasmonean Dynasty

You shall have no other gods before me.

Exodus 20:3

When the empire of Alexander the Great fragmented, Palestine fell neatly between the Ptolemaic realm based in Egypt and the Hellenistic Seleukids of Syria. Battles between these two prominent powers were frequently played out on Palestinian soil.

The Judaeans lived passively until the accession of the Seleukid Antiochus IV in 175 BC (also known as Antiochus Epiphanes meaning "god manifest"), who was intent on religious reform. He effectively banned Judaism and installed in its place the pagan cult of Zeus. Not content with scrapping dietary laws and forbidding circumcision, Antiochus moved into Jerusalem in 168, built a fortress called the Akra, and took Zeus into the Temple.

This sacrilegious act finally provoked the Jews into a rebellion, which was ignited when an outraged priest named Mattathias Hasmoneas killed one of the king's agents sent to ensure proper Greek worship was taking place. Mattathias and his five sons fled to the hills to escape a bloody retribution. Soon they became the focus of a burgeoning Jewish opposition movement, which trained in guerilla warfare and prepared for a showdown to save their faith.

Below: In this 19th-century engraving by French artist Gustave Doré, Judas Maccabeus is seen exhorting the Israelites in front of the Seleukid army commanded by the Greek general Nikanor near Emmaus.

Intrigue and murder

Judas, the third son and the commander of the new force, was known as Maccabeus (the hammer). The expected confrontation with the Seleukid Greeks occurred not once but on numerous occasions across Palestine, with Judas employing canny tactics to outwit his more experienced enemy. The heat was often taken out of the war when venomous power struggles diverted the attentions of the Seleucid leaders. Antiochus Epiphanes and Judas Maccabeus died within a year of one another.

Their successors, Alexander Ephiphanes and Judas' brother Jonathan forged a peace treaty of sorts. Jonathan then set about consolidating Judaean power and extending its boundaries once more. He became high priest in Jerusalem, a move that alarmed some conservative Jews who protested that only descendants of Aaron, Moses' brother, could aspire to such a title. One group, the Essenes, retreated to a cave complex near Qumran in disgust. They are the authors of the Dead Sea Scrolls.

Jonathan was betrayed and murdered by an ally, to be succeeded by his brother Simon, who also adopted the mantle of high priest. Simon was assassinated in 135 BC along with two of his sons, but not before reaching an agreement with Rome that guaranteed Jews unrestricted rights in Palestine. His son, John Hyrcanus, became ruler of

Judaea and head of the Hasmonean dynasty, also called the House of Maccabees. He mounted several campaigns to regain important centers including Shechem and Samaria.

John Hyrcanus's reign was rocked by conflict between the Sadduccees and the hostile Pharisees. The Pharisees—although not members of any religious hierarchy—were still pious in the extreme. They obeyed God's laws, then created their own rank of religious legislation to ring-fence those laws. At the time of Jesus there were about 6,000 Pharisees. The Sadducees were fewer in number but more influential, and usually connected to a priesthood. They were less obsessive about reviewing and reinforcing old laws and traditions and were strong supporters of the Hasmonean dynasty.

A Hasmonean penchant for kingship, first seen in John Hyrcanus's son and a hallmark of the dynasty thereafter, further aggravated Orthodox Jews. While the borders of the country were being pressed outward, the new model Judaea was on the brink of civil strife. Bickering between sibling rivals continued, creating a perfect opening for the Romans when they chose to march into Palestine in 65 BC. While one faction retreated to the Temple

Above: Fragments of the Dead Sea Scrolls discovered near Qumran included early texts of the Hebrew Bible from c.200 BC. The scrolls, probably written by the dissenting Essene sect, were hidden from invading Romans.

Mount to fight, another opened the gates of Jerusalem to usher in the Romans. In 63, a siege erupted into appalling bloodshed with some 12,000 Judaean casualties.

The Roman commander Pompey showed characteristic wisdom in immediately ordering the cleansing of the Temple so that worship and sacrifice could resume. However, he also dismantled the empire accrued by John Hyrcanus and his son Alexander Janneus, creating free cities throughout the region.

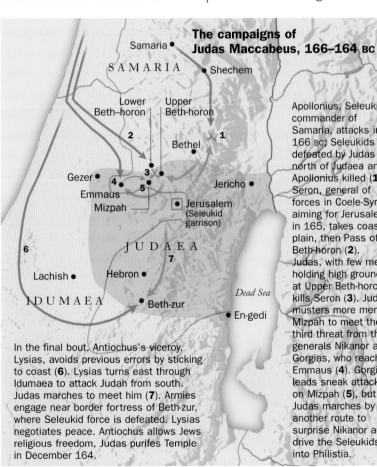

The campaigns of Judas Maccabeus, 166–164 BC

Apollonius, Seleukid commander of Samaria, attacks in 166 BC; Seleukids defeated by Judas to north of Judaea and Apollonius killed (**1**). Seron, general of forces in Coele-Syria, aiming for Jerusalem in 165, takes coastal plain, then Pass of Beth-horon (**2**). Judas, with few men holding high ground at Upper Beth-horon, kills Seron (**3**). Judas musters more men at Mizpah to meet the third threat from the generals Nikanor and Gorgias, who reach Emmaus (**4**). Gorgias leads sneak attack on Mizpah (**5**), but Judas marches by another route to surprise Nikanor and drive the Seleukids into Philistia.

In the final bout, Antiochus's viceroy, Lysias, avoids previous errors by sticking to coast (**6**). Lysias turns east through Idumaea to attack Judah from south. Judas marches to meet him (**7**). Armies engage near border fortress of Beth-zur, where Seleukid force is defeated. Lysias negotiates peace. Antiochus allows Jews religious freedom, Judas purifes Temple in December 164.

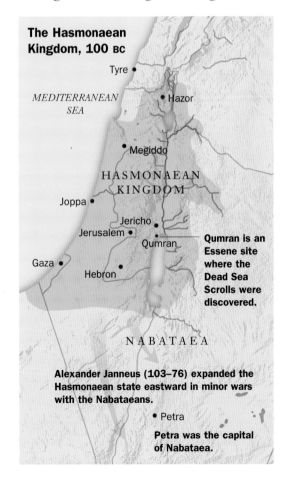

The Hasmonaean Kingdom, 100 BC

Qumran is an Essene site where the Dead Sea Scrolls were discovered.

Alexander Janneus (103–76) expanded the Hasmonaean state eastward in minor wars with the Nabataeans.

Petra was the capital of Nabataea.

The Holy Lands, 1180–530 BC.

Sardis

Lydia

T U R K E Y

Cappadocia

Armenia

Lake Van

Lake Urmia

Caria

Xanthos

Cilicia

Rhodes

M E D I T E R R A N E A N   S E A

Cyprus

Aleppo

Nineveh

Arbil

Assyria

Euphrates

Ugarit

S Y R I A

Arvad

Mari

LEBANON

Byblos

Phoenicia

Sidon

Tyre

⊙ Damascus

The Sea Peoples settled near Gaza after being defeated in a naval battle of 1180 by Ramesses III.

Acre

Megiddo

Jordan

ISRAEL

Jerusalem ⊙   ⊙ **Jericho**

Gaza

Palestine

Dead Sea

J O R D A N

I R A Q

Opis

Sippar

Babylon ●

Nippur

Babyloni

Babyloni

Tanis

Avaris

Lower Egypt

Heliopolis

Memphis

E G Y P T

KINGDOM OF EGYPT

Nile

Herakleopolis

→ migration of Sea Peoples, c.1180

Babylonian Empire, 597

Achemenid Persian Empire, 530

Kingdom of Egypt, 530

modern border

IRAQ modern country

Arabia

S A U D I   A R A B I A

El-Amarna

Asyut

Akhmin

Abydos

R E D   S E A

Upper Egypt

Thebes

L O W E R   N U B I A

Votive table relief of Urnanshe, King of Lagash, c.2500 BC. The city-states of Sumer were in a constant state of war during this period, especially Lagash. This encouraged the growth of professional standing armies. It would not be long before they sought to take war toward the west.

U P P E R   N U B I A

S U D A N

K U S H

CHAPTER FOUR

Key Biblical Cities

...and all the store cities that Solomon had, and the cities for his chariots, and the cities for his horsemen, whatever Solomon desired to build in Jerusalem, and in Lebanon, and in all the land of his dominion.

1 Kings 9:19

The Bible is full of people whose faces, voices, and physical appearance we can only imagine. But the places they came from and traveled to are frequently mentioned in the Old Testament so it is these sites we must explore to get a better picture of the personalities and events we are seeking to know.

Many of the primary cities are in existence today. At the time of Abraham the city of Ur was at its peak in terms of influence and power. Lying southeast of Babylon it was not, strictly speaking, in the Holy Lands but it was from here that the Patriarch hailed. Using Ur as an anchor on the map we can see the great length of Abraham's journey into Canaan.

Jericho is best remembered as the town where Joshua and his marching men brought down the walls at the blast of a trumpet and a mighty shout. The Bible wants us to believe that faith was responsible for the astonishing feat. Whatever the truth of the story, it is accurate to state that Israelites of the day would have visited Jericho, a city that had already existed for thousands of years by this time and is indeed one of the world's oldest permanent settlements.

Damascus likes to stake its claim to be the oldest inhabited city in the world. It certainly features frequently throughout the Bible, as a site of King David's victory over the Assyrians, as an ally of Judah against Israel, and as the place where Paul sought shelter after his conversion to Christianity. But it was of secondary importance compared to Jerusalem, which was endowed with spiritual significance by King David in about 1000 BC. Thereafter, Jerusalem became the symbolic home of the Jewish people. By barring Jews from the city numerous tyrants reveled in a subtle yet devastating punishment.

Today, all of these cities have changed beyond recognition. The urban landscapes known prior to Jesus, for example, are now buried several feet beneath the modern conurbations, and are only revealed during the rare occasions when building works make archaeological excavation possible.

Media

IRAN

Elam

• Susa

KUWAIT

approximate position of ancient coastline

Persia

PERSIAN GULF

A Babylonian cylinder seal, c.1050 BC, shows a goddess or priestess leading a worshipper before deified King Ur-Nammu (*see page 61*), first of a dynasty of rulers who made Ur into a nation.

QATAR

Maka

UNITED ARAB EMIRATES

OMAN

1. Jerusalem

But the Jebusites, the inhabitants of Jerusalem, the people of Judah could not drive out, so the Jebusites dwell with the people of Judah at Jerusalem to this day.

Joshua 15:63

Jerusalem is a vital center of faith for Jews, Christians, and Muslims. Solomon built a temple here, long gone but still revered by Jews. Jesus was condemned to death in the city and crucified just outside its walls. And it was from Jerusalem that the Prophet Mohammed embarked on his inspiring Night Journey. Given the religious battles that have been waged over the city, it is hardly surprising that Jerusalem is known today as much for its religious conflict as for its sacred sites.

This divided but beautiful city—variously known in later times as City of David, Aelia Capitolina, Zion—has been in existence since about 3500 BC. Early settlers were probably drawn to it by the Gihon Spring, a healthy water supply that would sustain Jerusalem's future population through several sieges. The site also promised security, having valleys on three sides.

Jerusalem is identified in Egyptian records of about the 19th century BC by the name Rushalimum. Soon afterward its name appears as the coming together of two Canaanite words, *yru*, meaning foundation, and *Slm*, the name of a local god. Abraham, meanwhile, knew it as Shalem. According to the Tell el 'Amarna letters of the 14th century BC it was Urusalim and it is known by a similar word early in the Bible.

Joshua was unable to conquer the city, which was occupied by Jebusites who had constructed a sophisticated water storage system. Called Warren's Shaft, for Charles Warren, the 19th-century engineer who discovered it, its remnants are on the tourist trail today. Fortifications from the Jebusite age are visible in the vicinity. However, this same shaft may have been the weak spot David exploited when he captured the

Right: King David leading the procession of the Sacred Ark into Jerusalem. Detail from a 19th-century AD painting by Luigi Ademollo. The symbolic arrival of the Ark of the Covenant in the city conferred a capital status on Jerusalem, which afterward became known as the City of David.

city. David had promised great things of the first man to enter Jerusalem, and *2 Samuel 5:8* tells us that "Whoever gets up a tunnel and kills a Jebusite…" would receive the reward. Joab was the first, and was made Israel's general.

David united Jerusalem and the surrounding lands under one kingdom. After conquering the city, David made it his capital, and brought with him the Ark of the Covenant containing the Word of God, conferring sacredness on Jerusalem. Thereafter Jerusalem became religiously crucial, even more so after David's son Solomon built the First Temple.

When the realm divided into Israel and Judah, Jerusalem remained the capital of Judah. It withstood attacks by Shishak, pharaoh of Egypt, in 925 BC (*see page 38*) and Sennacherib, king of Assyria, in 701 BC (*see page 39*). To fend off the Assyrians homes were torn down and the stones used to fortify the city. Remains of the Broad Wall can still be seen today.

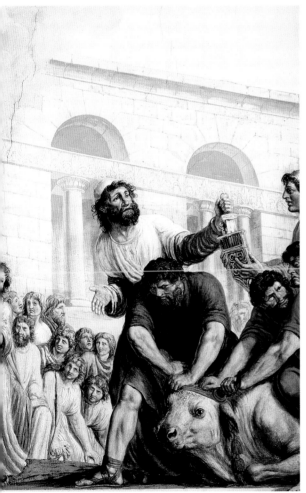

King Hezekiah commissioned another defensive measure against the Assyrians, one that diverted irrigation from the valley beyond the city into the fortifications and denied the Assyrians access to a fresh water supply. Accordingly a tunnel measuring 1,750 feet was constructed, cut from both ends simultaneously, to connect the spring with a large new storage pool. An inscription was discovered in 1880 relating to this astonishing engineering feat. "The hewers hacked each toward the other, ax against ax, and the water flowed from the spring to the pool, a distance of 1,200 cubits…" The inscription was itself hewn from the rock and is now held in a museum in Istanbul.

But despite the steps taken, Jerusalem was not sufficiently protected to fend off the acquisitive King Nebuchadnezzar of Babylon during his extensive forays in the Middle East in 586 BC (*see page 40*). Nebuchadnezzar burned down the First Temple and forcibly removed the Jewish population, condemning them to years of misery abroad.

Above: A tourist clambers down steep steps in the entrance to the top of Warren's Shaft (seen in plan below) which connects the Gihon Spring to the city of Jerusalem. This was in use by the time of David and may have been the route used to assault the Jebusite city. Its water supply may also have been the reason why Joshua was earlier unable to win a siege of Jerusalem.

entrance

Jebusite wall

cave

water level

Warren's Shaft

Gihon Spring

Jerusalem—Crossroads of Culture and Religion

I was glad when they said to me, "Let us go to the house of the Lord!" Our feet have been standing within your gates, O Jerusalem! Jerusalem built as a city that is bound firmly together.

Psalm 122:1–2

Below: A Christian Holy Bible sits on a corner ledge overlooking Old Jerusalem. The image neatly sums up the importance of the city to many faiths: Islamic mosques jostle with Greek Orthodox and Roman Catholic basilicas and spires, most sitting atop ancient Hebrew sacred centers.

In Jerusalem the differences between the three monotheistic faiths are striking. Additionally, each one acts as an umbrella for numerous offshoots. The Orthodox Jews, for example, have quite different practices to Reform Jews. The Druze, originally from Lebanon, hold views that are distinct from those of mainstream Muslims, while the sects of Christianity in the city include Lutheran, Armenian, Coptic, Ethiopian, Syrian, Russian, and Greek. Represented within the city walls is the spiritual life of many forms of the Abrahamic faiths, and their places of worship.

Architecturally Jerusalem is also a blend of different times and trends. The city has been conquered at least 18 times and has probably witnessed more destruction over time than any single location in the world. It had already been rebuilt on many occasions by the time of Jesus.

By 538 BC Persia had come under the enlightened kingship of Cyrus the Great who organized the re-population of Jerusalem. Its walls were rebuilt and daily life resumed its rhythm. In 515 BC the Second Temple was consecrated, giving Jerusalem a fresh spiritual impetus.

It is said that Alexander the Great visited the city in 332 BC. Certainly the Hellenistic influence infiltrated, giving a new slant to its culture. Jerusalem came under fire again in 169 BC, this time from Antiochus IV Epiphanes, King of Seleukid Syria, who plundered and pillaged at will, ultimately outlawing Judaism. Two years later the Maccabean revolt brought about a new lease of life for the Temple and its faith. Just over 100 years later Pompey brought in the Roman army, permitting Jewish worship and customs but nonetheless stamping Roman political authority upon the city.

Under Herod the Great, the Jewish king installed by Rome, vast building plans were instigated, not least at the site of the second Temple. He enlarged and elaborated the existing building, extending the Temple Mount on which it stood. A Biblical source claims it took 46 years to finish the job. This opulent and overwhelmingly extravagant building was the Temple visited by Jesus, who witnessed with horror the sacrifice of animals, the payment of the annual Temple tax, and the additional

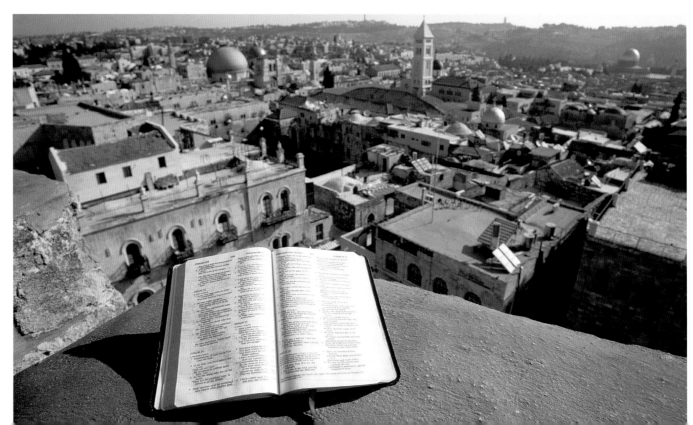

"second tithe," offered by pilgrims. Its courtyards jangled with the sound of shekels being counted.

Jerusalem may have been stifled by rigid religious laws and under occupation but it was still relatively peaceful and productive. But new scars were inflicted with the Jewish Revolt that began in AD 66 and culminated in the siege of Jerusalem four years later. The Temple was leveled, leaving only the Western Wall as a token place of pilgrimage for Jews. The Western—or Wailing—Wall, standing at some 59 feet high remains a focus of a Jewish faith that still mourns the loss of its most holy venue. Afterward, the role of the synagogue in Jewish worship was radically elevated in terms of maintaining the faith's identity and continuity.

Roman and Byzantine city

A further rebellion in AD 135 prompted the Emperor Hadrian to close Jerusalem to the Jews. He renamed it Aelia Capitolina and it became a model Roman city. Between the second and sixth centuries the city was tattooed with grid-like thoroughfares, known as the Cardo. Like other Roman roads, there were accompanying colonnades. Excavations have turned up street paving and pillars. In the fourth century the Roman Empire embraced Christianity and, although the empire split in two, Jerusalem remained under Christian control for more than 300 years during which time a plethora of churches marking its associations with Jesus, his family, and other martyrs were put up. Numerous pilgrims visited the city and there was also a great building program of monasteries.

Among the finest of the Byzantine churches was the Nea (New) church built for the Byzantine Emperor Justinian (r.527–65). One account of it left to history says: "The size of this holy building, its radiant glory, and the richness of its decorations are too monumental for me to describe." Completed in 543, its fate is unknown, except to say that it crumbled to earth. Historians became aware of its existence only through literature and the Madaba map. But when tenements built for Jews in 1862 were damaged in the 1967 war, artifacts of the Nea church were discovered. While archaeological finds from the church have been limited workmen have traced the church outline,

measuring 328 feet by 171 feet.

The Cathedral of St. James, the holiest place of worship for the (dwindling) Armenian community, is said to stand on the spot where Herod Agrippa I, grandson of Herod the Great, beheaded St. James with a sword. The building dates from Crusader times. The Armenian Patriarch resides next-door.

Above: Solomon's Wall, oil painting by Jean-Leon Gerome c.1870. After the Roman closure of Jerusalem to Jews, Solomon's (or the Western) Wall became known as the Wailing Wall, an enduring focus of Jewish faith.

Left: A Roman relief on display in the Jerusalem Museum depicts the sack of Jerusalem by Titus's troops in AD 70. The Romans can be seen bearing away the holy menorah of the Temple.

Jerusalem—Temple Mount and Dome of the Rock

Now the Passover of the Jews was at hand, and many went up from the country to Jerusalem before the Passover to purify themselves.

John 11:55

Below: The Dome of the Rock was erected between AD 690–92 by the Umayyad caliph 'Abd al-Malik for three reasons: first to claim Abraham for Islam; second to symbolize the defeat of the Byzantine and Persian empires; third to inform both Christians and Jews that Islam had superseded their revelations, and was the Final Truth.

After the destruction of the temple the site was left as wasteland. Christians were keen that it should be so because Jesus had prophesied to Jews: "Behold your house is left unto you desolate."

Julian the Apostate (r.AD 361–3), a close relative of Constantine the Great but an avowed pagan, gave permission for Jews to rebuild the temple. His aim was to destabilize Christianity, which he regarded as destructive. To encourage the Jews he promised to build and populate Jerusalem "which for many years you have yearned to see settled by yourselves, and together with you I shall give glory to the very great God." Despite attracting investment and manpower aplenty, the project came to nothing.

It is said Jews on-site were scared off by a conflagration (probably caused by combustible gases that had collected in underground chambers and ignited on being released). The death of Julian shortly afterward consigned the scheme to failure. After this the site of the temple became a dumping ground for the city's refuse until the arrival of Islam.

Byzantine designers and craftsmen built the Dome of the Rock, or Haram-es-Sherif, meaning the noble sanctuary. As desert nomads, the Arabs lacked the necessary expertise. The bluish building is octagonal, with each outer wall measuring 67 feet, matching precisely the Dome's diameter and its height from the base. It is decorated with mosaics and tiles, some of which are originals and some replacements lovingly copied by the craftsmen of Suleiman the Magnificent in 1545.

The Dome looks the same today as it always has, a beautiful example of architecture with a reflective dome that is immediately identifiable on the city skyline. On the outside the Dome

was originally colored by copper but is now covered in gold leaf, thanks to the late King Hussein of Jordan. Within, the Dome's décor is elaborate and exotic, with inscriptions dedicated to Saladin, who helped to restore the masterpiece following the Crusades.

While the city is not mentioned in the Koran, this is the third most holy site of Islam, after Mecca and Medina. The Dome encloses a mighty rock from which, say Muslims, the Prophet Mohammed departed from earth to heaven upon his steed al-Burak at the end of his "night flight." This same boulder is thought by Jews to be the Foundation Stone, the symbolic bedrock on which the world was created and the place where Isaac was bound by his father Abraham for sacrifice. Theories also exist about it being the last spot on earth touched by God's foot and that Adam is buried beneath it.

Thus the Dome's site is riven with duality. Built on foundations laid by, or prior to, Herod, many of those who visit the Dome feel the shadow of the Temple upon them.

The Dome of the Rock overshadows its fellow mosque, the nearby silver domed El-Aqsa, although they were built only 20 years apart. The first El Aqsa mosque was wooden but it was replaced in the early eighth century by the Ummayad Caliph el-Walid, subsequently damaged by an earthquake in AD 747, then rebuilt by the Abbasids. In 1099, to the consternation of Muslims, crusaders occupied the mosque. First the Christian kings stayed there, then it was handed over to the elite Knights Templar, a pious group formed to protect pilgrims on their journey to the Holy Land. They built a façade that was altered by the Egyptian Mamluks when they took control of the city after 1265. Inside there are ranks of marble columns donated by 20th-century Italian fascist dictator Benito Mussolini. A carved *minibar* (pulpit) dating from Saladin's time went up in flames in 1969 at the hands of an arsonist. A further three mosques stand on Haram-es-Sherif, or what Jews know as Temple Mount.

Crusader atrocities

When crusaders captured Jerusalem in 1099 they slaughtered Jewish and Muslim residents, such was Christian intolerance at the time. The slaughter was partly inspired by their passion for Jerusalem, as revealed in William of Tyre's

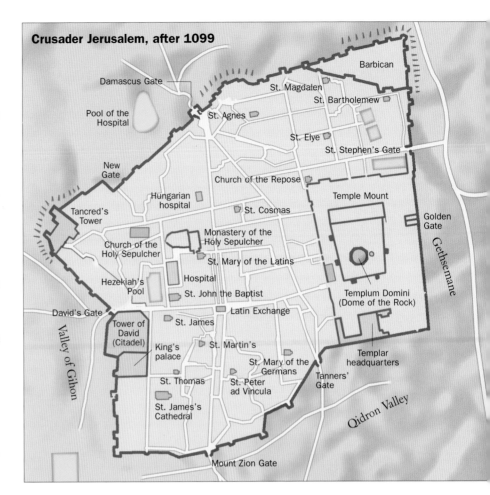

Crusader Jerusalem, after 1099

description of their reaction on arrival. "When they heard the name Jerusalem called out they began to weep and fell on their knees, giving thanks to Our Lord with many sighs for the great love which He had shown them in allowing them to reach the goal of their pilgrimage, the Holy City. It was deeply moving to see the tears and hear the loud sobs of these good folk."

In crusader times Jerusalem was marked by four main gates according to a description by an anonymous pilgrim written in about 1150 and bequeathed to future generations in the Cambrai manuscript. "In the city of Jerusalem there are four principal gates, in the shape of a cross, one opposite the other... David's Gate faces west and stands exactly opposite the Golden gate which faces east... this gate belongs to the Tower of David and is therefore called David's Gate." He confirmed that, as today, the road between the Tower of David and the Golden Gate is called David Street.

At the moment eight gates are discernible in the Old City walls, including Damascus Gate, built by Suleiman the Great in the 16th century. However it seems likely the impressive edifice was constructed at a point that had long been used as an entrance or exit to the city. One gate has been symbolically walled up by Muslims to prevent a Jewish Messiah from entering.

Sacred to Mohammed

There are problems with the generally accepted view that the Dome of the Rock was built to commemorate the Prophet Mohammed's miraculous night-time journey from Mecca to Jerusalem, where he prayed before his ascension to Heaven on the celestial animal Buraq. Many early Islamic scholars simply did not accept that the place where the Prophet prayed that night was, in fact, Jerusalem.

Jerusalem—Stations of the Cross

…and [Jesus] said to them, "Thus it is written, that the Christ should suffer, and on the third day rise from the dead, and that repentance and forgiveness of sins should be proclaimed in his name to all nations, beginning at Jerusalem."

Luke 24:46–47

Below: A Good Friday procession enters the Church of the Holy Sepulcher. The church also incorporates a Greek Orthodox monastery on the roof.

So important to Jews was Jerusalem, that Jesus knew it was imperative to take his teachings into the city. Likewise, he was sure there would be conflict with the authorities that could spell his doom.

The Via Dolorosa, or Way of Sorrows, is allegedly the route taken by Jesus from his trial before Pontius Pilate to Calvary, where he was crucified. However, a cloud of doubt hangs over the claims that the Via Dolorosa is the authentic route. Pilgrims keen to follow in Christ's footsteps are undaunted by the fact that the supposed path has changed several times over the centuries, for at least it remains a reflection of the final journey taken by Jesus and adequately demonstrates images of the suffering involved.

The route has 14 Stations of the Cross, each linked to a part of the story, and stretches between the Muslim and Christian quarters of the city. Jesus was told at the Roman fortress that he was to die. The site became the Monastery of the Flagellation and is now within the boundaries of a Mamluk college, Madrasa el-Omariyya, which is the First Station.

Then comes the emotive point where Jesus took up the cross, having been flogged and crowned with thorns. This, the Second Station, falls outside the Monastery of the Flagellation, a Franciscan complex containing a striking chapel designed in the 1920s by the Italian architect Antonio Barluzzi. (The Chapel of Condemnation nearby, which dates from the 20th century, was constructed on the site of a medieval chapel once commemorated as the spot where Christ was given the capital sentence.)

At the Third Station, where Jesus stumbled beneath the weight of the cross, there is a small chapel, while at the Fourth, the point where he met his mother, Mary, there is the Armenian Church of Our Lady of the Spasm, built over an earlier crusader church. A Franciscan oratory marks the Fifth Station, where Simon of Kyrene was ordered by frustrated soldiers to heave the cross onward. The Chapel of St. Veronica denotes the Sixth Station, named for a woman who wiped Jesus' labored brow with a cloth and came away with an imprint of his face.

Another Franciscan chapel, this one containing a Roman column, marks the Seventh Station, where Jesus fell a second time. A cross on the wall of a Greek Orthodox monastery indicates the Eighth Station, where Jesus comforted the weeping women of Jerusalem. At the third spot, where Jesus fell, there now stands an Ethiopian monastery.

Rock of Golgotha

The final five Stations all fall within the Church of the Holy Sepulcher, perhaps the most important church in the Christian world. The Roman Emperor and Christian convert Constantine built a sprawling basilica between AD 326–35, at the urging of his devout mother, Helena. Tradition dictates that Helena (who later became a saint) found the True Cross at this site. Within its walls lay the probable Rock of Golgotha, which is Hebrew for "place of the skull," where stood the crucifixion cross.

The First Station

Critics believe a more likely starting point for Jesus' final journey is the Citadel, sometimes known as the Tower of David or Herod's Palace. At the time it was a royal palace and the likely residence of Pontius Pilate. No one knows just what it looked like through Jesus' eyes. It had been constructed in the second century BC by the Hasmonean dynasty but was modified beyond recognition after that. Herod the Great built a defensive tower that existed at the time of the Crucifixion but it was demolished by Hadrian in AD 135, only to be rebuilt 12 centuries later. There are Byzantine contributions to the walls, Islamic additions by the Mamluks, and a triple-arched gateway from the 16th century.

There is also the tomb of Christ, marked by a marble slab installed in 1555 during the reconstruction of a shrine that had long since marked the spot.

Constantine's beloved building was destroyed by Islamic forces in 1009 but subsequently rebuilt in the 1040s by a Byzantine emperor. His project was enlarged by the crusaders until their expulsion from Jerusalem in 1170. A fire in 1808 and an earthquake in 1927 means that today's church is a damaged building, although still impressive in appearance. A Muslim holds the keys to the church, a tradition rooted in history.

No one has proved for sure that this is indeed the site of the crucifixion but archaeology has indicated that it once lay outside the city walls, as a place of execution surely would have done. Golgotha was brought within the city walls after building work carried out in AD 43. There is archaeological evidence that rock-cut tombs were made here during the first century.

Left: Small stores line the Via Dolorosa near the Church of the Holy Sepulcher.

Stations of the Cross, numbered in map below
1 Jesus is condemned to death
2 Jesus receives Cross
3 Jesus falls 1st time
4 Jesus meets mother
5 Simon made to bear Cross
6 Veronica wipes Jesus' face
7 Jesus falls 2nd time
8 Jesus meets women of Jerusalem
9 Jesus falls 3rd time
10 Jesus stripped of garments
11 Jesus nailed to Cross
12 Jesus dies on Cross
13 Jesus taken down from Cross
14 Jesus laid in tomb

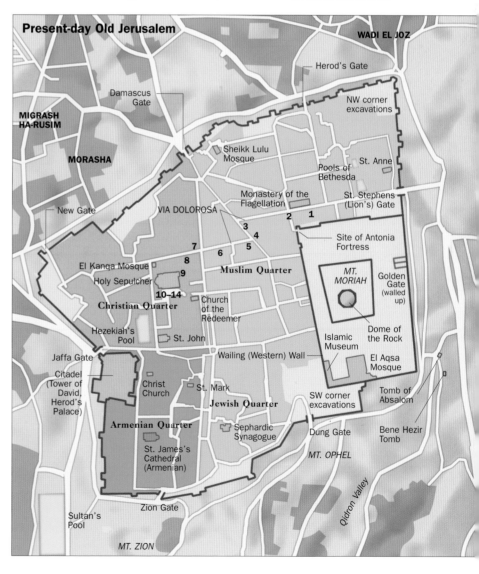

Jerusalem—Outside the City Wall

Then they returned to Jerusalem from the mount called Olivet, which is near Jerusalem, a Sabbath day's journey away.

Acts 1:12

Below: Mishkenot Sha'ananim was the first Jewish district established outside Jerusalem's city walls in the modern era. Completed in 1860, it was a symbol of the Jews' desire to return to their homeland. Photographed in the 1870s, a tinsmith works with his young apprentice.

Jerusalem has become a by-word for everything great and glorious. Through the ages it was lionized for the history that lies within its city walls. Its reputation overseas was enhanced by crusaders and pilgrims alike, although there was probably nothing exalted about living in the Old City in medieval times.

There is history in abundance lying outside the sun-bleached stone walls. There is the Tomb of Absalom, a magnificent monument in the Qidron Valley, supposedly built by Absalom, son of David. The Biblical reference is in *2 Samuel 18:18: Now Absalom in his lifetime had taken and set up for himself the pillar that is in the King's Valley, for he said, "I have no son to keep my name in remembrance." And he called the pillar after his own name, and it is called Absalom's monument to this day.* The Bible also states that Absalom was not buried there. Absalom was the rebellious son who has earned the contempt of Jews, Christians, and Muslims alike. Consequently passers-by would throw stones at the monument until it was virtually submerged. In 1925 the stones were cleared away and the monument restored.

There are numerous examples of rock-cut tombs around Jerusalem, like the Bene Hezir Tomb, also in Qidron Valley. An inscription in Hebrew identifies members of the priestly family of Hezir and it is presumed they were the occupants. Dated from the second century BC, the entrance is defined by two columns, and there are five burial chambers within. Local people believe this may be the place to which Azariah retired after contracting leprosy.

Landmarks for three faiths

The Garden tomb, lying northeast of the Damascus Gate, is thought by some Protestant denominations to be where Jesus was crucified and buried, but just who was laid to rest in these tombs is a matter of conjecture. There is an ancient tomb on the Mount of Olives which Jews are convinced belongs to Huldah the prophetess who lived in the time of King Josiah. Christians are certain it is where a converted dancing girl from Antioch known as Pelagia the Penitent was buried, while Muslims are sure a ninth-century holy woman of Islam is buried there.

The first Jewish neighborhood established outside the city walls was finished in 1860, one of the first concrete expressions of the Jewish desire to return to their homeland. The funds for construction at Mishkenot Sha'ananim came from Judah Touro, an American Jewish philanthropist, who paid for 16 apartments and two synagogues. There was a communal lavatory block and oven as well as a windmill to assist self-sufficiency. Alas, innovator Sir Moses Montefiore, who drew up the plans, failed to take into account the lack of wind in the Holy Land, which rendered the mill idle most of the time.

Olive trees live for hundreds or sometimes thousands of years, their gnarled barks winding slowly up through silver green leaves to weather storms and time. These same trees cling to the sides of the Mount of Olives and bear fruit in the Garden of Gethsemene, where Jesus spent his last hours before being arrested. The trees are almost, but not quite, outnumbered by the chapels and churches that today mark the Garden's religious links.

Above: In the Qidron Valley (*see map on previous page*) stands the Tomb of Absalom, son of King David, left, and the Tomb of Bene Hezir, right. This is also sometimes referred to as the tomb of the Old Testament prophet Zechariah. Beyond lies the vast Jewish cemetery which dominates the Mount of Olives. The Garden of Gethsemane is just to the north (left of picture).

2. Damascus

An oracle concerning Damascus. Behold, Damascus will cease to be a city and will become a heap of ruins.
Isiah 17:1

Is this the oldest city in the world? The argument about the "most ancient" title rages on, with Jericho, Aleppo, and Damascus (or Dimashq) slugging it out, wielding claim and counter claim. Concerning Damascus, the evidence is compelling.

An urban center appears to have been in existence as early as the fourth millennium BC at Tell as-Salhiyah, to the southeast of the present city. Pottery dating from the third millennium has been found in the Old City, while there is evidence of an irrigation system in place by the second millennium. Some authorities suggest that settlement dates from the seventh millennium BC. However, there is no archaeological evidence to yield detail about those early days. It is probably all buried beneath existing monuments that are too ancient and valuable to be tampered with.

In the days of Abraham, Damascus was evidently a busy and important city. Egyptian records from the 14th and 15th centuries BC reveal "Dimashqa" listed as a conquered territory. The tribesmen living there were the Semitic Aramaeans, their language being Aramaic. Historically, Damascus was an enemy of Israel.

Ancient armies belonging to Assyrians, Babylonians, and Persians came and went. Like most of the surrounding swathes of land, Damascus fell to Alexander the Great and his arrival signaled 250 years of Greek domination.

Although the locals adopted Hellenistic customs there is little in today's city that marks its Greek associations. The Nabataeans and Armenians snatched brief spells of mastery in Damascus before Roman conquest in 64 BC. As an important Roman city Damascus knew sufficient stability to swell and prosper.

Cradle of Christianity

It was to this booming Damascus that Saul went in AD 34, a Pharisee or Orthodox Jew who had witnessed the stoning to death of Stephen in Jerusalem, and was intent on crushing the new Christian religion before it gained more converts in the city.

Famously, on the road that led to Damascus Saul encountered Jesus himself, was blinded by the great light, and converted to Christianity. Shortly afterward he was baptized with the

name Paul in the city by a resident called Ananias, who also cured his blindness. Later, when the Orthodox Jews discovered Paul had become a Christian they sought revenge. Paul became a fugitive and was lowered from the top of the city walls to safety. An Abyssinnian

Right: Funerary mask of the 1st century AD from the Damascene Roman period.

Facing above: A manuscript illumination of 1526 depicts St. Paul escaping Damascus by being lowered from the walls in a basket.

Facing below: Godfried Kempesen's map of Damascus, c.1580, showing the major buildings.

guard, already converted to Christianity, helped Paul and was subsequently put to death. The tomb of this man, now canonized as St. George of Abyssinia and revered by Christians, lies close to the city walls.

Roman Damascus was distinguished by a large thoroughfare known as the Via Recta or Straight Street, going from east to west between grand arches. Sadly, the arches crumbled along with Roman hegemony (although Arab gates replaced them), as did much of the colonnade that ran alongside. It is interesting to note that the ground level of the city has risen some 15 feet since Paul's time on the rubble of its former glory. Only when workmen demolish houses are the remains of Roman architecture discovered and retrieved.

Probably the oldest monument standing in Damascus is the Roman Gate of the Sun, built in the early third century AD. The lower parts of the city walls belong to Roman times while upper parts were added later by Arabs and Ottomans. Under Byzantine rule, a clutch of churches was built but the remains of only six are obvious today.

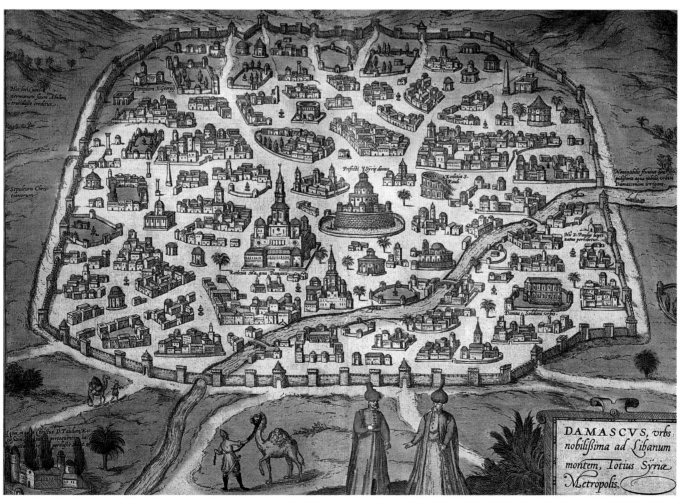

Damascus—A City Worth Fighting For

And when the Syrians of Damascus came to help Hadadezer king of Zobah, David struck down 20,000 men of the Syrians.

2 Samuel 8:5

Damascus is close to the border of Israel and Lebanon, and also the Syrian Desert. Nestled in a fertile valley as befits an oasis, the city is picturesque with orchards and gardens, prompting local Bedouins to call it "Pearl of the East" or "Necklace on the Throat of Beauty."

Perhaps for this reason Damascus was among one of the first conquests of Islam. In AD 636 Khaled Ibn al-Walid, "Sword of God," and his men marched into the city. Residents were so weary of the squabbling empires and border wars that the invaders were welcomed. The Ummayad Caliph was so delighted with his new acquisition that he made Damascus the capital of the Muslim world.

But when the Ummayads were eventually deemed too self-indulgent, a new dynasty rose to power, the Abbasids, and took over. They transferred the capital status to Baghdad, leaving Damascus exposed to the attentions of Muslim dynasties, tyrants, and empires. Before doing so they tore down many of the Ummayad buildings, the memory of which is left only in written records. Despite this, there was a surprising amount of religious tolerance and all the key faiths survived in the city.

The changing nature of faith is amply illustrated in Damascus. A temple dedicated to the Roman god Jupiter was built on the site of a shrine to Hadad, a Babylonian god of storm. The Roman temple gave way to a Christian church in honor of John the Baptist. Now a

Below: Courtyard of the Umayyad Mosque, also known as the Great Mosque, in Damascus. The building has undergone many alterations since it sat at the heart of the earliest Arabic empire.

mosque built in the early eighth century, shortly after the Dome of the Rock, occupies the spot. Once outrageously ornate, the mosque's construction took seven years' of state revenue. When the governor was shown the financial record, carried on the back of 18 camels, he stoutly said: "Truly we have spent this for Allah and we will make no account of it."

Unfortunately much of the costly mosaic work was lost when the courtyard was re-tiled in the 11th century and repaved with marble in the 19th century. The Great Mosque has been subject to fire and assault yet still stands proud in the city.

If only it could talk, the mosque would tell of riots and revolutions, rivalry and invasion—and all this before the crusaders rolled up in the Middle East in the last half of the tenth century. Damascus was besieged during the Second Crusade—although the initiative failed at the city gates—then the city became the headquarters of Saladin, scourge of the crusaders, who was buried in Damascus following his death in 1193.

Mongol onslaught

Successors among the Ayyubids, the dynasty Saladin founded, were unable to emulate his decisive rule and were riven with petty disputes. Damascus was so weakened it was left unable to withstand an assault in 1260 by the Mongol Tartars, who were themselves shortly driven out by the Egyptian Mamluks under the command of Baibars. The Mamluk general defeated the Mongols at the cataclysmic battle near Nazareth of Ain Jalut (Goliath's Spring, the traditional site of David's victory over the Philistines).

Almost all the architectural additions by the Ayyubids and the Mamluks were reduced to cinders in an onslaught by the Mongol warlord Tamerlane in 1401. He left only when the

Above: This fine example of the incised decoration known as Damascene is from the Byzantine period. The chalice is decorated with images of Christ and Mary.

surviving residents rallied a ransom of one million pieces of gold. He then took the city's skilled artisans in bondage back to his capital of Samarkand. Even the Citadel was badly damaged although it was substantially restored in the 20th century.

Exhausted by the excesses of Tamerlane, Damascus proved easy pickings for the Ottoman Empire, which took control in 1516 and did not relinquish the reigns of power there until 1918. Politically the city was weak but commercially it went from strength to strength. From the Ottomans the city gained the Tkiyyeh mosque, designed by the same architect as the famous Suleimaniye in Istanbul, and the Azem palace, built in 1749 on a grand scale by Assad Pasha al Azem, Ottoman governor and bon viveur. Assad also built some of the khans or warehouses still visible in Damascus.

However, Ottoman rule did not end the city's history of bloodshed. The Indian Mutiny of 1857 against British rule inspired the Muslims in Syria to attempt a revolution of their own. In 1860 more than 6,000 Christians were slaughtered in Damascus, with numerous women and girls being taken as sex slaves. Three hundred people who sought sanctuary in the church died when it was burned to the ground. The church was later rebuilt as the Greek Orthodox Patriarchal Church of the Virgin Mary. It took a French force comprising 10,000 men to restore order.

An Arabic proverb insists that art was born in Egypt, grew in Aleppo, and came to Damascus to die. The craftspeople of Damascus have long been famous for their etching and inlaying in gold and silver. *Damascene* is still used to describe this excellent workmanship. Damascus also has a reputation for making pearl jewelry and embellished lace.

3. Ur of the Chaldees

…they went forth together from Ur of the Chaldeans
to go into the land of Canaan.

Genesis 11:31

TURKEY
IRAQ
SYRIA
SAUDI ARABIA

ZAGROS MOUNTAINS
IRAN
• Bagdhad
AKKAD
Tigris
• Babylon
• Susa
Lagash •
ELAM
SUMER
Ur ○
IRAQ
**Approximate
position of
ancient
coastline**
KUWAIT
*PERSIAN
GULF*
SAUDI ARABIA
Euphrates

T he city identified by the Bible as Abraham's original home is Ur, now in southern Iraq. In the Bible it is known as Ur of the Chaldees after the powerful dynasty that settled there and helped destroy the Assyrian Empire in about 900 BC. But in Abraham's day (c.1900 BC) it was a wealthy, cosmopolitan city of the Mesopotamian region coveted by perpetually warring kings.

Long before Abraham migrated west to establish the Hebrew nation in Canaan, Ur was a thriving independent kingdom. The city was founded c.5000 BC by settlers known as Ubaidians but this population gradually absorbed Semite tribes from the Syrian and Arabian deserts and Sumerian immigrants from the northeast. It was this last group that became dominant, bequeathing the region its main language, the cuneiform writing system and, according to some historians, the wheel. The limited evidence crediting Sumer with this invention comes from a picture symbol dating to c.3500 BC which shows a wheeled sled.

Ancient superpower

Sumerian records reveal three royal dynasties at Ur which, over seven centuries, controlled the region to a varying extent. The first was the warrior king Mes-Anni-Padda who came to power about 2670 BC. He was an enthusiastic builder and it was his heir A-Anni-Padda who constructed the magnificent temple of the goddess Ninhursag at Tell al-Obeid, some five miles northeast of Ur. The successors of these

Right: Ziggurats were the preferred form of Sumerian religious architecture. They are made of mud bricks and appear as giant, stepped mounds topped by a temple or sanctuary. The best preserved is this ziggurat of Ur-Nammu at Ur which honored the city's principal deity, the moon god Nanna. Erected in 2100 BC, it was extensively remodeled by the last king of Babylonia, Nabonidus, in the mid-6th century.

kings were overthrown by the Akkadian Empire.

Very little is known about the second royal dynasty but by the emergence of the third, c.2100 BC, Ur was approaching the zenith of its wealth and influence. Under the first king of this era, Ur-Nammu, it became a flourishing center of art, architecture, and literature and with what was then the adjacent outlet of the Persian Gulf (due to silting, Ur now lies some 150 miles from the sea), it increased trade opportunities. Ur-Nammu's dynasty lasted until shortly before 2000 BC when Elamites from what is now the Iranian province of Khuzistan took control (*see next page*).

Much of our knowledge of Ur comes from the spectacular discoveries of Sir Leonard Woolley, a British archaeologist who excavated its royal, religious, and residential buildings between 1922–34, and his colleagues from the University of Pennsylvania. There was much excitement when, during one deep sounding, Woolley came across the remnants of huts and decorated pottery belonging to the city's first, sixth millennium BC inhabitants. These finds were buried in a six-foot thick layer of river silt and were seized on by some Biblical historians as proof of the Great Flood and the story of Noah's Ark.

The problem with this theory is that

The Tower of Babel

Ziggurats represent the holy mountains of worship—heights closer to God—of nomadic wanderers. When Mesopotamia became settled and urbanized, these temples were raised high above the alluvial plain. To the still-nomadic Hebrew tribes, the towers were anathema. *Genesis* tells us that after the Flood, all people spoke the same language, and raised a tower to reach Heaven to symbolize their co-operation. But this arrogance displeased Yahweh and he confused their language so they could no longer understand one another. Then he "scattered them thence all over the world and they stopped building their city" (*Genesis 11:8*). *Babel* (Gate of God) probably refers to Babylon, but is also a Hebrew pun on *balal*, which means "to confuse." To the Jews, the story illustrated the futility of humankind's attempts to challenge God's supremacy. It also explains the existence of many different languages.

hundreds of subsequent digs across the Middle East have failed to find an all-encompassing flood strata in the soil. This indicates that the flood at Ur was very much a local disaster. Most archaeologists now believe the silt was deposited by the Euphrates changing its course along the marshy estuary plain. However Mesopotamian mythology also carries stories of a Great Flood and arguments over this are now more about the scale, frequency, and location of floods rather than the literal truth of the Bible.

Ur—Ritual Killing and Sacrifice

By faith Abraham obeyed when he was called to go out to a place that he was to receive as an inheritance. And he went out, not knowing where he was going.

Hebrews 11:8

Below: The historic purpose of the Standard of Ur, c.2500 BC, is unknown, but it received its name from Woolley, who thought it was carried on a pole as a standard. Its four panels depict soldiers leading prisoners to their king, and commoners bringing the fruits of their labor as gifts.

Sir Leonard Woolley's greatest work at Ur focused on the Royal Cemetery—a series of underground, vaulted caverns entered via a pit or ramp. Here he laid bare the extraordinary wealth of the city rulers who, fortunately for archaeologists, demanded that their most prized possessions accompany them to the grave and the afterlife. This convention extended to slaves and servants—even horses—all apparently sacrificed as part of the burial ritual.

One grave contained the remains of 68 female and six male attendants, laid neatly in rows, still wearing their finest courtly garments. Another tomb had its outer entrance protected by sacrificed soldiers carrying weapons and drivers placed with oxen and carts. Nine women with gold headdresses were slaughtered and arranged in the burial chamber to attend to the king's personal needs. However tempting the promises of glory, their thoughts as they assembled in the death-pit are not difficult to imagine.

Among the most important tombs were those of Meskalamdug, Akalamdug, the queen Pu-abi and other monarchs of the mid-third millennium BC—all identified by stone cuneiform etchings. The fabulous objects arrayed beside them attest to the wealth and influence that Ur then enjoyed, the skills of its craftsmen, and the wide reach of its trading links.

Priceless artifacts

The most celebrated items recovered are the so-called Standard of Ur, an inlaid wooden panel in which scenes of war and peace are portrayed in lapis lazuli (a blue gemstone) and

mother-of-pearl, and the electrum helmet of Meskalamdug. Woolley restored one lyre decorated with a gold bull's head and another which depicted animals playing musical instruments. Alongside these priceless artifacts lay many fine examples of gold and silver jewelry, ostrich eggs inlaid with asphalt, seals made of semi-precious stones, cosmetic jars, and intricately inlaid gaming boards.

Bible scholars make much of Abraham's faith in leaving behind a city of comparative comfort and security to journey with his wife Sarah, father Terah, and nephew Lot into the unknown. Faith there may well have been, but the idea that Ur was a safe haven at the start of the second millennium BC is questionable. Even allowing for the unreliability of Bbiblical dates we know that throughout this period it was a prize coveted by rival powers.

In c.2004 BC, the Elamite army captured Ur's ruler, King Ibbi-Sin, and sacked the city. It was rebuilt soon afterward and became part of first the Isin, then the Larsa kingdom. Later it was incorporated into Babylonia and was an important religious center under the Kassites.

The last Babylonian king, Nabonidus (r.556–39 BC), made his eldest daughter the city's high priestess and lavished much of his wealth on temple-building, remodeling the ziggurat of Ur-Nammu (*see previous page*) to rival even Babylon's magnificent temple of Marduk. But by the fourth century BC Ur's influence had waned and it became little more than an outpost of the Persian Empire.

Though most historians agree that Woolley's team unearthed ruins of the "real" Ur, there remains some debate over the legitimacy of this location. The Bible offers little help; apart from the Chaldean link the only additional information comes from St. Stephen, who implies that the city is in Mesopotamia. Other ancient texts identify the city with Urfa, near the Armenian tablelands, Warka, 120 miles southeast of Babylon, and a settlement known to the Greeks as Orchoe. Like so many sites on the edge of written history, Ur guards its secrets jealously.

Above: Constant war between Sumer's city-states spurred development of military technique far beyond that found elsewhere at the time. The first war for which there is any detailed evidence was between Lagash and neighboring Umma in 2525 BC. Afterward, Eannatum of Lagash erected a stele (Stele of Vultures) to celebrate his victory. This panel shows that Sumerian troops fought in phalanx formation, suggesting training and discipline.

4. Jericho

> As soon as the people heard the sound of the trumpet, the people shouted a great shout, and the wall fell down flat, so that the people went up into the city…
>
> *Joshua 6:20*

The conquest of Jericho by Joshua and his invading Israelite army is among the Old Testament's most compelling stories. Most Christian schoolchildren learn how the Israelites marched seven times around the city walls before demolishing them with a shout and the blast of a trumpet. The cause of the collapse involves the usual, irreconcilable, battle of faith versus skepticism; either you believe the hand of God was at work or you suspect more prosaic causes, such as earthquakes, sabotage, or fanciful storytelling.

The archaeology of the city pre-dates the Old Testament by many thousands of years. The site was first settled at the end of the last Ice Age—roughly 10,500–8500 BC—when the Stone Age Natufian culture was dominant in Palestine. These people were among the first experimental farmers, using wheat and barley to supplement their traditional hunter-gatherer lifestyle. Their characteristic round dwellings consisted of a single room partly dug into the ground and they built semi-permanent villages housing several hundred people.

The Neolithic (New Stone) Age, began around 8500 BC and heralded advanced stone tool technology with polished axes. For many years archaeologists believed that pot production and farming emerged side by side but evidence from Jericho and other early sites worldwide shows that crop cultivation sometimes got under way before pottery was invented. To highlight the apparent anomaly of food-growing people who had no pots, this period became known as Pre-Pottery Neolithic (PPN). This has in turn been sub-divided into PPN-A (8500–7300 BC) and PPN-B (7300–6300 BC).

Right: One of the painted, clay-encased skulls found in Jericho.

Excavations by Dame Kathleen Kenyon (*see next page*) of PPN-A Jericho produced some remarkable discoveries. She unearthed an 11.8-foot-high stone wall surrounding the 10-acre settlement along with a 30-foot-high tower constructed from solid stone and entered via a central staircase. This kind of engineering was completely unexpected and reshaped our perceptions of Neolithic society. Although Kenyon believed the stonework was essentially a defensive structure, recent theories link it to flood protection.

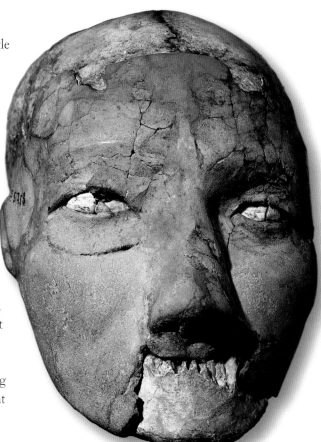

Israelite invasion

Early 20th-century archaeology has concentrated on establishing a date for Jericho's biblical destruction, since this would also fix the approximate time of the Exodus from Egypt and the Israelite invasion of Canaan. According to most Old Testament interpretations, the city's fall occurred sometime between 1400–1200 BC. Yet the chronology of Egypt and the Holy Land is notoriously insecure and the Bible itself gives contradictory accounts of what took place.

Right: The over-building of continuously populated Neolithic sites created low mounds (Tel). At the time of the Israelites' arrival Jericho's old walls had been enlarged. A massive bank of earth was raised on a supporting stone wall. The bank was as much as 66 feet wide and 46 feet high in some places. A mud-brick wall topped the rampart, which was faced with a layer of plaster to make a steep, slippery surface. A section of supporting wall—all that is left—can be seen in the picture below.

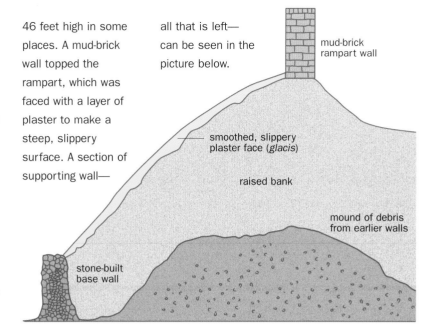

mud-brick rampart wall

smoothed, slippery plaster face (*glacis*)

raised bank

mound of debris from earlier walls

stone-built base wall

The book of *Joshua* tells how Joshua, as successor to Moses, led the twelve tribes of Israel across the Jordan to invade Canaan and claim the Promised Land. *Joshua 10:40* states: "So Joshua smote all the land, the hill country, and the South, and the Lowland, and the slopes, and all their kings; he left none remaining; but he utterly destroyed all that breathed."

Including Jericho? The above verse seems unequivocal. Yet in *Judges 1:27-33* a different picture emerges. Here we read how the Israelites left many cities untouched—among them Beth-shean, Taanach, Dor, Ibleam, Megiddo, Gezer, Kitron, Accho, Zidon, Ahlab, Achzib, Aphik, and Beth-shemesh—and lived in peace with the occupants. Most academics now believe the *Judges* account indicates no sudden conquest and that the Israelites were a semi-nomadic desert people who infiltrated Canaan over several generations, leading to occasional local conflicts. A third theory advocates a "peasants' uprising"— effectively a series of local revolutions against exploitative overlords (*see panel below*).

Unfortunately, repeated digs at Jericho have not produced a definitive answer. Palestinian history is heavily politicized and there are plenty of scholars prepared to make a slanted case either for or against Jewish claims. Of the evidence collected, four excavations, discussed in more detail overleaf, have set the agenda for future debate.

Exploited farmers

The derivation of the word *Hebrew* gives strength to the third argument of the "conquest" of Canaan by the Israelites, that this was an internal revolt by disaffected elements of the rural population. The Hebrews appear to have been associated with the *habiru*, a term that denotes groups that were in some (unknown) way outside society.

Jericho—Reconstructing the City

"Hear, O Israel: you are to cross the Jordan today, to go in to dispossess nations greater and mightier than yourself, cities great and fortified up to heaven."

Deuteronomy 9:1

Below: By the mid-19th century, when Charles Warren began exploratory excavation, Jericho was a village of little consequence. This photograph of c.1860–65 shows Jericho and the Jordan valley, looking north.

The words of Moses above seem designed to prepare Joshua's Israelites for a formidable enemy. Jericho was the first major Canaanite stronghold west of the Jordan, and the city's sky-high walls must have been a daunting prospect. Here was a fortress that could not be ignored. Its strategic position at the gateway to Canaan's heartlands demanded that it be taken.

If what the Bible says is true, archaeologists should have found abundant evidence of the sack of Jericho at Joshua's hands. Certainly they did find ruined walls and a thick layer of soot indicating a great fire. Yet the key question remains: can this material be dated to the period of the Israelite invasion?

Jericho was one the first cities in the Holy Land to be excavated. Some preparatory work was carried out in 1868 by a Victorian engineer called Charles Warren, and in 1907 two German archaeologists, Carl Watzinger and Ernest Sellin, began a three-year study which they hoped would validate the Biblical story of the tumbling walls. Initially they believed they had achieved this goal. Only in a subsequent analysis did they conclude that Jericho had long been a deserted ruin in the time of Joshua.

Twenty years later a new expedition was launched by the British archaeologist John

Garstang. Garstang uncovered a network of fallen walls which he dated to about 1400 BC—the time he believed the Israelites had invaded. He was dismissive of Watzinger and Sellin's main findings and stated categorically that archaeological evidence confirmed Biblical accounts of the fall of Jericho. "As to the main fact, then," he noted, "there remains no doubt: the walls fell outward so completely, the attackers would be able to clamber up and over the ruins of the city.

Garstang's arguments might hold more weight today if the excavation techniques he employed had been more sophisticated. His work also suffers from comparison to the meticulous studies of another Briton, Dame Kathleen Kenyon

Careful excavation

Kenyon's investigations at Jericho between 1952–58 remain a model of scientific analysis. She conducted a minute examination of the soil, carefully recording its stratification. She excavated a deep, narrow pit to produce a cross-section of the city's entire history. And where a large area had to be dug—say, the ground floor of a house—she kept within measured sample squares, ensuring that the strips between them preserved the original archaeological layer. Of the damaged areas she wrote: "The destruction was complete. Walls and floors were blackened or reddened by fire and every room was filled with fallen bricks."

Her work at Jericho provided a new insight into early farming settlements. She discovered a deeply buried tomb containing the beautifully painted clay-clad skulls of Neolithic inhabitants (*see page 64*). Crucially, she located the earliest, 10,000-year-old, walls and presented evidence to show that they had been re-built or repaired at least 17 times down the years, probably as a result of earthquake damage. The most recent wall—dated to 1400 BC by Garstang—was, she argued, actually 900 years older. According to Kenyon, Joshua's army would have found only a blackened, deserted shell of a city.

Kenyon's study, however admirable, has not settled the Jericho problem. In 1990, her findings were reviewed by the archaeologist Bryant Wood who insisted that she had overlooked the importance of an abundance of pottery shards found in the city. These matched pots known to be popular in 1400 BC. Moreover, carbon-14 tests on charcoal recovered from the old city produced a date of 1410 BC—right within Joshua's timeframe. While this proves nothing in itself, it is not yet possible for archaeology to dismiss the Biblical account of Jericho's demise.

Below: Archaeologists continue to work on Old Jericho. Here, pieces of papyrus have been uncovered by the leader of an Israeli dig.

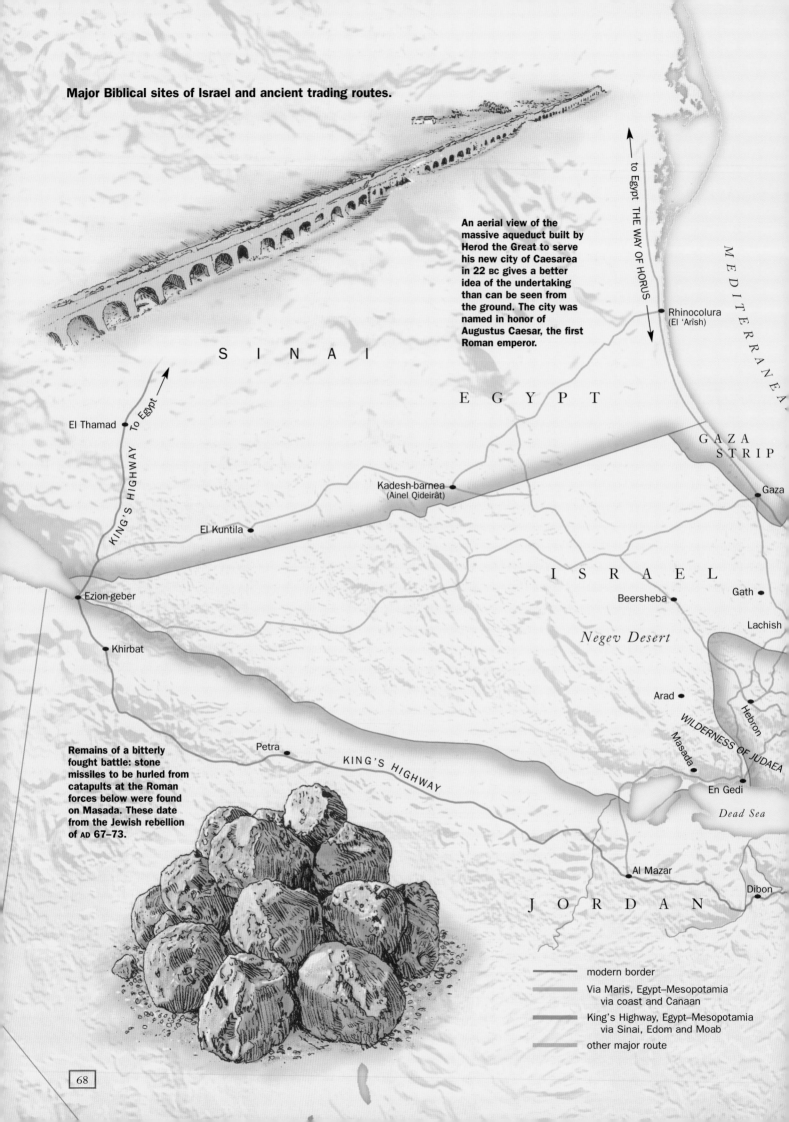

Major Biblical sites of Israel and ancient trading routes.

An aerial view of the massive aqueduct built by Herod the Great to serve his new city of Caesarea in 22 BC gives a better idea of the undertaking than can be seen from the ground. The city was named in honor of Augustus Caesar, the first Roman emperor.

M E D I T E R R A N E A N

to Egypt THE WAY OF HORUS

Rhinocolura
(El 'Arîsh)

S I N A I

E G Y P T

To Egypt

El Thamad

KING'S HIGHWAY

Kadesh-barnea
(Ainel Qideirât)

G A Z A
S T R I P

Gaza

El Kuntila

I S R A E L

Beersheba

Gath

Lachish

Negev Desert

Ezion-geber

Khirbat

Arad

Hebron

WILDERNESS OF JUDAEA

Masada

Remains of a bitterly fought battle: stone missiles to be hurled from catapults at the Roman forces below were found on Masada. These date from the Jewish rebellion of AD 67–73.

Petra

KING'S HIGHWAY

En Gedi

Dead Sea

Al Mazar

Dibon

J O R D A N

modern border

Via Maris, Egypt–Mesopotamia
via coast and Canaan

King's Highway, Egypt–Mesopotamia
via Sinai, Edom and Moab

other major route

CHAPTER FIVE

Israel Gazetteer

After the death of Joshua, the people of Israel enquired of the Lord, "Who shall go up first for us against the Canaanites, to fight against them?"

Judges 1:1

Israel is a story in two elongated episodes. There is the ancient tale of Israelites moving into Canaan at the bidding of an omnipotent God and their trials, tribulations, and triumphs in doing so. Then there is modern Israel, the realization of a Zionist dream when it was formed in 1948 that evolved into a nightmare of unending troubles. Both halves of the saga are marked by acts of unspeakable horror. Conflict in the region is age-old and the Palestine has been a battleground for tyrants and empire-builders from three continents; Europe, Africa, and Asia.

At the heart of the modern state of Israel's claim to the Holy Land is the ancient covenant with God, set out in the Old Testament, an agreement that goes unrecognized by the region's Arabs who have lived there for generations. There is also a humanitarian case for the creation of Israel. Jews suffered anti-Semitism for centuries and had no nation of their own until a modern Jewish state was formed to receive them. This is cold comfort to Palestinians who remain without a country to call their own.

Despite the prominence and importance of religion, Israel remains a secular state. There is a fundamentalist section of society that would like to see everyone living strictly by the laws laid down in the Torah. Indeed, some groups do live according to what they perceive to be the Word of God, flouting civil law in the process. But there are many more liberal-minded people who have shrugged off the age-old laws of Judaism that extend into the present from a bygone age in favor of a modern and pragmatic approach to faith. They have respect for the history of Israel and the sufferings of its people but are not weighed down by the burden.

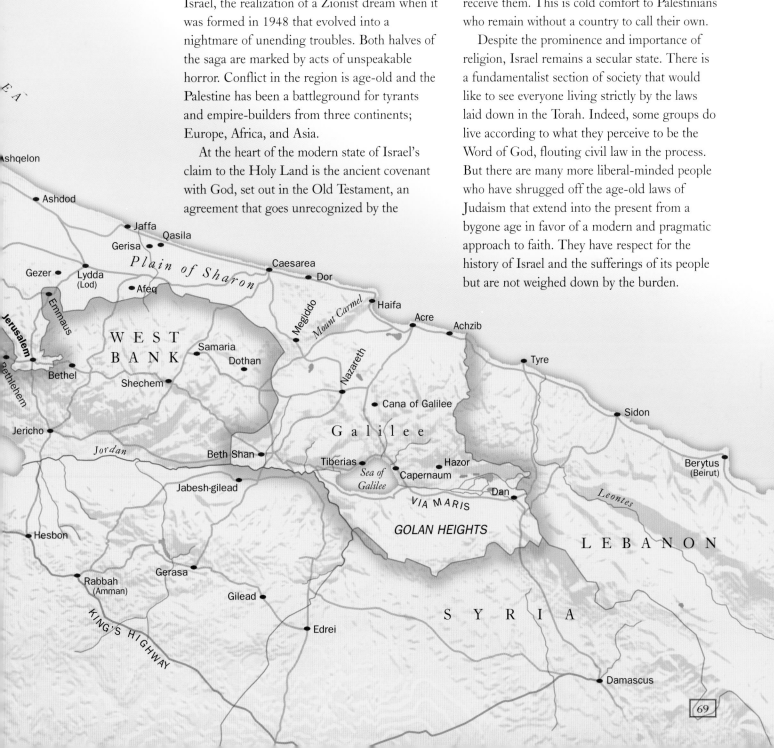

5. Acre

Asher did not drive out the inhabitants of Acco, or the inhabitants of Sidon, or of Ahlab, or of Achzib, or of Helbah, or of Aphik, or of Rehob.

Judges 1:31

Acre ('Akko, Acco, Akka) has a long and illustrious heritage, mostly for its command of the coast between Egypt and Syria. Mentioned in the book of *Judges*, Acre is also identified in ancient Egyptian documents including the Book of Curses, which dates from the 19th century BC. But the proud position it has held as harbor and fortified town has also made it vulnerable to attack. Thus control of Acre has been fluid through history.

It was originally a fortified Canaanite city that probably survived the influx of hostile Israelites following the death of Joshua. But it could not hold out against the marauding Assyrians and in 701 BC it was conquered by King Sennacherib.

Political changes rang out again with the arrival of Alexander the Great who wrought a Greek influence upon the region. Under his direction the settlement moved to the coast and was renamed Ptolemais. The Romans quickly appreciated the strategic advantages offered by Acre and seized on it with glee, transforming it into a major naval base. For the first time in its history there was Jewish settlement of the area, although many perished in the subsequent Jewish revolt.

However, those Jews that survived remained and later thrived. Acre became a beacon for Jewish scholarship and was visited by eminent

rabbis of the era, including Rambam in AD 1165 and Alharizi in 1212. Its position was all the more unusual because by now it was in the hands of crusaders, for once tolerant of an established Jewish population. But for its overt Christian associations it became a target for the Egyptian sultans and was finally conquered and destroyed in 1291.

Crusader legacies include the remains of a breakwater, fortress, and lighthouse as well as the Crypt of St. John, an underground Gothic hall used for ceremonial purposes and to bury eminent knights. (At first archaeologists believed the crusaders constructed their city entirely underground, because of its labarynthine qualities. However, it became apparent that Al Jazzar, the Arab ruler responsible for the city's reconstruction, simply built atop the crusader site.)

It took decades for the city to be recolonized, but once again Jews became a significant proportion of the new population. The political climate was uncertain until the 18th century when the Bedouin leader Dahir el 'Amr chose the city as his capital. He stabilized the situation and invited Jewish people to live alongside loyal Arabs.

Strategic city

With the advent of the Ottoman Empire Acre might have expected a period of peace and prosperity. In fact, it remained at the forefront of conflict, attracting the unwelcome attentions of everyone from Napoleon to Ibrahim Pasha. Indeed, Napoleon later claimed that had Acre fallen to him "the world would have been mine."

However, the lasting legacy of the Ottomans is the fine Turkish-style mosque with its emerald dome at the entrance to the Old City, completed in 1791. Its attractive courtyard contains columns

Below: Once the scene of bitter fighting between crusader forces and victorious Mamluks, modern Akko basks under the Mediterranean sun.

taken from Caesarea. According to Arab legend, the mosque sponsor, Ahmed al-Jazzar, buried a treasure trove beneath the building to ensure there would be sufficient funds to rebuild it should it ever fall. Although an earthquake shook its foundations in 1927 the theory hasn't been tested. In a green cage there is a shrine which, according to tradition, contains hairs from the beard of the Prophet Mohammed.

In 1918 Acre came under British control. Tensions were running high for several decades between Britons, Arabs, and Jews. A series of riots in the years before the Second World War convinced most of the Jewish population to quit. However, in 1948 the Haganah, Jewish freedom fighters and the forerunner of the Israeli army, took control. The citadel, once used as a prison, is now a museum devoted to the memory of the Jews who lost their lives during the British mandate of the territory.

Significant in the histories of the Jewish and Arab peoples of Palestine, Acre is holiest to the Bahá'í faith founded in Persia in 1863. The Bahá'ís believe that Mirza Husain 'Ali (1817–92), also known as Bahá'Allah is one of God's prophets, and his body is buried at a mansion surrounded by stunning gardens in Acre, attracting thousands of pilgrims each year.

Above: Massive walls shelter crusader Acre on its promontory, but they were unable to keep out the Sultan Baibars in 1291.

Left: Beautiful gardens surround the most important shrine to the Bahá'í faith, which is in Acre.

6. Galilee and Tiberias

And Jesus returned in the power of the Spirit to
Galilee, and a report about him went out through all
the surrounding country.

Luke 4:14

Galilee is a region of three parts. There is
the upper area with its high peaks and
forested escarpments, and frequent deluges of
rain. Then there is lower Galilee, delineated
from its sister region by the narrow Beth
Hakerem Valley. It is less spectacular to look at
but less harsh to live upon. The Jewish historian
Josephus, who became governor of the
region in AD 66, noted 204 villages and
towns in Galilee, so it was a densely
populated area at the time. Once a
major spiritual center, the Jewish
population was almost eliminated at the

time of the crusaders and did not recover until
the end of the 19th century.

The third piece is, of course, the Sea of Galilee
itself (Lake Gennesaret, Lake Kinneret, Sea of
Tiberius, Lake of Tarichaeae, Sea of Chinnereth),
fed and drained by the Jordan and a frequent
backdrop in tales relating to Christ. A
freshwater lake some 13 miles long and seven
miles wide, it was here that Jesus walked on water,
according to the *Gospel of St. Matthew*. Thanks to
the New Testament we know the Sea of Galilee
was famed for its fierce storms and abundant fish.

In 1986 a fishing boat of Jesus' era was
discovered in the shoreline mud of the lake, the
first of its kind ever discovered. A two-month
drought had revealed its faint outline and some
sharp-eyed visitors spotted it. Subsequently, the
boat was retrieved and closely scrutinized.
The type of joints used in boat construction,
scientific tests on the wood, as well as artifacts

Right: A hotch-potch
of styles—Roman,
Arabic, Norman,
Egyptian, and many
since—the buildings
of Tiberias are a
testament to the
accretion of time.

found inside helped date the vessel to about the first century AD.

Massacre on the lake

According to Josephus, Jews and Romans went to war on the Sea of Galilee. During the revolt of AD 66–70 some Jews fled by ship from the city of Tarichae when it was taken over. They were followed and slaughtered on Galilee. "During the days that followed a horrible stench hung over the region," wrote Josephus. "The beaches were thick with wrecks and swollen bodies which, hot and steaming in the sun, made the air so foul that the calamity not only horrified the Jews but revolted even those who brought it about." The recovered boat may have been an abandoned fishing vessel or one of the ships used by the ill-fated Jews.

On the western shores lies Tiberias, another monument to Rome fashioned by Herod, this time dedicated to Tiberius (r.14 BC–AD 37), stepson and successor to the Emperor Augustus. At the time Jews, including Jesus, refused to go there because it was built on the site of ancient Jewish graves. But although there is scant mention of the place in the gospels, Tiberias rose to prominence following the destruction of Jerusalem in the Great Revolt when it became a major Jewish center, having been declared pure by a second-century rabbi. Afterward it was home to the most eminent clerics of the age and some of the Talmud was authored here.

This golden time ended with the arrival of the Persians in 614 and Muslims in 637—who were themselves defeated in the First Crusade of 1099. None were friends of the Jews, who departed in droves for Jerusalem and Babylon. Less than 150 years later it was the turn of the Mamluks, slave soldiers of Syria and Egypt, to claim Tiberias. They left it deserted and that is how it stayed until the time of the Ottoman Empire when Sultan Suleiman the Magnificent offered the town to a Jewish refugee. This brought life back to Tiberias and it has remained inhabited ever since. Today Tiberias survives as a pleasant resort town.

Many of the significant sites were destroyed during a major earthquake in 1837. The old city is in pieces while the 12th-century crusader castle provides only a sample of the town's previous grandeur. However, some of the greatest Jewish scholars are buried here, including Spanish-born Mamonides, whose body was allegedly brought here on the back of an unguided camel. His influence on Judaism was immense and his words are still revered.

Above: Galilee's changing landscape ranges from low, fertile hills to rugged mountainous terrain further north. Here, beyond the cliffs of Mount Abel, lies the Sea of Galilee.

7. Megiddo

In his days Pharaoh Neco king of Egypt went up to the king of Assyria to the river Euphrates. King Josiah went to meet him, and Pharaoh Neco killed him, as soon as he saw him.

2 Kings 23:29

Its very name inspires dread. Megiddo is the root of the word Armageddon where, according to *Revelations*, Christ will undertake his final apocalyptic battle against Satan. The prospect of this titanic clash fired the imaginations of generations of artists who have created numerous paintings of the predicted Armageddon.

However, it is unlikely that this place was chosen by chance. Megiddo was for centuries the site of pivotal battles between warring empires and it is surely this association that the Bible writers were exploiting.

Megiddo—founded at the end of the fourth millennium BC—is strategically positioned. On the well-worn route linking Egypt with Syria and Mesopotamia, it was a wealthy trading post in times of peace. But when it came to unrest the armies of the region frequently met at Megiddo for their earth-shattering clashes.

Of the early battles the most notable is that between Tuthmosis III (r.1504–1450 BC) and the Canaanite rebels of the region. This pharaoh of the 18th dynasty, in his first year of independent rule, was victorious and went on to conduct campaigns beyond the Euphrates. Subsequent Egyptian sources mention that Megiddo was under Egyptian control. According to the Bible Joshua and his armies defeated the king of Megiddo. (*Joshua 12:21*).

It was the site of conflict in 920 BC (caused once more by invading Egyptians) and yet again in 815 BC. In *Chronicles* we hear of another battle involving the Egyptians at Megiddo, this time against Josiah, the king of Judah, in 609 BC. Once again the Egyptians triumphed, following Josiah's death. If the battlefields were typical of the era then they would have been chaotic and corpse-strewn, thus lending Megiddo its woeful image.

Place of destruction

Given that it was built-up and burned down so many times, archaeologists can only speculate on the layout of Megiddo in ancient times as they ponder the 20 different layers of ruins identified on the site, dated between 3500 BC and the fifth century BC.

But we do know of a Canaanite temple dedicated to Astarte dating from the 20th century BC and that its appearance was overhauled in the days of King Solomon, who allegedly built two palaces there as well as a

monumental gate and numerous chariot stables. When King Ahab ruled he oversaw the installation of an impressive water supply system.

The Romans however did not take to Megiddo and abandoned it in favor of a newly built base some distance away. Even when St. John the Divine was pledging Megiddo as the site of the final battle (Har Megiddo is Hebrew for "Hill of Megiddo" and emerged as "Armageddon") the place was already deserted.

It was not however the end of Megiddo's history of violence. In 1918 a decisive battle was fought nearby between British and Turkish forces. On his victory, the British General Allenby was made Lord of Megiddo.

Above: An ancient Israelite trough and tethering post stand near the early Bronze Age temple at Megiddo, **facing**, which dates from the Canaanite period

8. Nazareth

In the sixth month the angel Gabriel was sent from God to a city of Galilee, named Nazareth.

Luke 1:26

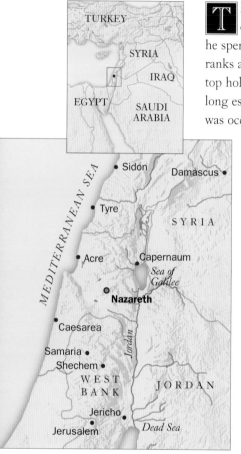

The Galilean town of Nazareth was, of course, home to Jesus and it is here that he spent 30 of his 33 years. For Christians it ranks alongside Bethlehem and Jerusalem as a top holy site. Indications are that the town was long established even in Jesus' time and that it was occupied as long ago as the early Bronze Age. So it seems strange that before the time of the New Testament there are few recorded references to Nazareth, despite the fact it was a thriving Jewish city.

There is evidence that the Jewish settlement continued after Jesus' day, but Jews of the region sided with the Persians in their war against the Byzantines in AD 614. Alas, they backed the wrong side and the triumphant Byzantines were swift and unforgiving in their revenge. Jews were slaughtered wholesale and Nazareth was destroyed.

The Islamic sweep through Palestine in the seventh century brought Nazareth into the Arab fold. Vengeful crusaders, conscious of its Christian relevance, were of course keen to incorporate it in their realm. This was done in 1099 by the Norman Prince Tancred (1078–1112) as part of the conquest of Jerusalem.

Nazareth became another victim of the religious wars that characterized the times when Arabs recaptured the town in 1263 and completely destroyed it. After this the site remained deserted and desolate for 350 years until a Druze ruler permitted Franciscan monks to move in to construct churches and monasteries. From then on its importance gradually increased, so much so that during the First World War the Turkish army made Nazareth its headquarters in the region

Today, contemporaries of Jesus would struggle to recognize the astonishing religious mix that makes up Nazareth. There are Arabs, Jews, Catholics, and Greek Orthodox Christians, all with their own distinct residential quarter.

Town of churches

Nazareth has abundant churches, as befits a place so characterized by its Christian associations, and it is these holy sites that attract pilgrims to this otherwise unremarkable looking town.

The most prominent church is perhaps the Basilica of the Annunciation, said to be built on the site once occupied by Mary's home and is thus where the angel Gabriel appeared to tell her she would bear a son. Although a church has existed on the site since the fourth century, the present building was constructed by Roman Catholics in 1955. Another church, built in 1914, is on top of the cave that Joseph is said to have lived in. Steps lead underground to what is termed "Joseph's workshop."

The Greek Catholic Synagogue Church chooses for its site the synagogue where Jesus preached in boyhood. The Greek Orthodox Church of St. Gabriel stands over the town's water source. The original church was built in AD 356 over the spring where Mary drew water and where the Greek Orthodox Church believes Gabriel appeared to her. The existing church dates from 1750.

In addition to all the above there are churches of the Russian Orthodox, Maronite, Syrian, Coptic, Armenian, and Protestant denominations as well.

Right above: A statue of the Holy Family sits in a wall niche in the Church of St. Joseph, Nazareth.

Facing: Situated in the hills to the northwest of the Valley of Jezreel—a major communications route between the northern coastal plains and the Jordan valley—modern Nazareth is a town of many churches and as many faiths.

9. The Rock of Masada

The Lord is my rock and my fortress and my deliverer, my God, my rock, in whom I take refuge, my shield and the horn of my salvation, my stronghold.

(Psalm 18:2)

Although the Rock of Masada is never mentioned in the Bible, its emergence as a symbol of Jewish resistance was surely in the mind of the psalmist who wrote these verses. The story of how some 960 men, women, and children held Masada for months against the fury of the Roman X Legion—finally committing mass suicide—is etched in the consciousness of every Israeli.

The Rock rises 1,440 feet above the western shores of the Dead Sea on the edge of the Judaean Wilderness. It is a mesa, or table mountain, on which the virtually flat plateau extends across 233,000 square yards and is flanked by sheer cliffs. The site is a superb natural stronghold—*masada* is the Hebrew word for fortress—and was the natural choice for Judaea's King Herod the Great as his refuge in times of crisis. Between 36 and 33 BC, Herod built two major palaces there along with defensive towers and a lookout station. To cope with the arid climate his engineers devised a system of damming valleys along the edge of the mountain, so diverting winter rains into specially built cliffside cisterns. From here slaves carried the water to a huge reservoir on the plateau.

Jewish tragedy

According to the Pharisee historian Flavius Josephus, the ramp-assault worked, the Romans advanced battering rams against the plateau walls, and the defenders, realizing their fate, took their own lives rather than suffer execution or slavery. Josephus says ten men were chosen by lot to kill the entire garrison after which the ten themselves drew lots to determine who would perform the final killings. In fact, Josephus claims, there were seven survivors who reported "everything that was said and done" to the Romans.

Archaeological investigations at Masada began in 1963 under the meticulous eye of the Israeli professor Yigael Yadin. Among artifacts recovered were Old Testament scrolls, two of which were hidden under the synagogue. Intriguingly the team also unearthed eleven *ostraka* (pottery fragments) carrying people's names. These might simply have been a way of identifying property, though some experts think they were the lots used to choose the garrison's killers.

Major questions continue to hang over Josephus's account and Yadin's work. Josephus says all possessions were gathered into a single pile and set alight, yet Yadin proved there were many piles and many fires. Josephus tells how everything was destroyed except food (illustrating to the Romans that the rebels did not succumb to starvation). Yet many storerooms did contain traces of burned rations. There are also questions of how the seven survivors saw so much yet still survived the butchery.

Yadin dismisses the discovery of 25 skeletons in an inaccessible cave below the fortress as bodies "irreverently" tossed away by the Romans. This seems unlikely in the extreme. A more objective view is that these people were hiding when they were killed by either Romans or fellow Jews. Perhaps not all Masada's defenders sought a martyr's death.

The background to the siege begins with the AD 66 Jewish Revolt. Zealots known as Sicarii captured Masada from the Romans and the garrison soon became a rallying point for others fleeing the oppression of Rome. The last refugees arrived in AD 70 and helped build a synagogue, public hall, and two ritual baths. They survived until the full deployment of the X Legion in AD 72 and then held out for several more months while the besiegers worked on a plan of attack. The Romans first encircled the entire mountain with a two-mile-long wall, constructed eight siege camps, and then built a massive earth ramp up the western side, using Jewish forced labor to dissuade the rebels from hurling down stones.

Left: This aerial view of Masada from the northwest, with the Dead Sea beyond, shows Herod's palace complex. Later Roman fortifications can be seen on lower ledges in the foreground. It took the Romans more than two years to breach the extensive walls.

Above: Inside the bath house of King Herod, which is currently being excavated. Here the Judaean King would live in a similar degree of opulence to his political masters in Rome.

10. Lachish

And the Lord gave Lachish into the hand of Israel, and he captured it on the second day, and struck it with the edge of the sword, and every person in it, as he had done in Libnah.

Joshua 10:32

At times the written evidence of the Bible is at odds with texts and documents from other sources. There are other occasions when all sources agree, with one historical source complementing the next. The story of Lachish has archaeology at its heart with Biblical accounts filling in around the edges, for one source convincingly reflects the other.

Tel Lachish, the mound on which the city was built, is in the Judaean hills, some 30 miles southeast of Jerusalem. At the beginning of the second millennium BC it was a Canaanite city, a wealthy settlement situated by the Philistine coast road. Its fortifications included a wall and a glacis, a bank of earth smothered with a lime plaster, similar to that of Jericho. A royal palace was constructed on the acropolis, although a later building has obliterated some parts of it. There were two temples in use and the indications are that both were ornate.

Records from Egypt dating from the 14th century BC reveal that Lachish was an eminent urban center and the property of the pharaohs. However, a wealthy city was inevitably the envy of others and it was destroyed at the end of the 12th century BC. The Bible states that the Israelites under Joshua were responsible for this. However, it is worth remembering that many of the details of Joshua's campaign in the Biblical texts have not been archaeologically substantiated. There is another theory that Philistines were the marauders in this instance. A fitting for the main gate bears the name of Pharaoh Ramesses III, so the destruction came no earlier than his reign, which began in 1184 BC.

Lachish was rebuilt to become an important frontier town in the Kingdom of Judah. Two lines of enormous mud brick walls stood on stone foundations, and in places the defenses were six feet wide. The city gate is one of the biggest and stoutest known of the era.

Remains of siege

A palace was rebuilt on the acropolis, probably as a residence for the governor serving the king of Judah. Once again its glory was turned to ashes, this time by the Assyrian King Sennacherib (r.704–681 BC). The siege and attack are described in the Bible. Further, a stone relief depicting the event was commissioned by Sennacherib and was discovered at his palace in Nineveh (*see pages 39, 147*). Archaeologists have

Right: All that remains of the once proud city of Lachish is this huge mound, itself resembling one of the lower Judean hills in which it sits.

been able to confirm that the attack was launched from the southwest and that a ramp was built containing thousands of tons of rubble so the battering ram could be moved into position. It is the only surviving siege structure from the period. Debris left scattered on the floor, including hundreds of arrowheads at the foot of the city walls, reveals that the battle was fierce. A mass burial site was discovered in caves nearby, containing the bodies of some 1,500 people.

Phoenix-like, Lachish rose once more from the ashes, although it failed to reach the proportions it had previously known. Its patron this time was King Josiah (r. c.640–609 BC), presumably acting with the defense of Jerusalem in mind.

Lachish fell victim to battle and invasion for a third time with the arrival of the Babylonian army in 587 BC. Texts discovered on pottery sherds buried in a courtyard give a poignant insight into the last few hours of the city defenders, scanning the horizon to see the lights of towns go out one by one as they were overrun and destroyed. Presumably written from an outpost to a Lachish commander one reads: "And may my lord know that we are watching for the signals of Lachish according to all the signs that my lord gave. For we do not see Azekah." The book of *Jeremiah* testifies that Lachish and Azekah were the last cities prior to Jerusalem to fall.

The *ostraka* were written in ink in a Hebraic script. Known as the Lachish Letters they are valuable evidence of Israelite life in the First Temple period. Other finds include a seal indicating the ownership of an item by "Gedaliah, Royal Steward," who is mentioned in the second book of *Kings*.

11. Hazor

And this is the account of the forced labor that King Solomon drafted to build the House of the Lord, and his own house, and the Millo, and the wall of Jerusalem, and Hazor, and Megiddo, and Gezer.

1 Kings 9:15

Twenty-nine centuries before the birth of Christ, the city of Hazor was already in existence in Upper Galilee. It expanded, prospered, and was wiped out before some other ancient places had even been founded. The city was so ancient, in fact, that within 20 years of the foundation of Rome Hazor was recorded as wreckage on the *Via Maris* highway. Its existence was but a memory at the time the First Temple was plundered and destroyed.

In the Bronze Age, Hazor had a population about 20 times the size of Jerusalem, which was then in Jebusite hands. It extended across some 200 acres, twice the size of Megiddo and about four times the size of Lachish.

So this was a huge city for its time.

Hazor is mentioned on at least seven of the 25,000 tablets discovered at Mari accross the Syrian desert on the Euphrates. One reveals that Hazor was so important to Hammurabi of Babylon that he installed not one but two ambassadors there. The king, famous for his law-making, may even have lived in Hazor for a while. Another tablet emphasizes the importance of tin trading in Hazor (this was prior to the Iron Age, when tin was vital for the production of bronze weapons). Evidence from Egypt supports claims to Hazor's importance. It was sought after by successive pharaohs, who co-ordinated military campaigns in Canaan.

The Bible, too, makes much of the eminence of Hazor. According to the book of *Joshua* Hazor, led by King Jabin, was at the head of a coalition of kingdoms that opposed Joshua. It seems Hazor was destroyed in the 13th century BC, perhaps by Joshua, although the Israelite invasion may have happened much later. At the moment it is impossible to say which of the theories, if either, is right.

Whichever is true, the city was rebuilt,

Facing: Tel Hazor stands out starkly against the Galilean hills. The lower city is to the left, upper section on the right.

Right: A groove ringing the stone base of an olive press at Hazor once caught the oil and fed it through a small spout into a jar embedded in the ground.

possibly on the orders of Solomon (gates of a particular design assigned to the reign of Solomon have been discovered at Hazor, Gezer, and Megiddo), but later theory points to King Omri being the architect. Hazor was destroyed a second time by Tiglath-pileser III of Assyria in 732 BC. Mud-brick walls, turned red by the heat of the blaze, still stand six feet tall.

Hazor was first identified in the 1930s and investigations carried on for decades, yielding rich rewards. An array of items was extracted from the ruins of the temples and palace, although the hoped-for archive of cuneiform tablets is as yet undiscovered. There are two distinct areas of Hazor, the upper city high on the Tel, where at least 23 strata have been identified, and a larger, enclosed lower city. One of its most fascinating aspects is the underground water system quarried during the reign of Ahab (874–853 BC) which can still be reached by descending 123 steps.

The battle that never happened

One of the largest settlements in Israel was called Ai in the Bible and has been linked to Khirbet et-Tell, northeast of Jerusalem. The city was fortified and covered an area of some 25 acres. Excavations undertaken between 1933–35 revealed a large temple and other remains dating from the third millennium BC.

In the Bible we are told that Joshua burned down the city, and slaughtered its inhabitants after they fell into a tactical trap. Archaeologists say the evidence contradicts this, and that settlement had ended there by 2400 BC, long before the era of Joshua, with only fleeting recolonization occurring among the ruins in 1200 BC. The name *ai* means "ruin."

12. Beersheba and Dan

So David said to Joab and to the commanders of the army, "Go, number Israel, from Beersheba to Dan, and bring me a report, that I may know the number."

1 Chronicles 21:2

L ying on the edge of the Negev desert, it was near Beersheba that Hagar and her son by Abraham came close to death from thirst. According to *Genesis* God produced a well of water that saved young Ishmael from dying of thirst. Here too, Abraham dug a well and planted a grove. He made a covenant with Abimelech, the king of Gerar. This was the man who had kidnapped Abraham's wife Sarah as part of a dispute over the well and was visited by God in a dream with a warning to reunite husband and wife.

Like Abraham, the residents of Beersheba were for years nomadic by nature and their impact on the region was slight. Although the exact site of the dwelling place of Abraham is unknown, there is archaeological evidence of small ancient settlements at several locations in the immediate area. Later, there emerged a fortified and bustling settlement, lying to the east of the present city, whose potency was probably at its height in the time of David and Solomon. In this era the phrase "from Dan to Beersheba" was commonly used as a way of referring to the whole kingdom of Israel, from north to south. Archaeologists have discovered the remains of a house dating from the eighth century BC and a Roman fortress built in the second century AD.

For an unknown reason, the center of population switched from its former site to the present one during the Second Temple period. The Romans later erected defenses in the area and the town was Christianized during the Byzantine era.

Its history was peaceful during Arab and Turkish domination in the second millennium but became a flashpoint in the Israeli war of independence. After being captured by the Israeli Defense Forces in 1948 it was transformed from a small Bedouin town into a city suitable for administration, industry, and commerce.

Today it is known as Be'er Sheva' and is Israel's fourth largest city. It still proudly displays Abraham's well. Aspects of Bedouin

Right: Around the modern city of Beersheba there are remains of several earlier settlements, including these ruins from Nabataean, Roman, and Byzantine occupations at Avdat.

life are celebrated in Be'er Sheva' through its weekly market established a century ago and a museum dedicated to a culture that is fast disappearing. The city constantly encroaches on the Negev desert as the government invests in its expansion.

Dan (Leshem, Laish)

The city of Dan takes its name from the tribe that moved there following the Israelites' arrival in Canaan. These were apparently the

descendants of Dan, the son born to Jacob and Bilhah, maid of Rachel. According to the Bible it became a focal point for idolatry, and at Dan a "high place" for cult worship has indeed been excavated.

Given its northerly position, Dan was exposed and vulnerable to conquerors. It is known that King Hazael of Syria took the city in the ninth century BC since an inscription relating to a victory over the Israelite kingdom was discovered. On the stele Hazael justifies his invasion by claiming "the king of Israel entered previously in my father's land." It is thought that Hazael rebuilt Dan and other cities that he flattened in battle. Syrian glory came to an abrupt end, however, thanks to the menace of the Assyrians.

Israel eventually recaptured Dan, smashing the stele and using the fragments for construction. But they too felt the powerful wrath of the Assyrians who attacked and destroyed Dan in 721 BC. The Danites, who included Samson among their number, became one of the ten lost tribes of Israel. Fascinating legends sprang up about their fate and they were supposedly sighted at exotic locations all over the globe. In reality, their populations probably assimilated with those of the invaders and other migrants until they became ethnically indistinct.

Above: A fragment of a tablet uncovered during excavations at Tel Dan bears an inscription which includes the phrase "House of David."

13. Caesarea

...and as he passed through he preached the gospel to all the towns until he came to Caesarea.

Acts 8:40

For years the town that would become Caesarea lurked in anonymity as a Phoenician port giving shelter to boats plying the routes between Syria and Egypt. Then Herod the Great embarked on an ambitious construction project, and piers, theaters, baths, a stadium, and an aqueduct were constructed.

The city was named for Herod's benefactor, the Roman Emperor Augustus Caesar, who allocated it to him. Even today it appears breathtaking in its scale and grandeur. Astonishingly, the huge Roman city was completed in as little as 12 years. Had Herod not been inspired by paranoia and ordered widespread infanticide at the time of the Nativity, his name would have been forever linked with greatness rather than infamy.

Belated in its prominence, Caesarea was for centuries known as Straton's Tower and was dominated by the seafaring Phoenicians. Only after it was captured by the Hasmonean king Alexander Jannaeus in 96 BC were Jews allowed to settle there.

Herod seized on the port's potential in 22 BC. Artfully adopting Roman-style architecture, Herod attracted the support and favor of the empire overlords by making this Palestinian port a bastion of Rome. It was in modern, magnificent Caesarea that Paul was detained for 20 years before meeting his fate in Rome.

One of the city's triumphs was an eight-mile-long aqueduct bringing spring water from Mount Carmel into the heart of the city. The name Caesarea Maritima (Caesarea on Sea) was adopted to distinguish it from Caesarea Philippi, another Herodic showpiece for Rome in northern Israel.

Perhaps not surprisingly, the ruling Romans endorsed the city's success by making it an administrative capital. A plaque at the theater indicates that Pontius Pilate, the Roman governor who condemned Jesus to death, was resident in the city at some stage. Alongside Jews lived numerous Greeks and Syrians. It became significant for Christians for a variety of reasons; Peter converted the Roman centurion Cornelius in Caesarea, Philip the Evangelist lived and preached there, and as previously mentioned, Paul was a detainee.

Jewish Revolt

If the city's creator Herod was in the thrall of the Romans, the majority of the Jewish population was not. They resented the confines of Roman hegemony and lashed out against it. An extreme example of the problems that ensued was the slaughter of some 20,000 Jews on a single day in Caesarea in AD 66, as related by the historian Flavius Josephus (c.AD 38–100). This incident sparked the six-year Jewish Revolt.

Dark days continued for the Jews as Caesarea became a garrison town for the Roman army, now at war with Jerusalem. Jewish captives were brought back in triumph to the city to be

paraded in chains on its streets and pitched against gladiators or even wild animals in the arenas at a time when the Roman Hippodrome could hold 30,000 baying spectators. In the Bar Kokhba revolt of AD 132 numerous Jewish martyrs were killed in Caesarea, among them Rabbi Akiva, one of the great sages who was allegedly torn apart by iron combs.

It was also here that Christianity made great strides and by the end of the second century it had a bishop in place, assisted by Church elder Origenes, who fashioned a famous school and library there. From the school came an early translation of the Bible called Hexapla.

After Christianity became firmly established toleration of other faiths in Caesarea diminished, so that the Samaritans became marginalized and disgruntled. During a Samaritan revolt in 555 the city was badly damaged. Byzantine emperor Justinian responded by killing thousands of insurgents

By the time the Arabs overran Caesarea it was at the peak of its influence and power. Legend says a Jew named Joseph let the invaders into the fortress city through a secret passage. Appreciating its value, they refrained from razing it and its prosperity continued.

Given its Roman heritage and strategic value, the crusaders made it an important center early in the second millennium. Rather than restoring the old fortifications, they constructed new ones, many of which are still in evidence today. In a raid on a mosque crusaders discovered a goblet which they deemed to be the Holy Grail, subsequently sent to Italy. In 1170, according to the diarist Benjamin of Tudela, there were just ten Jewish families and some 200 Samaritan families in residence, with the vast majority of the population being Christian.

Saladin took Caesarea in 1187, massacred many of the Christians, and then lost the city again to invading crusaders. When the Crusades finally collapsed in Palestine and the Levant in 1291, Caesarea was razed by a ruling Sultan to deter a seaborne invasion and it retained only a shadow of its former glory.

Below: The Romanized King Herod the Great embarked on an ambitious construction plan for an obscure Phoenician seaport in 22 BC, which he named Caesarea after Augustus Caesar, first emperor of Rome. A testament to the sound building techniques of Roman architects, many of the public structures, like this massive aqueduct, still survive.

14. Capernaum

And they went into Capernaum, and immediately on the Sabbath he entered into the synagogue and was teaching.

Mark 1:21

On the northwestern shores of the Sea of Galilee is the site of the ancient fishing town of Capernaum (Kefar, Nahum, Talhum), deserted since the eighth century. It was here that Jesus recruited his first disciples among the local fishermen. These were, the *Gospel according to St. Matthew* tell us, Simon, called Peter, his brother Andrew, James, and his brother John.

Soon after, Jesus began healing in the city and nowhere did he perform more miracles than in Capernaum. Among those to benefit were Simon's mother-in-law, a paralytic, a man possessed by the devil, and numerous other afflicted folk. Further, he raised from the dead the daughter of Jairus, a synagogue official. The miracles are related in the *Gospel according to St. Mark*. So closely linked was Jesus to the place that Matthew's gospel calls it "his own city."

Fishermen like Peter traded at Capernaum and the town taxed those passing through on the *Via Maris* highway (the vital trade link between Egypt, Syria, and Mesopotamia). According to the Bible Levi was a tax collector until he became a disciple and adopted the name Matthew. However, many in Capernaum were dismissive of Jesus' message and were issued a strongly-worded warning by Jesus.

A visitor to the empty, echoing streets of old Capernaum now will find it hard to imagine the town as it must have been nearly 2,000 years ago, thronging with people eager to catch the words of an exciting new preacher, or disdainfully gossiping about him. Residents of this place formed the earliest of Christian congregations and Peter the Apostle was born here. Yet it never assumed the same importance in the Christian psyche as Bethlehem or Jerusalem.

Significance rediscovered

When it was abandoned centuries later, following Muslim invasion, nature quickly encroached on the ruins and it became a jungle of shrubs and thorns. Only in 1838 did American explorer Edward Robinson identify the site as Capernaum. Initial excavations were

Right: A relief carving from the Synagogue of Capernaum depicts the Ark of the Covenant borne along on its wheeled carriage.

made but it was not until the area had been purchased by a Franciscan order that wholesale investigation could begin. If it had not been for the efforts of 19th- and 20th-century archaeologists Capernaum might still be a place name recalled only in Bible stories rather than developed into a modern town with homes, shops, and a synagogue.

Archaeologists discovered that Capernuam had been settled since the second century BC and that, as a small, unfortified town, it did not take part in the Jewish wars against the Romans and thus escaped unscathed during this era. It was probably at the height of its greatness in the fourth century AD but had already declined by the time of the seventh-century Arab invasion.

One of its archaeological treasures is a white stone synagogue, dating from the third century, situated at the highest point in the town. Its elaborate appearance suggests a wealthy Jewish population at the time of construction. Almost certainly it was built on the site of the synagogue known by Jesus.

There is speculation that a church existed enclosing what is now known as "the house of Peter" (no one knows if Peter really lived here but it is likely that a strong oral tradition inspired the legend, indicating that it probably is true). It seems this building was for years a hostel-style residence until one room was improved with a limestone floor and a plaster coating on the wall. Its roof was arched and it is tempting to believe it was this building seen by the nun Egeria who visited Capernaum between 381 and 384 and identified both a church and a synagogue. In the middle of the fifth century this first house was pulled down and replaced by an octagonal church. Inscriptions and fragments found on the site suggest strong early Christian connections.

Above: The ruins of the 3rd-century AD synagogue are elaborate, indicating a wealthy Jewish population at the time of its construction. It almost certainly stood above the remains of the synagogue in which Jesus preached.

CHAPTER SIX
Lebanon Gazetteer

They gave money to the masons and the carpenters, and food, drink, and oil to the Sidonians and the Tyrians to bring cedar trees from Lebanon to the sea, to Joppa, according to the grant that they had from Cyrus king of Persia.

Ezra 3:7

W ith one side of its land flanked by mountains and the other lapped by the sea, Lebanon appeared a land of limited potential. But that did not deter the Phoenicians who settled there in about 2500 BC and set about exploiting the possibilities open to them.

The coastline is rugged—but that made for excellent anchorage. Inland there were dense cedar forests, ideal material for a fleet. Those two factors combined to give the Phoenicians excellent trading opportunities, which they approached creatively. They did not restrict themselves to one commodity or specialize in a specific craft. Phoenicians mined gold, silver, and tin and became accomplished metalworkers. They created glass and pottery, carved ivory, and manufactured furniture. They were even fashionable dressers, so much so that Homer was moved to comment on their tunics.

Given their multitude of skills, Phoenicians made ideal allies or mercenaries. For this reason they traversed the Holy Lands in the ancient

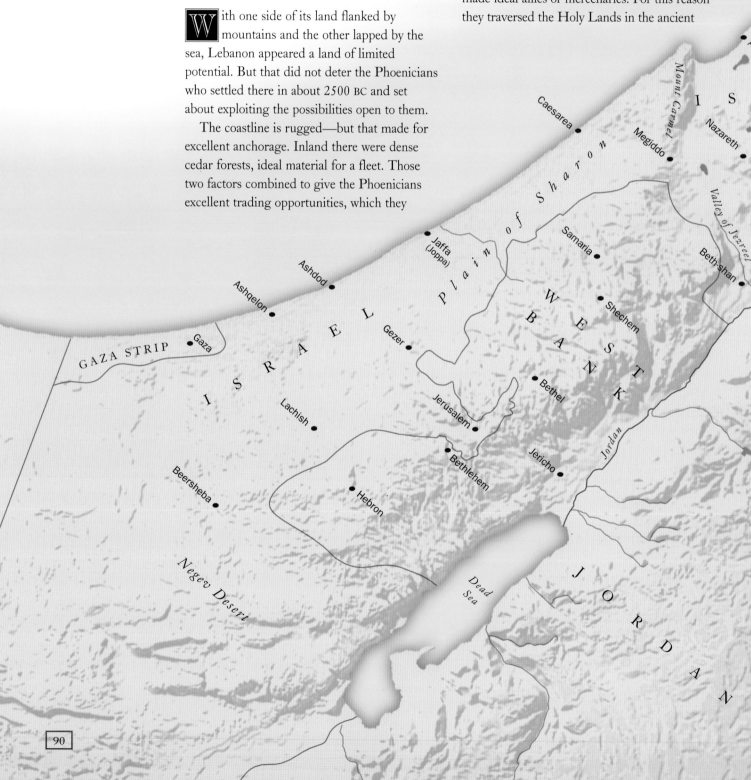

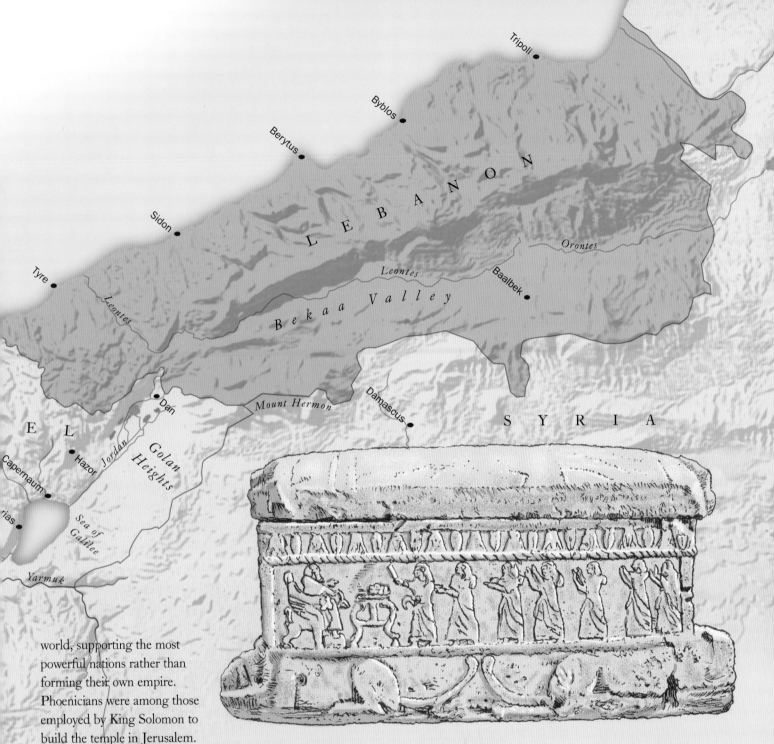

The map shows locations including Tripoli, Byblos, Berytus, Sidon, Tyre, LEBANON, Orontes, Leontes, Baalbek, Bekaa Valley, Dan, Mount Hermon, Damascus, SYRIA, Hazor, Jordan, Golan Heights, Capernaum, Sea of Galilee, Yarmuk, Leontes, EL.

world, supporting the most powerful nations rather than forming their own empire. Phoenicians were among those employed by King Solomon to build the temple in Jerusalem.

But perhaps one of their greatest contributions to history is one that is often glibly ascribed to others. For it was this talented people who first produced a recognizable alphabet of 22 symbols, each representing a single consonant. Further, the characters were arranged in a definite order so that they could be memorized. The purpose behind the invention of the alphabet was not to produce great Phoenician literature—there is little evidence of great tales or philosophy emerging from the region—but to keep trading accounts. For this reason they encouraged the use of ink and paper.

The Greeks went on to refine the alphabet—it was one of many things, including some mythology, that they borrowed from the Phoenicians and adopted as their own. So while the Greeks are remembered as the classical civilization, it was the Phoenicians, lurking in the shadows of history, that provided one of Western civilization's cornerstones. Over time, the Phoenicians became more obscure and indistinct as a people, especially after Aramaic became the region's main language.

Since the beginning of Christianity Lebanon has been viewed as a refuge for the religiously persecuted. A Christian sect went there in the seventh century AD to avoid conversion to Islam and its members became known as the Maronites. Similarly Muslim Shi'ites who were persecuted in the ninth century withdrew to Lebanon, and 200 years later they were followed by the Druze.

The sarcophagus of Ahiram, who was king of Byblos at some point between the 13th–12th centuries BC. The relief shows couriers, hands raised in worship, while their leader makes an offering to the king, who is seated on his throne. A winged sphinx stands beside him.

15. Sidon

And he came down with them and stood on a level place, with a great crowd of his disciples and a great multitude of people from all Judaea and Jerusalem and the sea coast of Tyre and Sidon, who came to hear him and to be healed of their diseases.

Luke 6:17

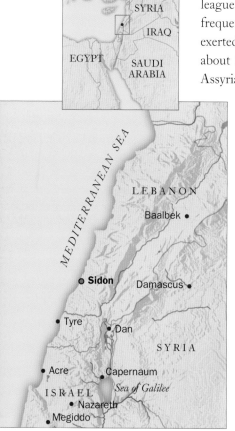

At least as old as neighboring Tyre, Sidon (Zidon) vied for premier position in the league of coastal cities. Its ambitions were frequently curbed by the Egyptians, who exerted a military influence in the region from about 1450 BC. In the ninth century BC, the Assyrians were the aggressors and, after 539, the Persians were in charge.

The Sidonians remained restless at their role of pawn in the game of empires being played out in the region during Biblical times. There were uprisings and rebellions—one against the Persians, which ended in the suicide of 40,000 of the city's inhabitants who preferred death to submission. Such was their abiding hatred of Persians thereafter that the people of Sidon openly welcomed Alexander the Great on his whirlwind invasion of the region, unlike the neighboring Tyrians, who suffered for their defiance (*see next page*).

Alexander, through the deputed services of his trusted friend Hephaistion, installed a king in Sidon, a man who had previously worked as a gardener. It is thought to have been this individual who ordered the construction of the marble marvel that is the Alexander Sarcophagus, found in exquisite condition in Sidon and bearing carved reliefs relating to the lifestyle and leisure pursuits of Alexander. It did not, however, contain his body. The great warrior was buried in a gold sarcophagus in Alexandria.

Right: Detail of a man's head carved on the lid of a Phoenician sarcophagus of the 5th century BC, found at Sidon.

Facing: Fishing nets dry in the sun against the background of the crusader castle of Sidon.

Crossroads of armies

Despite all the invasions, the Phoenicians never let the political outlook hamper their trading opportunities. Like the rest of Phoenicia, Sidon was condemned in *Ezekiel*, in which there was a threat of God sending "pestilence and blood into her." The warning goes on; "…and the slain shall fall in her midst, by the sword that is against her on every side." (*Ezekiel 28:23*)

Later came the Seleukids, the Ptolemaics of Egypt (successors to Alexander's North African empire), the Romans, European crusaders, Saladin, the Mamluks, Turks, the French; a seemingly endless list of conquerors each making a mark on Sidon. By the time St. Paul visited Sidon on his way to Rome, the city's best days were already behind it. Its descent into an

untidy urban blot took centuries. Yet there still remains the Temple of Echmoun, just outside the town, built in the seventh century BC in honor of Sidon's favored god, Echmoun, who is linked to healing and medicine. This is the most complete Phoenician site in existence today. It features the Throne of Astarte, carved from granite and flanked by two sphinxes. The town itself features some intriguing crusader ruins, including a castle built on an offshore island and connected to the mainland by a causeway.

16. Tyre

And Hiram king of Tyre sent messengers to David, and cedar trees, also carpenters and masons who built David a house.

2 Samuel 5:11

If cities had lucky colors, Tyre's would be purple. If they could choose a mascot creature, this coastal enclave would surely pick the humble sea-snail. For here was a city which in Biblical times enjoyed great wealth from the export of a purple dye derived from the *murex* sea-snail. Purple became associated with imperial greatness, and aspiring emperors, especially Roman, were keen to possess a ready supply. Even in the times of Emperor Diocletian (r.AD 284–305) two pounds of purple-dyed silk sold for six-and-a-half pounds of gold.

All the eastern Phoenician bases employed the art of dye-making but Tyre was best known for its production. It took 300 snails to produce a single ounce of dye. Each snail contains a yellowish sac that turns purple when exposed to light. Every silver lining has a cloud, and for Tyre it was the malodorous residue of the dye-making process left heaped along the shoreline. The mounds of half-empty mollusk shells rotted in the midday sun, causing such a smell that it moved the Greek geographer Strabo (c.64 BC–c.AD 21) to remark that Tyre was the most evil-smelling town he had come across.

Probably starting life as a colony of nearby Sidon, Tyre went on to surpass its neighbor in terms of wealth and influence. Tyre was in effect two islands (they were later made one) joined to the mainland by King Hiram I (r. 969–36 BC). In doing so he created ideal harbors, endorsing a seafaring tradition. Keen on engineering feats and an ally of Israel, Hiram assisted Solomon in the construction of the first Temple in Jerusalem. In return he received tribute and territory in Galilee. Together they sent a fleet to Arabia and Africa, which returned with gold, myrrh, ivory, and (curiously) baboons.

However, the Phoenicians were not habitually supportive of the Israelites and there is little in the Bible that praises them. Tyre's Biblical notoriety was confirmed with the fact that Jezebel, the wicked wife of King Ahab of Israel and a worshipper of Baal, was the daughter of a king of Tyre and Sidon. The prophets Ezekiel and Amos condemn the Phoenicians of both cities. Hebrew disapproval did little to dent Tyre's success at the time. It was clearly an important city for many centuries with its wealth rooted in trade.

The earliest Phoenician coinage yet found was minted at Tyre in the mid-fifth century BC. The city witnessed many traumatic events, however. Tyre was subjected to a 14-year siege by King Nebuchadnezzar from 586 BC and its defenders were compelled to retreat to the island's citadel, behind newly fortified walls said to have been 150 feet high.

Alexander's wrath

At the time Alexander the Great began his conquest in 334 BC, the Tyrians were allied with the Persians, his sworn enemies. Tyre's people endured a seven-month siege by the Greek forces and retired again to the island fortress. But Alexander refused to be thwarted. He knew the Persians could be kept afloat by their sea-faring allies, the Phoenicians, and it was his avowed intention to destroy this threat. To do so he razed much of Old Tyre on the mainland and used the rubble to build a

causeway out to the island. It measured 2,600 feet in length and was some 900 feet at its widest point. He finally took the city in August 332, and wreaked a terrible revenge. Tyre's buildings were destroyed, 10,000 men slaughtered, and a further 30,000 people sold into slavery.

Alexander's causeway remained intact and turned the island into a peninsula. Tyre returned to glory under the Greeks and Romans—the largest Roman hippodrome ever built is sited there. Paul stayed there for one week on his return to Jerusalem from his third mission. It later became a key crusader city. Triumphant Muslims found little use for it, except to use its ancient stones for other building projects.

Today Tyre appears a shadow of itself, in what has become a depressed part of Lebanon since the closure of borders with Israel, a dozen miles to the south. In 1984 UNESCO named it a world heritage site in a bid to preserve some of its antiquities. Continuing aggression in the region has done little to help the cause of revitalizing the city.

17. Baalbek

And Cain knew his wife; and she conceived, and bare Enoch: and he builded a city, and called the name of the city after the name of his son, Enoch.

Genesis 4:17

Baalbek has witnessed the rise and fall of many religions, as the masonry and monuments left behind attest. The city was founded in the fertile Beqaa valley by the Phoenicians and became a center of worship for their principal god, Baal, from which the city's name was derived. Scores of tombs cut into the rocks around Baalbek date from Phoenician times. Baalbek appears in the Bible as Baalath and references to it in *Kings* and *Chronicles* indicate its prominence at the time of King Solomon.

Alexander the Great arrived with his forces in 332 BC and subjected the town to the process of Hellenization. Baalbek became Heliopolis, City of the Sun. and there were changes in the deities worshipped there, from Canaanite to Greek. Further changes were made when Julius Caesar made it a Roman colony in 15 BC, and it is from theis period that Baalbek is noted.

Caesar called the place, rather longwindedly, Colonia Julia Augusta Felix Heliopolitanus. Its significance lies with the Temple of Jupiter Heliopolitanus, planned by Caesar and quite simply the largest place of worship in the Roman Empire. Its length is a monstrous 290 feet while the width is 160 feet. It was surrounded by 54 columns, each with a diameter of seven feet and a height of 70 feet—the equivalent of a six-storey building. Six of the giant columns still stand. Apart from its scale the detail of its decoration is breathtaking, since the carved relief is exquisite.

Work on the temple continued for more than 150 years and it was never completely finished. The extraordinary sights at Baalbek do not end with this magnificent temple, however. There is one circular temple dedicated to Venus and another to Bacchus, and a short distance away Mercury is honored.

Feat of engineering

Beyond these architectural spectacles there is an enigma that has made Baalbek famous. In the

temple complex is the *trilithon*, a row of three mighty building blocks, among the largest ever used anywhere in the world. Each block measures almost 70 feet in length, 14 feet in height, and is 10 feet thick. In a limestone quarry a short distance from the temples lies a fourth stone, even larger, called Hajar el Gouble (Stone of the South) or Hajar el Hibla, (Stone of the Pregnant Woman). This is a full three feet longer than the others and weighs an estimated 1,200 tons. The process of cutting the block was never completed and it remains attached to the quarry at its base.

Just how the stones of the *trilithon* were sculpted from the earth and maneuvered into position—so accurately that it is said there is barely a pin's width between them—remains a mystery. Their colossal size dwarfs the project of installing the fine temple columns. Six large

blocks measuring about 35 feet in length lay beneath the *trilithon*. It is assumed the technology dates from the Roman era although there is no reference to it in contemporary writings.

Local people offer a different explanation. The original Baalbek was, they say, built before the Great Flood by Cain, the son of Adam and murderer of his brother Abel. Although the deluge destroyed the city, it was rebuilt by Nimrod, son of Ham and grandson of Noah using the labors of a race of giants. Various rather more scientific theories have been put forward, but none has been proven.

Ruins at Baalbek were scrutinized by archaeologists in the 19th and early 20th centuries but the town has gone off limits since becoming a base for the Islamic extremist group Hezbollah, prompting numerous military adventures in the region by Israel.

Above: An aerial view of the Julius Heliopolitanus complex at Baalbek shows the enormous size of the largest of Roman temples ever built. But scale is not the only surprise, the quality of the relief carving is among the finest in the Roman Empire. The example shown here, **facing**, is of a lion-headed water spout on the entabulature of the Temple of Bacchus (left in picture above).

The Phoenicians

They made all your planks of fir trees from Senir: they took a cedar from Lebanon to make a mast…The inhabitants of Sidon and Arvad were your rowers…
Ezekiel 27:5, 8

Also known as the Canaanites, the Phoenicians are among history's unsung heroes. The Phoenicians were adept navigators and tradesmen, and had developed an alphabet centuries before their rivals, achieving a greatness that equaled and occasionally outstripped the neighboring Greeks (who adopted the Phoenician alphabet) and Egyptians. But there are no pyramids or Parthenon to remember the Phoenicians by, and the discovery of Phoenician artifacts has occurred only relatively recently. Monuments to Phoenicia's glory days are decidedly small-scale and their empire lacks the glamor that would carry it into today's schoolbooks.

Their indisputable talents were not even appreciated by Biblical figures. Phoenicia was criticized in *Ezekiel* for the worship of Baal, the god of a pagan faith that for a while rivaled Judaism in popularity around the Holy Land.

The Phoenicians arrived on the eastern coast of the Mediterranean in what we know today as Lebanon during the second millennium BC. No one is certain just where they came from although it is possible that, as Greek historian Herodotos (c.484–425 BC) believed, they were from the Persian Gulf.

Their most important settlement was at Byblos (Jubayl today), which is identified in Egyptian records from the 14th to the 10th century BC that chronicle trading links of the time. Byblos became known as a supplier of papyrus. Such was its fame that it became associated with the written word, and we derive the words bible and bibliography from the city's name.

There are crushed limestone floors in Byblos that date back to Neolithic times, or the fifth millennium BC, some of the earliest building remains that exist in the world today. They make their neighbors, the Roman colonnade and theater, and the crusader fortress look juvenile by comparison.

Empire builders

When the thin strip of land in the control of the Phoenicians proved insufficient they took to the Mediterranean Sea to search for new provinces to settle, in ships made from local wood. Carthage was founded on the coast of North Africa about 814 BC. Tradition dictates that it was Dido, sister of the Phoenician king, who established the outpost after ambitious plotting against her sibling and his priesthood failed. When she fled to North Africa she took with her boatloads of Phoenician treasure. Carthage went from strength to strength and it was from there that Hannibal mounted his challenge against the might of Rome in the third century BC. The Romans utterly destroyed and then rebuilt the city. It was again destroyed, by the Muslims, in the seventh century AD.

But Carthage was not the only colony in the Phoenician Empire. It is believed that at the time of Solomon, Phoenician power had radiated as far away as Spain. Along the way they took in Cyprus and Sardinia, and numerous bases around the Greek domains. Rather

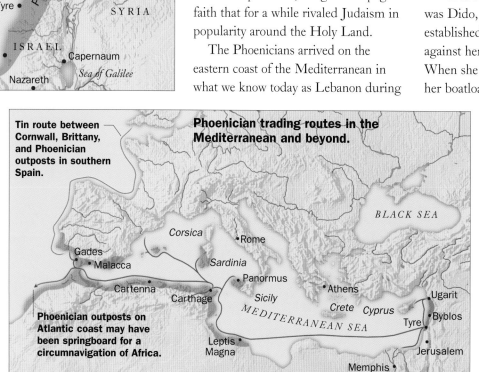

Tin route between Cornwall, Brittany, and Phoenician outposts in southern Spain.

Phoenician trading routes in the Mediterranean and beyond.

Phoenician outposts on Atlantic coast may have been springboard for a circumnavigation of Africa.

than fashion a political union out of the far-flung colonies the Phoenicians were content for each to be independent and work as part of a federation. A similar pattern was adopted by the Greek city-states, but less successfully because they were more warlike. The Phoenicians preferred making money to making war and consequently traded with all the major powers in the region, including the Egyptians, the Persians, and the Greeks. Thus there was no dramatic imperial rise to power nor was there a catastrophic fall from grace. Instead the Phoenicians provided economic stability in the region.

Key to Phoenician success was its seafaring tradition. So potent was the Phoenician fleet that by the seventh century BC it had almost total control of the Mediterranean, operating between bases set up along the African coast. Ships carried cargo including precious stones, metalwork, wood, and raw materials. According to Herodotos, the Phoenician sailors were so adventurous that in the sixth century BC they ventured through the Straits of Gibraltar and circumnavigated the African continent. Although this cannot be proved, it is known that the Phoenicians were technologically capable of carrying out such an expedition.

Carvings recovered from the era of Phoenician power have revealed the shape and dimensions of the ships fashioned by them for trade and adventure. They jealously guarded control of the sea, particularly against the Greeks who for centuries were their biggest rival.

Below: Roman ruins at Byblos—the columns in the background—are young compared to the ancient Phoenician city walls, right, and even older houses in the foreground.

CHAPTER SEVEN

West Bank Gazetteer

Now after Jesus was born in Bethlehem of Judaea in the days of Herod the king, behold, wise men from the east came to to Jerusalem.

St. Matthew 2:1

The West Bank is a relatively new term for an area of longstanding Biblical significance. Old Testament characters knew the region better by the names of Samaria and Judaea, both areas great battlegrounds over the millennia. But the imperial or dynastic struggles that have long since faded into history have been replaced by today's political tensions between

Israelis and Palestinians. Small but immensely important, this region was the Patriarchs' back yard and the home ground of such key figures as Abraham and Solomon. It is the heart of the Holy Land.

Geographically, the West Bank lies alongside Jerusalem and includes Biblically sacred towns including Bethlehem and Hebron. The region is an archaeologist's dream, but due to the ongoing conflict there is much work that cannot be carried out. Not for the first time in world history, religious and political dogma has kept human endeavor at bay. Students must depend on information gleaned years ago rather than enjoying the fruits of modern archaeological studies made using the latest scientific techniques. Only peace in the West Bank will bring the opportunity to uncover fresh evidence on some of the Bible's most intriguing mysteries.

Philistines briefly captured the Ark of the Covenant near Afeq.
(*1 Samuel 4:1–2*)

Tel Qasila
Tel Aviv-Yafo
Yarqon
Tel Afeq
Jaffa

Tel Ashdod **Ashdod**

Tel Ashqelon

Ashqelon

Tall al Ujul

Tel Gezer

Tel Miqn (Ekron)

VIA MARIS—EGYPT TO MESOPOTAMIA

to Alexandria THE WAY OF HORUS **Gaza**

GAZA STRIP

Tall Gaza

I S R A E L

Lower Beth-ho
Upper Beth-horon

Ram Alla

Jerusalem

Tel Nagila (Gath)

Tel Lachish

Solomon's Pools

Bethlehem

Beersheba

Kellah

Khirbat Zif

Hebron

Hasmonaean treasure house and fortress, was torn down by the Romans, to be rebuilt by Herod the Great as a prison. It became a monastery in AD 492.

Herodium

Hyrcan

Be'er Sheva'

Negev Desert

W I L D E R N E S S
O F   J U D A E A

Dead Sea

The Dead Sea is the lowest point on earth. Its high concentration of mineral salts, which makes the water unable to sustain life, gives its other name of Salt Sea. Both parts of the lake, once joined, have shrunk because of Jordanian and Israeli water diversion projects.

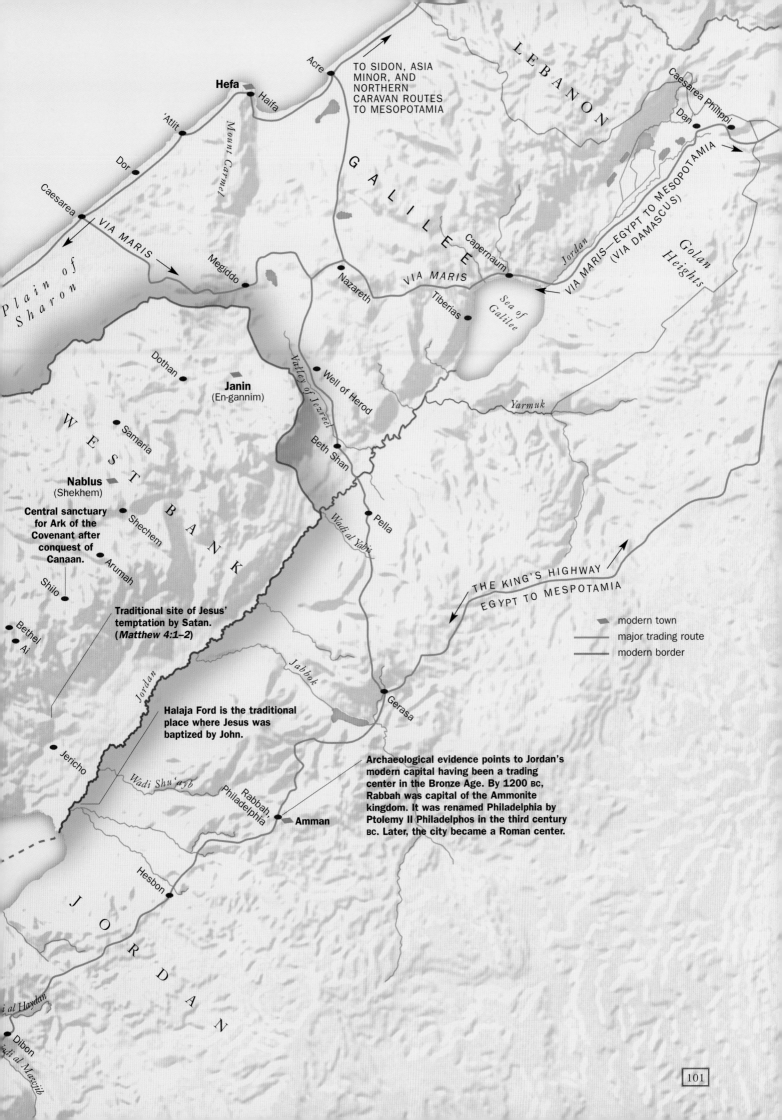

TO SIDON, ASIA
MINOR, AND
NORTHERN
CARAVAN ROUTES
TO MESOPOTAMIA

LEBANON

Caesarea Philippi

Dan

VIA MARIS—EGYPT TO MESOPOTAMIA
(VIA DAMASCUS)

Golan
Heights

Acre

Hefa

Haifa

'Atlit

GALILEE

Capernaum

VIA MARIS

Dor

Mount Carmel

Jordan

Caesarea

VIA MARIS

Nazareth

Tiberias

Sea of
Galilee

Plain of
Sharon

Megiddo

Yarmuk

Dothan

Janin
(En-gannim)

Well of Herod

Valley of Jezreel

Samaria

WEST BANK

Beth Shan

Nablus
(Shekhem)

**Central sanctuary
for Ark of the
Covenant after
conquest of
Canaan.**

Shechem

Pella

Wadi al Yabis

Arumah

Shilo

**Traditional site of Jesus'
temptation by Satan.
(*Matthew 4:1–2*)**

THE KING'S HIGHWAY
EGYPT TO MESOPOTAMIA

Bethel

Ai

Jordan

Jabbok

**Halaja Ford is the traditional
place where Jesus was
baptized by John.**

Gerasa

Jericho

Wadi Shu'ayb

**Archaeological evidence points to Jordan's
modern capital having been a trading
center in the Bronze Age. By 1200 BC,
Rabbah was capital of the Ammonite
kingdom. It was renamed Philadelphia by
Ptolemy II Philadelphos in the third century
BC. Later, the city became a Roman center.**

Rabbah,
Philadelphia

Amman

modern town
major trading route
modern border

Hesbon

JORDAN

i al Haydan

Dibon

adi al Mawjib

101

18. Gaza

> He struck down the Philistines as far as Gaza and its territory, from watchtower to fortified city.
>
> *2 Kings 18:8*

Just as Gaza (Ghazzah, 'azzah) is a vital area in the Middle East today so it was for ancient Egypt more than 3,000 years ago, standing at the north end of the treacherous Way of Horus. This was the route along which pharaohs marched their troops for campaigns in and around Canaan. According to the records of the warmongering Tuthmosis III his footsoldiers traveled between the eastern delta and Gaza—a distance of some 150 miles—in ten days. In preparation for such route marches the Egyptians peppered the Way of Horus with forts, granaries, and wells to provide sustenance for troops. A map from the time of Seti I, around 1300 BC, engraved on a wall in the temple of Amon at Karnak illustrates the supply points and at least one fort has been located and excavated.

The arrival of the Sea Peoples (who, as settlers of Canaan, were later called Philistines) ended Egyptian dominance in the area of Gaza. It was one of five cities strung out along the coastal plain that defined their realm. Gaza under the control of the Philistines is the setting for one of the most famous Biblical stories, that of strongman Samson and the treacherous Delilah. Samson was an Israelite who was famous for his strength, and a sworn enemy of the Philistines. However, when he fell in love with Delilah, a Philistine, he revealed to her the secret of his strength, which lay in his uncut hair. As he slept, she sheared his locks and, as a weakling, he was thrown into prison and had his eyes gouged out.

Captive in Gaza, Samson spent his days grinding grain. This was, of course, one of the most time-consuming tasks of ancient times that usually fell to the women of the household. It is likely that incapacitated prisoners like Samson would have been put to work with a pestle and mortar in grinding houses, providing flour for the elite.

According to the *Judges*, Samson was brought

Right: Much of Gaza's multi-colored history is now buried beneath the ruins of the modern city. Decades of war and Israeli punitive missions have helped to pile more rubble on top of any archaeological sites. The Beach Refugee Camp pictured here now obscures most of the historical harbor.

before the Philistine leaders during a religious ceremony. They failed to notice that his hair had grown again, thus his awesome strength had been restored. Standing between two pillars, Samson flexed his muscles and toppled the temple supports. The building collapsed, killing thousands of Philistines and Samson himself, giving Israel the opportunity to reverse her fortunes in the on-going conflict.

Two temples believed to have belonged to the Philistines have been excavated by archaeologists, one at Tel Qasila in northern Tel Aviv and one at Tel Miqne, the site of ancient Ekron. Both appear to have been designed with a roof supported by two central pillars made of wood and resting on stone bases. The pillars stood about six feet apart. Findings seem to provide justification for the Biblical story—a strong man might be capable of heaving such posts down and collapsing a Philistine temple.

Strategic strip

Gaza's gateway status between Asia and Africa attracted all the conquering empires of ensuing generations, permitting little peace for its beleaguered inhabitants. After Alexander the Great met with some surprisingly prolonged resistance here he, sold the residents into slavery as punishment. For him Gaza was a stepping stone between troublesome Tyre and Egypt, where he would be called Pharaoh. Three centuries later when the Romans arrived, the vital trading artery that Gaza stood astride became known as the *Via Maris*. When Muslim armies took the area in AD 635 it was renamed the Road of Sultans.

Gaza did not rely solely on this sought-after passage. There was a harbor, too, built in the seventh century BC just outside the settlement. Thanks to this facility trading ships were regular visitors throughout history, so commercial links around the Mediterranean were maintained. Today the Beach Refugee Camp largely conceals the historic harbor.

Control of Gaza switched from Arab to Christian hands with the onset of the Crusades. However, in 1187 the crusaders were ousted once and for all. Gaza was absorbed into the Ottoman Empire in the 16th century.

Archaeological work begun during the British Mandate has been left unfinished. The best finds so far are mosaics but there is a strong suspicion that more items of interest lie beneath the overburdened modern city.

Above: In a kinder time, the Victorian artist David Roberts R.A. captured this view of old Gaza, and hinted at the historical treasures that once lay about. The Scottish painter (1796–1864) had already gained a fine reputation before he traveled in 1838 to Egypt and Palestine to paint the monuments, architecture, and people. On his return to London, the results were published as lithographic sets, and were an immediate success. His eye for detail has given us the most accurate glimpse of ancient monuments before the arrival of photography.

19. Shechem

Joshua gathered all the tribes of Israel to Shechem and summoned the elders, the heads, the judges, and the officers of Israel. And they presented themselves before God.

(Joshua 24:1)

T oday Shechem (which sits close by Nablus, aslo earlier known as Shekhem) is a heap of stones, undeniably ancient but not overtly impressive. Yet once this was a vital city of the Holy Land. Archaeology has confirmed that Shechem is one of the oldest cities in the region and, according to the Bible, it became a regular meeting place of the Patriarchs.

According to *Genesis*, Abraham built the first altar in the Promised Land in the vicinity of Shechem and Jacob also built one there. Shechem, a young prince presumably named after the city, raped Jacob's daughter, and its residents were killed by her vengeful brothers. According to the book of *Joshua*, it was here that Joshua gathered together the tribes of Israel to renew the covenant between them and God. Joseph's bones were brought out of Egypt by the children of Israel to be buried in Shechem on land bought by Jacob for 100 pieces of silver. (Today the ancient tomb known as Joseph's is within a domed construction at the foot of the mound on which Shechem stood).

There is independent verification of Shechem's early importance from Egypt. Documentation dating from the 19th century BC identifies Shechem as a center of resistance against Egyptian rule.

Despite the early takeover by the Israelites, the place wasn't immune to the spread of Canaanite religion, which rivaled that of the Israelites. It was here, says *Judges*, that a temple known as the House of Baal-berith was later established. Indeed, the remnants of a temple are clearly identified in excavations. The temple included a large *mazzebah*, or standing stone, often installed for Canaanite worship.

Right: The modern town of Nablus, the largest Arab town of the West Bank, sprawls across the valley under Mount Gezerim—sacred to the Samaritans—and incorporates the remains of Shechem and Samaria.

Melting pot

Turning once again to the Bible, we discover that Shechem faded from the limelight after the kingdom of Israel chose a different capital. With Assyrian ascendancy came a broad mix of peoples brought together from across a mighty empire. They may have mingled with the remaining Israelite population to become the Samaritans, although Samaritans themselves tell a different tale (*see pages 110–11*). At first they were allies of Alexander the Great. Although they later rebelled against him, they nevertheless won his permission to build a temple at Mount

Gerizim, southwest of Shechem.

In 197 BC, Shechem was razed by John Hyrcanus I, the high priest of Israel whose military and political exploits compelled most of the residents of south Judaea to adopt Judaism. Advancing Romans chose a nearby site to build a town they called Flavia Neapolis, now known as Nablus. Christianity was soon established in Flavia Neapolis and by the fourth century AD it was sufficiently important to rank as an Episcopal see. Yet when Jesus was alive the Shechem known by the Israelites was already obsolete. Thanks to the Bible, it was gone but not forgotten.

For centuries scholars could only pore over the Good Book, speculating on the city's whereabouts, until 1903, when German explorer Professor Hermann Thiersh at last pinpointed its position. It was a further decade before the first expedition reached the crumbled ruins at Tel Balata, east of Nablus. Excavations were hampered by the outbreak of the First World War and, when they restarted, they yielded disappointingly little information. The haul has included a cuneiform inscription, an Iron Age seal alongside city walls and towers. The Roman designs were laid waste by an earthquake in 1927.

Pilgrims might also want to visit Jacob's Well on the outskirts of Shechem, where Jesus asked a Samaritan woman for water (*John 4:5–26*). It is at the center of an unfinished church, begun under the auspices of the Russian Czar but a victim of the 1917 Revolution.

20. Bethlehem

For this purpose I was born and for this purpose I have come into the world—to bear witness to the truth.
(John 18:37)

Bethlehem (Bayt Lahm today) was home to the humble harp-player David, destined to be king of the 12 tribes of Israel, who was tending sheep here when he received the first intimations of greatness. It was also here that Rachel, wife of Jacob and mother of two of his sons, was buried. Bethlehem lies some 2,500 feet above sea level, perched on the edge of the Judaean desert. It was prominent in ancient times for its proximity to the main route through the region, linking Beersheba, Hebron, Jerusalem, and Bethel, known as the Way of the Patriarchs. However, archaeological excavations have barely begun in the pretty town. Most of our information about it is derived from literary texts, primarily the Bible.

Chronologically, the first of its sacred sites is the Tomb of Rachel, significant to both Jews and Muslims. Rachel was the best-loved wife of the Patriarch Jacob and died giving birth to Benjamin, her second son. Her firstborn was Joseph, remembered for his decorated robe and vivid dreams, who was later sold into slavery by his jealous brothers. According to *Genesis 35:20*, Rachel died in Bethlehem and "Jacob set a pillar over her tomb. It is the pillar of Rachel's tomb which is there to this day." Although there is some contradiction later in the Bible about the exact whereabouts of her burial this spot seems the most likely.

The fort-like structure marking the grave today is a remodeled version of the one built by the occupying Ottomans in about 1620. Like the Virgin Mary some centuries later, Rachel is seen as a mother figure and women are attracted to the tomb to pray for fertility.

The Church of the Nativity is central to the Christian pilgrimage to Bethlehem. Appearing more like a defended fortress than a place of

Above right: The Chapel of the Milk Grotto where, according to tradition, a drop of Mary's milk spilled while she was suckling the baby Jesus. Legend has it that the white, chalky rock is supposed to increase a woman's milk if eaten.

worship, it is a sixth-century construction that has been modified and modernized. The present structure replaced a tumble-down church dating from AD 326—one of the first three ever built—surrounding the grotto where Jesus was born. The writings of St. Justin the Martyr in about AD 160 reveal that the cave had long been a venerated site.

Targeted holy site

A mosaic depicting the Magi on the church façade ensured its survival when the Persians invaded in 614. Although they had razed other churches in the region, the soldiers recognized the garb of fellow countrymen and showed mercy. Its glory years were during the Crusades, when Christian warriors lavished it with care and money. Of the 44 columns in the church, 30 still bear the paintings of saints commissioned during this era. It was here on Christmas Day 1100 that French nobleman Baldwin of Boulogne was crowned the first king of Jerusalem six months after the ruling Muslims had been ousted. However, the church degenerated when the political balance of the region shifted. It was the target for assaults by rival religious sects and was further undermined

by an earthquake in 1834 and a fire in 1869. Its restoration has been a long, drawn-out affair.

Another sacred site is the Milk Grotto nearby. It was here that the Holy Family is said to have taken shelter during Herod's reign of terror following the birth of Jesus. As the baby fed from his mother's breast a drop of milk is said to have splashed onto the floor, turning it white. A belief widely held by Christians and Muslims says that the chalky deposits in the grotto can benefit nursing mothers. In 1871 Franciscan monks built a church over the site. On sale in the souk are the delightful nativity scenes carved out of olive wood by local craftsman. For centuries these mementos have been famous across the region. Bethlehem's population today is a blend of Jews, Christians, and Muslims. The town is is under the nominal authority of the Palestinians, although recent Israeli-Palestinian tensions have resulted in several incursions by the Israeli army, during which, in early 2002, Palestinian irregulars were besieged in the Chruch of the Nativity, an affair which—for once—ended with little loss of life.

Left: The Church of the Nativity was built by Constantine the Great in AD 330. He was the first Roman emperor to embrace Christianity; his church was constructed over the site of Jesus' birth as an act of worship and as a sign that the Roman Empire had adopted Christianity as the state religion.

Below: Bethlehem awaits detailed archaeological investigation to confirm the wealth of textual information we have about the town.

21. Hebron

> After this, Abraham buried Sarah his wife in the cave of the field of Machpelah east of Mamre (that is Hebron) in the land of Canaan.
> *Genesis 23:19*

Perched high in the Judaean hills, Hebron (Mamre, al-Khalil, Hevron) is believed to be one of the oldest continuously inhabited cities in the world. If the Bible is to be believed, it was a settlement seven years before the creation of Zoan at the top of the Nile in Egypt—and that has been dated to the 18th century BC.

Hebron won its religious significance in ancient times for being the burial place of the following Matriarchs and Patriarchs: Abraham, Sarah, Isaac, Rebekah, Jacob, and Leah, all of whom are sacred to Jews, Christians, and Muslims. Legend also claims Adam and Eve are buried here but that is now thought to have emerged from an early misinterpretation of the Bible.

Today the burial cave is hidden from view by towering walls probably built by Herod (r.37 BC–AD 4). At the time they enclosed a building or shrine but that has long since fallen into dust. A marbleized mosque now stands on the site, with a crenellation and a minaret added to Herodian handiwork. Its main entry is by two flights of stairs dating from the 14th century.

The caves that lie beneath the mosque are still something of a mystery. Before the era of Arab dominance there was some incomplete investigation by monks. Subsequent studies have been severely limited and there is little of scientific substance on record.

Uneasy co-existence

Conflict over who has a right to worship at the tombs caused feuding between the faiths down the centuries. Arabs who took over Hebron in the seventh century were prepared to share the right. However, crusaders took exception to both Muslims and Jews, expelling the latter from the city. The Mamluks, who pushed the crusaders out of the Holy Land, permitted Jews to return to Hebron but banned them from the Cave, a prohibition that remained in force for some 700 years until the Six-Day War of 1967. Muslims and Jews now enter by different doorways to pray to the Patriarch.

Much is made by the Jews of the fact that Abraham bought the Cave of Machpeläh from Ephron the Hittite. This much we know from the Bible. The implication is that he intended to preserve the place as a Jewish sanctuary. Muslims take issue on the subject and believe they have right of tenure as the new faith. There are other sites in the city strongly linked to Abraham, including an ancient oak tree and a well.

Joshua fought against the king of Hebron and, according to Biblical tradition, slaughtered the city's population during a bloodthirsty campaign through the Holy Land. King David was advised by God to go Hebron and there he stayed, as king, for seven and a half years. His sons were born there and David established a power base before moving on to Jerusalem.

Both the Arab name for Hebron (al-Khalil) and the Hebrew name (Hevron) translates to "friend," reflecting the reputation Abraham had for hospitality. Yet today Hebron is inextricably associated with violence and intransigence. Following the Six-Day War in 1967, in which Israel triumphed over a coalition of Arab neighbors, nationalistic and religious settlers decided to claim more of the Holy Land for themselves. There had been no Jewish representation in Hebron since an evacuation in 1929 by the ruling British after 69 Jews were killed by rioting Palestinians. Reclamation began in Hebron and it is from here that Jewish fundamentalists made in-roads on Palestinian land ownership.

In 1994 U.S.-born doctor Baruch Goldstein burst into the Mosque of Abraham and killed 29 praying Arabs, and was beaten to death as a consequence. International condemnation was colored by approval from some quarters of Israel and Baruch was hailed as a saint.

Facing: The Cave of Machpeläh, traditional burial site of Abraham, lies beneath a mosque which was added to the massive Herodian building. Jews, Christians, and Muslims have fought bitterly over the centuries as to who owns the site sacred to all three religions.

22. Samaria

And Omri slept with his fathers and was buried in Samaria, and Ahab his son reigned in his place.

1 Kings 16:28

The city of Samaria (Shomron, Sebaste, Sabastiya), which shares its name with the surrounding area, is one of the archaeological treasures of the Holy Land. Founded in the ninth century BC by King Omri and called Shomeron after Shemer, the owner of the land on which it was built, it was the chosen capital of successive kings of Israel. Excavations have uncovered palace walls and pieces of carved ivory which associate it with the "ivory house" talked of by King Ahab in *1 Kings*. So the assumption is that this was a prosperous place full of merchants and monuments—just the sort of city that might attract the attention of a jealous rival.

Sure enough, in 721 BC Samaria fell to the Assyrians who deported its population and brought in new residents from foreign lands. It remained a political heavyweight, however, being the provincial capital for several empires over the succeeding years. A gentile city, it was duly conquered and destroyed by John Hyrcanus as he stormed through the region. One of his successors encouraged resettlement by Jews.

Right: This aerial view shows the archaeological site of ancient Tel Sebastiya, part of the structures that comprised Samaria. The foundation work of this part of the town appear to date from about 100 BC, but it was greatly expanded by Herod the Great a hundred years later.

New life was breathed into the city when Herod spotted its potential. He embarked on one of his ambitious architectural projects, as usual in the Roman style and of course in honor of a Roman dignitary. He called it Sebaste, derived from a word meaning magnificent, the term commonly used for Caesar Augustus. Sebaste was characterized by numerous temples dedicated to Roman gods, alongside a stadium, theater, and forum. Later a marvelous colonnaded road was built through the city.

Its glory was short-lived. In the Jewish revolt against the Romans the city was destroyed. It rose again from the ashes during the Byzantine and crusader eras but declined in later centuries. Only after archaeological digs carried out between 1908–10 and 1931–35 was Samaria once again recognized for its importance.

Within its walls is the oldest standing Hellenistic tower. In addition to the remains of Herod's grand plans there is the crusader church, built over the ruins of a Byzantine structure and later converted to a mosque by Arabs. Perhaps the most impressive of the ruins are those belonging to the old kings of Israel.

According to Arab tradition, one of the tombs in the church is that of John the Baptist. His parents are believed to be buried nearby and this is also said to be the last resting-place of the prophets Elisha and Obadiah.

Good Samaritans

The people of ancient Samaria were known as the Samaritans and were made famous in one of Jesus' best-loved tales. The story of the Good Samaritan is about a man who was robbed and wounded and left for dead by a priest and a Levite. The only person who cared was a Samaritan. The subtext is that Jews like Jesus were traditionally enemies with Samaritans. Jesus chose them as an example to illustrate his "love thy neighbor" doctrine.

Samaritans maintain they are descendants of the Manasseh and Ephraim tribes of Israel. They split from mainstream Judaism in Old Testament times over their literal interpretation of Mosaic Law. Hostilities between Samaritans and Jews were at their height prior to the birth of Jesus, when John Hyrcanus destroyed the sacred Samaritan temple on Mount Gerizim, just outside Samaria, the holiest of the sect's sites. They believe this is the real Mount Moriah where Abraham prepared to sacrifice his son Isaac (contrary to the widely held belief that the event occurred in the vicinity of Jerusalem), and also that the broken tablets of the first Ten Commandments are buried here.

Today the Samaritan population has been reduced to mere hundreds, living in two communities; one in Nablus and the other outside Tel Aviv-Yafo.

Above: Dawn mists shroud the valleys of the Samarian hills and pale light illuminates the excavated ruins of the Samaritan temple complex on the summit of Mount Gezerim. The few remaining Samaritans still make regular pilgimages, especially at Passover, to worship on the sacred mountain, which lies two miles south of modern Nablus.

CHAPTER EIGHT
Jordan Gazetteer

And all the country of Judaea and all Jerusalem were
going out to him and were being baptized by him in
the river Jordan, confessing their sins.

Mark 1:5

As countries go, Jordan is a juvenile,
coming into existence shortly after the
foundation of Israel in the mid-20th century.
But archaeologists at work there are mining a
rich seam of antiquities, for the newly drawn
borders enclose some of the oldest Biblical sites
in existence.

The river Jordan divides Jordan and Israel,
with the former in control of the east bank. John
baptized Jesus in this river and there is
speculation that he was linked to a remote sect
living by the Dead Sea known as the Essenes.
In ancient times the area was the home of the
Amonites, the Moabites, and the Edomites
although it was largely conquered by King
David as he expanded his empire in the tenth
century BC. Empire after empire swept through
the region after the era of David and the balance
of power changed frequently.

Jordan's ties with Biblical history are many.
The remains of Moses lie in its territory,
although their whereabouts are unknown; the
oldest Old Testament in existence is there; it has
the oldest map of the Holy Land; and many
well-preserved Byzantine church mosaics, since
Jordan was a refuge for persecuted Christians in
Roman times.

In AD 542, the Jordan region suffered a
disaster of Biblical proportions when much of
the population was wiped out by the plague.
Centuries later the land became part of the
Ottoman Empire, and remained so until it was
allocated to the British at the end of the First
World War. Under British rule it was known as
the Emirate of Transjordan, and was run jointly
by the British and the Hashemite King
Abdullah, a 40th-generation descendant of the
Prophet Mohammed. Jordan gained full
independence at the end of the Second World
War, and is still governed by the Hashemite
family.

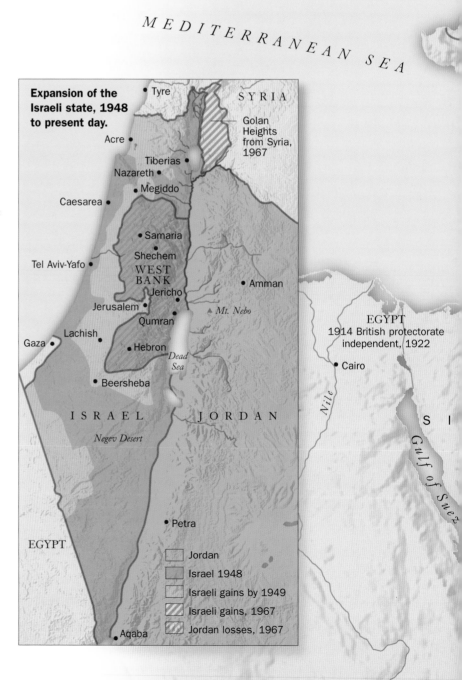

Expansion of the Israeli state, 1948 to present day.

MEDITERRANEAN SEA

SYRIA

Golan Heights from Syria, 1967

Tyre
Acre
Tiberias
Nazareth
Megiddo
Caesarea
Samaria
Shechem
Tel Aviv-Yafo
WEST BANK
Jericho
Amman
Jerusalem
Qumran
Mt. Nebo
Lachish
Gaza
Hebron
Dead Sea
Beersheba
ISRAEL
JORDAN
Negev Desert

EGYPT
1914 British protectorate independent, 1922

Cairo

Nile

EGYPT

Gulf of Suez

Petra

Aqaba

	Jordan
	Israel 1948
	Israeli gains by 1949
	Israeli gains, 1967
	Jordan losses, 1967

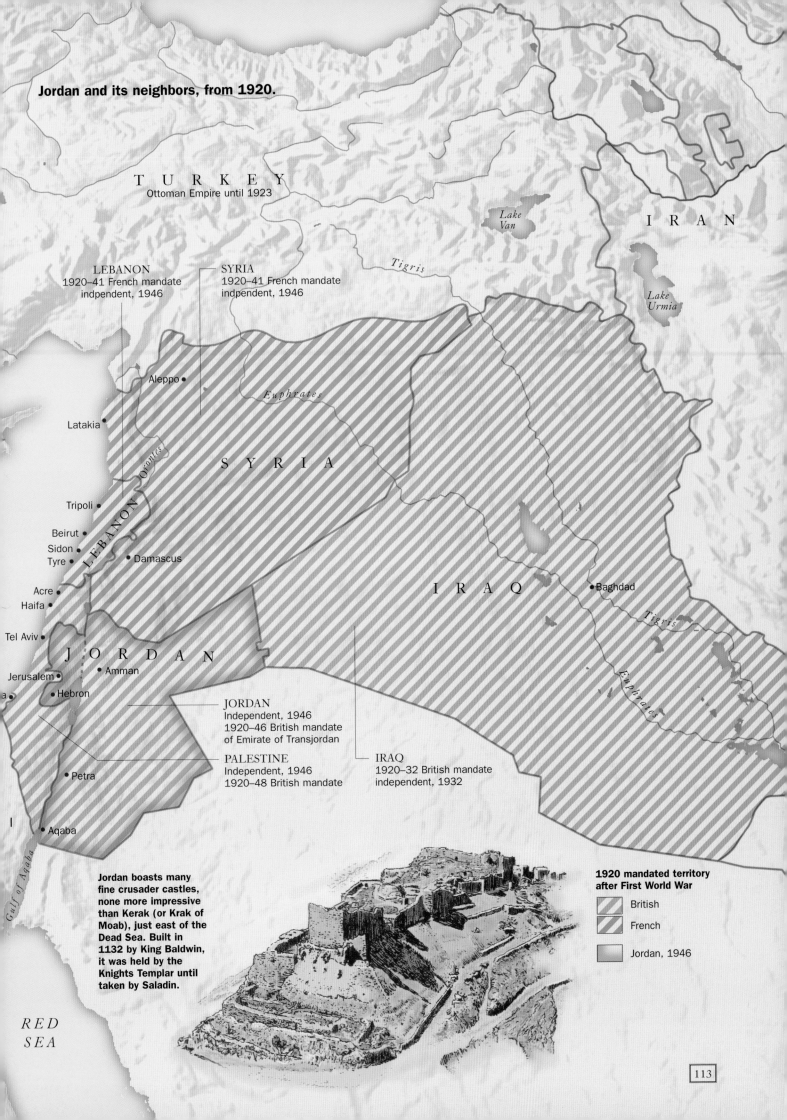

Jordan and its neighbors, from 1920.

T U R K E Y
Ottoman Empire until 1923

I R A N

Lake Van

Lake Urmia

Tigris

LEBANON
1920–41 French mandate
indpendent, 1946

SYRIA
1920–41 French mandate
indpendent, 1946

Aleppo •

Euphrates

Latakia •

Orontes

S Y R I A

Tripoli •

L E B A N O N

Beirut •
Sidon •
Tyre •   • Damascus

Acre •
Haifa •

I R A Q

• Baghdad

Tigris

Tel Aviv •

J O R D A N

Jerusalem •
a   • Amman

• Hebron

Euphrates

JORDAN
Independent, 1946
1920–46 British mandate
of Emirate of Transjordan

PALESTINE
Independent, 1946
1920–48 British mandate

IRAQ
1920–32 British mandate
independent, 1932

• Petra

l

• Aqaba

Gulf of Aqaba

Jordan boasts many
fine crusader castles,
none more impressive
than Kerak (or Krak of
Moab), just east of the
Dead Sea. Built in
1132 by King Baldwin,
it was held by the
Knights Templar until
taken by Saladin.

**1920 mandated territory
after First World War**

British

French

Jordan, 1946

*RED
SEA*

23. Qumran: The Dead Sea Scrolls

Then David arose, and all the people who were with him, and they crossed the Jordan. By daybreak not one was left who had not crossed the Jordan.

2 Samuel 17:22

Next to the discovery of Tutankhamun's treasure, the emergence of the Dead Sea Scrolls was the archaeological highlight of the 20th century. But the two could not be more different. When archaeologist Howard Carter first peered into the pharaoh's tomb in 1922 treasures lay all around, so he got an instant appreciation of the prizes stored within. In comparison, the Scrolls seem distinctly drab and downbeat. The arid atmosphere of the region had preserved some scrolls in reasonable condition but many more had fallen into fragments. It was years before the full worth of the find became apparent.

According to a well-worn tale, a Bedouin shepherd boy threw a stone into a cave near Qumran in the spring of 1947 and heard a crashing sound of shattering pottery. On further investigation he found a stack of jars containing the ancient manuscripts. Only when the first haul of scrolls was offered for sale to a part-time antiquities dealer did the find reach the ears of the world's Biblical scholars. A program of study and excavation was initiated that continues today, although by any standards it has been slow going.

It was not until 1949 that the cave that had stored the scrolls for centuries was identified. There followed an unseemly race between the world's top archaeologists and local people to comb through the area for more hidden caches. By 1956 a total of 11 caves in the area had yielded scrolls, manuscripts, and other archaeological items including wood, fabric, and pottery.

Painstaking analysis

The majority of the finds were put in the hands of a team of experts who published eight volumes of material in the subsequent four decades. The task ahead was colossal, with one cave alone containing no fewer than 520 texts, in 15,000 pieces. In total there were some 800 scrolls to analyze, the oldest dating from 200 BC and the most recent from AD 68. Nevertheless, criticism about the grinding pace of progress compelled the introduction of a fresh approach in the 1980s. For the first time Jewish academics were invited to scrutinize these scrolls, in a bid to gain further understanding of their content.

A final verdict about who wrote the scrolls and why is still some way off. There is a consensus about some aspects of their history, though. It seems the scrolls were part of a library maintained by a Jewish sect, most probably the Essenes. Although

Right: Painstaking restoration of the numerous and fragile fragments of the Dead Sea Scrolls was required. The results are now housed in the Shrine of the Book—a building designed to resemble the lid of a scroll jar—in Jerusalem. Work still continues.

not mentioned in the New Testament, the separatist Essenes were identified in other contemporary manuscripts, although mention of them is somewhat fleeting. They veered away from Orthodox Judaism when a Hasmonean king adopted the title of High Priest, a role they felt could only be inherited by a descendent of Aaron, Moses' brother.

One of the most fascinating facts thrown up by the scrolls is the likeness between today's Old Testament and that written two millennia ago. The scrolls contained copies of all the Old Testament books except *Esther* and are 1,000 years older that any other known. In addition there were hymns and prayers and assorted Jewish writings that appear to represent the theology of the writers. The languages used are primarily Hebrew and Aramaic, although some texts are in Greek.

Although the scrolls at first appeared unpromising, they have told the modern world more about how Judaism evolved during a turbulent time and the culture into which Christianity was launched than any other source.

The residents at Qumran, like the early Christians, held communal meals and practiced baptism, illustrating that both must have drawn on a common theme in Judaism at the time. It seems the Qumran community was overrun by Romans in AD 68, two years before the second Temple in Jerusalem was destroyed.

Above: The monastery at Qumran, ancient center of the Essene sect. The entrance to the caves where the Dead Sea Scrolls were discovered is circled in the photograph.

In the Wilderness of Judaea

The Essenes were wilderness dwellers, firm believers in baptism and in the Apocalypse. Some theological theorists place Jesus among the Essenes during his period in the wilderness, which may have colored his thinking about his coming mission. The Essenes were pious and disciplined, but their beliefs were considered heretical and it is thought that one of their leaders was put to death by mainstream Jewish priests in Jerusalem.

Perhaps they hid their texts in the caves on the outbreak of hostilities between the Jews and the occupying Romans in AD 66. Or maybe another group sought permission to use their remote settlement for the same purpose. The precise details of how the Dead Sea Scrolls were hidden will probably never be known.

24. Mount Nebo

The Moses went up from the plains of Moab to Mount Nebo, to the top of Pisgah, which is opposite Jericho And the Lord showed him the land…

Deuteronomy 34:1

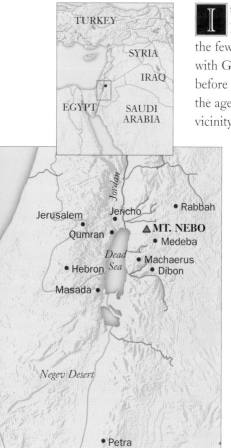

It was from a vantage point atop Mount Nebo (Jabal Naba) that Moses, one of the few men believed to have spoken directly with God, surveyed the Promised Land shortly before his death, which apparently occurred at the age of 120. He was buried somewhere in the vicinity although *Deuteronomy* states clearly that his grave was left unmarked.

That did not stop fourth-century Christians from attributing an empty cave discovered on Mount Nebo to being the last resting-place of Moses. A church already stood here when this tradition was cultivated, and the sect expanded to become one of the largest in the Holy Land. Unusually the church survived Persian and Arab invasions and continued to operate until about the ninth century. The site is now subject to continued excavation initiated by Fransican monks.

Facts combine to cause confusion about exactly where Moses was when his eyes fell on Canaan. Nebo is the name of the mountain but also of a nearby village. Peaks on the mountain ridge are known by different names. Clarity has not been helped by what must be an exaggerated account in *Deuteronomy* of what Moses could see as he gazed at the Promised Land from "Gilead as far as Dan," the implication being that he could even see the Mediterranean Sea.

Land of the Moabites

Mount Nebo is in Moab, a region that belonged to the Moabite tribe in Biblical times. The Moabites were descended from a son of Lot and a great nephew of Abraham. Although from similar ethnic stock as the Israelites, the Moabites worshipped Chemosh rather than Yahweh, and the two clashed culturally and territorially on a regular basis after about the 13th century BC. Despite the difficulties existing between the tribes, Ruth, a Moabite, married into an Israelite family and went on to become the great-grandmother of King David.

Evidence about the hostility is, however, threaded throughout the Bible and is corroborated, at least in part, in a fascinating independent source. The Moabite Stone—discovered in Dhiban (ancient Dibon) in 1868—harks back to the distant past when the King Omri if Israel (r.c.884–872 BC) conquered Moabite lands. Apparently authored by Mesha, the Moabite king, some 40 years later, it tells how this land had been won back again from one of Omri's successors, probably King Ahab. This remarkable archaeological gem is a black basalt boulder, measuring more than three feet in height, bearing 34 lines of text in the Moabite alphabet,

which was similar to that used in Canaan, and is the only written evidence that speaks for the Moabites. Smashed by criminals after its 19th-century discovery, it was restored and is now on display in the Louvre Museum in Paris.

The text mentions Nebo as the site of a slaughter of 7,000 Israelites by Mesha's men, carried out to curry favor from Chemosh. Other Old Testament cities are named, lending credence to Biblical accounts relating to Moab. If the Bible is to be believed, the Moabites suffered a terrible retaliation from Jehoram, the Israelite king, who destroyed every city in the region except one. According to the historian Josephus, the Moabites were driven out of their strongholds or killed in 582 BC following the Babylonian invasion.

There are other archaeological wonders in the vicinity, too. At Medeba, a town named in the

Israelites' travels, lies a marvellous mosaic map dating from the sixth century BC. Originally measuring some 72 by 23 feet, itd showed the Holy Lands from Byblos in the north to Thebes in the south. Alas, the portion showing Nablus to Egypt is all that remains. Still, it is the oldest map of the region and identifies places in the Negev that would otherwise be unknown. In 1965, some 80 years after it was first discovered, the mosaic was restored and photographed.

As part of his Holy Land building campaign Herod constructed a fortified palace at Machaerus, close to the Dead Sea. This is where his son Herod Antipas was enchanted by the dancing of stepdaughter Salome. When Herod Antipas promised to grant her dearest wish she asked for the head of the preacher John the Baptist. The Galilean ruler—frequently the target of John's criticisms—delivered it.

Above: The Promised Land can be seen from the snow-capped peaks of Mount Nebo. Moses' last resting place is nearby, although the exact location is unknown.

25. Petra of Edom and Nabataea

He struck down ten thousand Edomites in the Valley
of Salt and took Selah by storm and called it Joktheel,
which is its name today

2 Kings 14:7

Petra (Batra, Sela)—known as Selah in
Old Testament times—was in the heart of
Edomite country. Little is known of its ancient
inhabitants although remnants from the
Paleolithic and Neolithic ages have been found
there. According to the Bible, the Edomites are
descendents of Esau, hairy brother of the
smooth-skinned Jacob, and were thus closely
related to the Israelites. However, the Edomites
pursued their own faith with a chief deity, Qos
or Qaus, and a range of gods and goddesses.

Condemnation of the paganism that existed
in parallel to the worship of Yahweh is sparse in
the early books of the Old Testament; perhaps
because of a Biblical tradition that held God
himself came from Edom. Later there are harsh
words for the Edomite tribe but only after they
launched raiding parties and seized land
following the destruction of Jerusalem.

Right: The most
spectacular of Petra's
rock-hewn buildings is
the Khazneh, or
Treasury, so named
because it was
believed that looters
used it to stash their
treasures. Its large
scale—the frontage is
over 130 feet high—
suggests it may have
been a tomb for a
Nabataean king.

Edomites are mentioned in Assyrian literature of the eighth century BC as one of a number of subject nations to offer tributes.

Joash, the son of Jehoahaz and 12th king of Israel, conquered ancient Petra during a bloody campaign waged around the Holy Land after 800 BC, related in the *2 Kings* text. Edomites migrated westward and became known as Idumaeans.

The Nabataean Legacy

Petra knew another more glorious era, this time under the rulership of the Nabataeans, an Arab tribe that surged up from the south in about the sixth century BC and was dominant until AD 100 when they fell under Roman sway. During Nabataean rule, Petra was a vibrant entrepot on the spice route and the beating heart of a commercial empire. Merchants with camel caravans carrying goods from places such as China, Egypt, Greece, and India thronged in its streets and souks. At its peak the population was in excess of 30,000. To celebrate their city's success the Nabataeans carved stunning facades from the rock faces. Petra was stout enough to withstand and survive attack by Seleukid forces, still fresh from major victories under the recent leadership of Alexander the Great.

However, the Romans overwhelmed this city, like many others. Business went on much as before—it was still sufficiently vibrant and populous for the Romans to build a 7,000-seat theater—but changing trade routes and an earthquake in AD 551 finally relegated it to little more than an outpost.

Taken by Islamic forces in the seventh century, there is evidence that the crusaders made use of its astonishing natural defenses when they swept through the region 500 years later. But when the knights withdrew to Europe, Petra—despite its Bedouin population—effectively became isolated and a "lost city."

Imagine, then, the joy of Johann Ludwig Burckhardt (1784–1817), the Swiss-born explorer, when he became the first modern European to encounter the splendors of Petra, the "rose-red city," during his exploration of Arabia and northern Africa.

Today's tourists approach the city by treading the path of yesteryear's invaders, wending their way down a long gorge which narrows to nine feet in places with sheer walls of some 200 feet on either side, a corridor presumably created by earthquakes. Here Moses is said to have struck a rock and caused water to gush forth following the Exodus from Egypt.

Above: Monuments that draw the eye include the Ad-Dayr, or monastery, used in Byzantine times as a church (the painting by David Roberts R.A. captures the awe early European travelers experienced on seeing a city cut from rock cliffs). There is also evidence of a technologically advanced network put in place by the Nabataeans to transport water throughout the city. Archaeological work still contines at Petra, where there is grave concern over the effects of mass-tourism on the monuments.

CHAPTER NINE

Syria Gazetteer

And the Lord said to him, "Go, return on your way to the wilderness of Damascus. And when you arrive, anoint Hazael to be king over Syria.
1 Kings 19:15

To Herodotos, fifth-century BC Syria was "the Mediterranean coast of Arabia." It grew to be much more than this, incorporating the Taurus Mountains of Turkey, the Egyptian Sinai, and the hinterlands of the Euphrates. Indeed, Syria was a political entity that was comprised of a vast region of the Middle East. Today's national borders make it small by comparison.

Agriculture began in the region in about 9000 BC, and when food became abundant urban settlements developed. There followed trade, invasion, and the development of ships. But perhaps the vital contribution to mankind's advancement that came from the region was an alphabet. Characters began as lines and shapes gouged into clay tablets. After time, the system was refined by successive civilizations until the alphabet we know today emerged.

Syria became a reflection of whichever empire was strongest in the region. Like other areas of the Middle East, it prospered most under Roman rule, the 250-year *Pax Romana* permitting boundless trading opportunities. It was during this era that Palmyra came to eminence. When the ruins of Palmyra were discovered in the 19th century there was a flurry of excitement among archaeologists. Writing in the mid-20th century, author Agatha Christie was stunned by the place: "Palmyra—its slender creamy beauty rising up fantastically in the middle of hot sand. It is lovely and fantastic and unbelievable, with all the theatrical implausibility of a dream."

In Palmyra there are columns and carvings forged with white marble amid bowing palms trees, giving it a serene beauty. There are no links with the Bible here, however, for Palmyra, also known as Tadmor, was still little more than a desert trading post even in New Testament times. But later the Romans invested heavily in the city, and additional romance, as if any were needed, came in the form of Zenobia, the Palmyrene queen who briefly came to prominence in the east in AD 270.

The Syrian sun sets over Roman ruins at Palmyra.

26. Mari

And the Lord sent against him bands of the Chaldeans and bands of the Syrians and bands of the Moabites and bands of the Amonites, and sent them against Judah to destroy it, according to the word of the Lord that he spoke by his servants the prophets.

2 Kings 24:2

It seems impossible that a wall which is about 5,000 years old and bearing paintings could still be standing. In Syria, however, that is exactly what was discovered when the ruins at Mari came to light, an archaeological site now known as Tel Hariri.

Although Mari's fame and power was well known, 20th-century scholars had no idea where the city stood. Excavations were initiated at Tel Hariri, next to the Euphrates, in 1933 when a group of Bedouins seeking a boulder to mark a grave happened upon a massive statue of the sun god Shamash. Exciting though this find was, it was ultimately dwarfed by the array of buildings and treasures discovered there.

The ground floor of a second-millennium palace at Mari covered six acres and had 300 rooms. There was evidence of stairways too, making the size of the place even bigger. Amazing paintings were discovered on walls flanking one of two giant courtyards. One appears to relate to the coronation of a king. In four archive rooms 20,000 tablets were discovered, giving historians vast quantities of data, albeit in cuneiform script. Among them were letters—a significant proportion was royal correspondence—reports, diplomatic exchanges, accounts, and law decrees, expanding our knowledge of the ancient Assyrian culture enormously.

A room near the archives also appears to have been designated for schooling. There were baths and irrigation systems. In addition to wall paintings and sculptures there were cult objects as well as hundreds of everyday items, giving us a dramatic and accurate insight into life 2,000 years and more before the time of Christ.

Remains of a further palace dating from the third millennium were also evident. Scrutiny of the inscription on a statuette found here revealed that Tel Hariri was in fact the lost city of Mari. Six temples were revealed and it seems the population of Mari worshipped the pantheon of gods that characterized the Old Babylonian period. Worship in Mari was directed at Ishtar, goddess of love, and Dagan.

Mari appears to have been at its zenith in 2400 BC. The city poised between Egypt and Mesopotamia controlled vast tracts of surrounding countryside and a series of vassal

Left: The wall paintings found in many rooms of the palace at Mari are preserved in an astonishingly good state. In this panel, a priest pulls a sacrificial bull by a ring through its nose.

states. Its inhabitants were Amorites, referred to in the Old Testament, and they spoke a language related to Hebrew.

Saved as a time capsule

The Mari kingdom was wiped out by the Babylonians under the command of Hammurabi. In destroying the palace belonging to Mari's final king, Zimri-Lim, the violent Babylonians inadvertently preserved it. By knocking in its mud-brick walls the palace rooms were filled with earth and their contents were protected through time.

There is speculation that the ousted Mari population moved south to Canaan where they were known as the Hyksos. The first reference to the Hyksos in Egyptian records appears soon after the Mari kingdom was laid waste. Eventually, Hyksos would become pharaohs in Upper Egypt of the 15th and 16th dynasties, but they were ultimately crushed by a native

Egyptian revolution led by Tuthmosis III.

Perhaps the most compelling clue in the Mari saga was the discovery of a connection that links the Hebrews to Mari and Egypt. King Zimri-Lim himself uses the term "the *habiru*" to describe a people living in his kingdom. It is the same name given to Hebrews in the original Hebrew Bible (*see box, page 65*). Additionally, there is reference to the *habiru* in a scene on the tomb of Tuthmosis III, created in about 1500 BC, and on several further graves and monuments throughout Egypt, denoting manual workers. Perhaps, say critics, the word *habiru* merely referred to a class of slave. Or possibly it provides evidence of a Hebrew colony or slavery in Egypt in a time before the story of Moses.

Artifacts from Mari are distributed between the museums of Aleppo and Damascus in Syria and the Louvre in Paris.

Facing: This statue of a water goddess was found in the Court of Palms, part of the massive palace of Zimri-Lim at Mari. Clearly designed as a fountain piece, the room in which she was discovered was not connected to water, however. The horns on the headdress signify her status as a deity.

27. Ebla, Tall Mardikh

And Abraham took Sarah his wife, and Lot his brother's son, and all their possessions that they had gathered, and the people that they had acquired in Haran and they set out to go into the land of Canaan.

Genesis 12:5

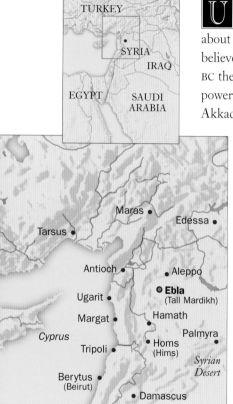

Up until the mid-1970s archaeologists made various—and wrong—assumptions about the lands mentioned in *Genesis*. It was believed that during the late third millennium BC the Near East was solely controlled by powerful Mesopotamian empires such as Sumer, Akkad, and Ur. The discovery of the Ebla tablets in 1975 turned this thinking on its head. It was one of those joyous occasions for archaeologists when they can truly claim to have rewritten history.

According to *Genesis*, Abraham was told by God to leave the city of Haran, on the upper Euphrates (*see pages 18–19*), and head south into Canaan. Biblical scholars generally agree that his rambling journey would have occurred around 2000 BC, taking in Shechem, Bethel (near Jerusalem), Hebron, and the Negev scrublands. During these wanderings he would almost certainly have passed through the kingdom of Ebla in the twilight years of its influence.

Ebla—modern-day Tall (or Tell) Mardikh near Aleppo, northwest Syria—was first excavated in 1974 by Paolo Matthiae and archaeologists from the University of Rome. The early findings were unremarkable; some moderately interesting Bronze Age temples and several well-preserved buildings were found, but that was all. Then they discovered a palace containing examples of Sumerian-style artwork in the form of woodcarvings, cylinder seals, and stone inlays. Unusually for the period, there was also a small quantity of inscribed clay tablets.

The following year, Matthiae and his team hit the motherlode. In an archive chamber they uncovered some 18,000 cuneiform tablets forming the day-to-day records of a palace official. Originally stacked on wooden shelves, long since decayed, some of the scripts now lay broken on the floor. Yet translation proved relatively straightfoward. The tablets were written in a Semitic tongue, more closely related to Hebrew and Arabic than Akkadian, and borrowed familiar symbols from the Sumerians. Some bore an incredible 3,000 lines of writing.

Records of state

The tablets carry mundane details of household matters, such as food and wine reserves, but there is also a fascinating glimpse of affairs of state. Here we find a powerful and wealthy kingdom, its economy based on agriculture, and a national flock numbering two million sheep. The vast quantities of wool produced were used in the textile industry, which in turn supported a healthy foreign trade. Precious metal and woodworking were also important and trade deals were regularly struck with other cities.

The archive recorded seed distribution, rations issued to workers, inventories of royal assets, official correspondence, and treaties. There were literary references to Mesopotamian mythology and an impressive range of proverbs, hymns, and incantations to a range of deities later identified with the Babylonian Empire. These included Dabir (the city's patron god), Marduk, Sipish, Hadad, Balatu, and Astarte. There were also accounts of a Great Flood and the Creation.

Many of the place names seem to have been linked to settlements as far away as Palestine, central Turkey, Lebanon, and northern Iraq. However some scholars suspect these refer to local towns within a smaller kingdom. Work is continuing on the tablets but the best guess so far is that, at the peak of its powers (c.2500 BC), Ebla controlled about 17 city-states and dominated northern Syria, Lebanon, and northern Mesopotamia. Kings were non-hereditary, governed for limited terms, and were appointed by a council of elders. Their military strength is unclear, though it is likely they relied heavily on mercenaries.

In the 24th century BC, Ebla faced a major

Right: In addition to cloth-making, smelting and alloying of gold, silver, copper, tin, and lead were important activities of Ebla. Finds, such as this necklace with disk pendants, indicate a high degree of artistic sophistication.

threat to its security from the Akkadian empire under the Semitic ruler Sargon I (r.c. 2335–2279 BC). Though Sargon may not have conquered the city as he claimed, his grandson Naram-Sin probably did burn it to the ground c.2240 BC. There then followed a long slow decline until the arrival of invading Amorites at the beginning of the second millennium BC.

Above: Ancient Ebla's excavations provided startling information about the Holy Lands.

28. Ugarit

And Hazael said, "What is your servant, who is but a dog, that he should do this great thing?" And Elisha answered, "The Lord has shown me that you are to be king over Syria.

2 Kings 8:13

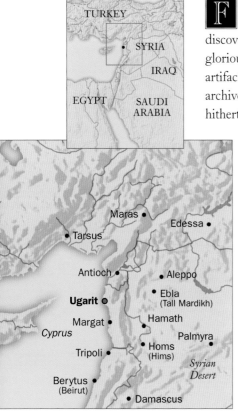

First uncovered by a peasant's plow, Ugarit (today's Ras Shamra) was from its first discovery an archaeological treasure trove. Its glorious palaces and temples were littered with artifacts, and it contained several libraries and archives containing a wealth of written material hitherto unknown. Excavations on the coastal site have been maintained virtually continuously since the whereabouts of the fallen city became known in 1929.

First settled in the seventh millennium BC, records from Ebla have revealed that Ugarit was a busy city in the early Bronze Age. By 2500 BC it was large, fortified, and held sway over the surrounding land. Its heyday occurred between about 1450 and its demise in 1185 BC. A sophisticated trading city, it did business overland with Anatolian merchants and by sea with the Aegean nations. Ugarit exported copper to Mesopotamia where there were no metal deposits to be mined. It sold trees to Egypt where few grew. The making of bronze became a specialty. In addition it dealt in ivory, semi-precious stones, foods, tin, and tools.

To record the deals, the Ugarit traders used cuneiform. There is also evidence that they were conversant in ten different languages and used five different scripts, one of which was something that approached an alphabet. The speculation is that this was developed in a local scribe's academy for use by workmen who found hieroglyphics too complex. Reflecting the local language, this appears to have been in use by Canaanites and is likely to have been the forerunner of the Phoenician alphabet, adopted by the Mycenaean Greeks, and, therefore, our own. It took scholars just over a year to crack the Ugarit cuneiform code.

Local gods appear to have been Baal, El, and Asherah of the Sea. Some of the tablets discovered in Ugarit contained apparently mythological stories that bore remarkable resemblances to the Biblical stories of the Patriarchs. That might mean that the events of the Bible were not only passed from generation to generation but were recorded soon after they happened.

Destroyed by Sea Peoples

The fact that Ugarit survived for as long as it did is a tribute to the diplomatic skills of its leaders. The city was squeezed between the expansionist Egyptians in the south and the Hittites to the north. The compromise was to become a vassal to the Hittite king, thus creating stability with a measure of independence.

Ugarit fell victim to the Sea Peoples, marauders who plagued the Mediterranean

Right above: This carved ivory head of a man, found at Ugarit, dates from c.1330 BC, during the city's classic period.

coasts and destroyed everything they came across. The identity of the Sea Peoples—ultimately defeated by the Egyptians—remains a mystery. Some believe they were Anatolian while others think they hailed from the Dorian invaders of the Aegean. Their raids occurred when Mycenaean culture, a towering influence in Greece, was in a terminal decline, probably caused by internal squabbling. Wherever they came from and whatever their aim, they wreaked havoc and collapsed several late Bronze Age empires.

A last desperate message has been found that was written by Ammurapi, the last king of Ugarit to his counterpart in Cyprus in about 1185 BC: "Ships of the enemy have come, some of my towns have been burned and they have done wicked things in our country. All my troops are deployed in Hittite territory, and all my ships are standing off the Lycian coast, so the country is at the mercy of the enemy. Seven enemy ships have appeared offshore and have done evil things. If there are more hostile ships on the way, please inform me and of what kind." Too late! The clay tablet bearing these words was still in the process of being baked when Ugarit went up in flames.

Ugarit is sited on a tel. Today's visitors are seeing the mound stripped down to the level corresponding to the 13th century BC. Ugarit builders used stone rather than mud so there is a fine array of ruins still in evidence.

Above: Many of Ugarit's stone-constructed buildings have survived the centuries. Here, the ruins of a fort date from c.1400 BC.

Below: A ceramic cylinder dating from c.1400 BC, is inscribed with cuneiform script. Ugarit scribes soon abandoned cuneiform for an alphabet.

29. Aleppo

And each struck down his man. The Syrians fled, and Israel pursued them, but Ben-Hadad king of Syria escaped on a horse with horsemen.

1 Kings 20:20

I n Arabic Aleppo (Halab, Halep) is fully titled Halab ash-Shahba, translating to "he milked the gray." It refers to the fact that Abraham is believed to have stopped atop the hill here as he traveled between Haran and Canaan and generously distributed milk from his gray cow. Aleppo, vying with its southerly neighbor Damascus for having the longest, proudest history, dates to at least the end of the third millennium BC. In the second century BC it belonged first to the Hittites, then the Egyptians, the Mitannis, and the Hittites once more.

It survived the invasion of the Sea Peoples as a Hittite state, then fell into the sphere of the Assyrians, followed by the Persians. With the arrival of Alexander the Great and Seleukid rule after 333 BC its name was changed to Beroia. This is not to be confused with the Beroia in Macedonia that Paul visited on his second missionary journey. However, its Biblical association occurred in that Hellenistic period when Seleukid king Antiochus V ordered the death of High Priest Menelaos here.

After the Greeks came the Romans (who became the Byzantines), then the Arabs. Its popularity with the empires of the era stems largely from the fact it was on a crossroads of important commercial routes, even when trade was in its infancy.

Yet the sum total of the architectural heritage from these diverse cultures extending from the depths of time to the golden age of Islam is astonishingly sparse. Apart from sections of city wall and the Greco-Roman style grid-system of streets there is little to denote its multi-faceted past. A Byzantine cathedral, believed to have been founded by St. Helena, the devout mother of Constantine the Great, has been greatly altered and little of it remains intact. Apart from that, Aleppo at a glance appears to have mislaid

Right: When the crusaders arrived in the Holy Land, the church of St. Simeon was already 700 years old. It was named after Simeon Stylites, the holy man who spent 37 years perched on a tall pillar, preaching Christianity to travelers and pilgrims from near and far. He died in AD 459.

a few millennia of history. Presumably, ancient ruins were largely recycled into new building by successive regimes, indicating that Aleppo had utility or outpost status.

However, the best was yet to come. In the tenth century AD the Hamdanid dynasty established the city as an independent principality, sparking a surge in culture. The Hamdanids were Arab refugees from Iraq who made the most of the prime trading position that Aleppo occupied. With the wealth they acquired they fostered the talents of poets and artists. They restyled the Great Mosque, devoted to Zachariah, the father of John the Baptist. His head is said to lie within. The court was within the citadel, which would later be impressively fortified to withstand crusader advances.

Waves of ruthless invaders

Aleppo became a frontline city during the Crusades, party to Islamic intrigues and Christian attack. The Muslim military hero Zengi and his son Nur ed-Din organized the defenses of Aleppo to repel the crusaders, which they did successfully, and also to keep rival Islamic factions at bay. But where the crusaders

failed in 1125, the Mongols succeeded less than 150 years later. Storming through the city's defenses, the Mongols slaughtered the inhabitants of Aleppo before moving south. The city fell into Mamluk hands until invasion by the Turks in the early 16th century.

As part of the Ottoman Empire, Aleppo had the opportunity to reorganize, having seen its valuable trading routes swallowed up or erased in the preceding centuries of strife. As testimony to the success of its efforts, the *khans* (warehouses) of the era are still standing and the streets of Aleppo host the most famous covered souks in the Middle East.

According to an early travel guide writer, John Green, writing in 1736: "Aleppo does not abound like Damascus in ancient and beautiful monuments but surpasses it in bigness, trade, and consequently wealth, which advantages have rendered it one of the most famous cities of the Turkish Empire." Trade was knocked once again when modern borders were drawn, and Aleppo found itself split from its neighbor Antioch and at the northern reaches of the Arab world. Today it has bridged the gap opened by trade losses through developing industry.

Above: The massive citadel of Aleppo dominates the city from its 150-foot defensive glacis. Built on the site of earlier defenses by Sayf al-Dawla al-Hamdani (r.c. 943–67), the castle became the headquarters of the Emir of Aleppo, who succeeded in resisting crusader incursions from the neighboring Principality of Antioch. The glacis was laid to stone and a huge, bridged gateway was added in 1203 by the Arabic Ayyubid ruler Malik az'Zahir.

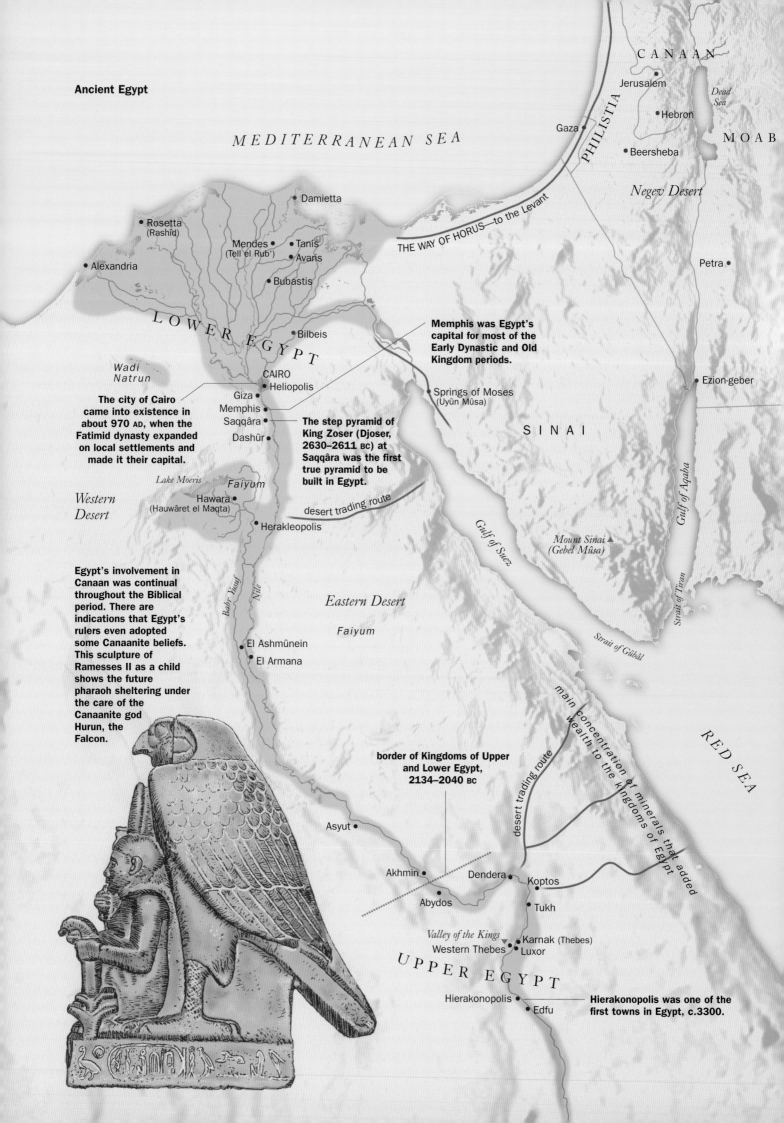

Ancient Egypt

MEDITERRANEAN SEA

CANAAN

Jerusalem

Dead Sea

Hebron

PHILISTIA

Gaza

Beersheba

MOAB

Negev Desert

Damietta

Rosetta
(Rashîd)

Mendes
(Tell el Rub')

Tanis

Avaris

THE WAY OF HORUS—to the Levant

Petra

Alexandria

Bubastis

L O W E R   E G Y P T

Bilbeis

Wadi Natrun

CAIRO

Heliopolis

Memphis was Egypt's capital for most of the Early Dynastic and Old Kingdom periods.

Ezion-geber

The city of Cairo came into existence in about 970 AD, when the Fatimid dynasty expanded on local settlements and made it their capital.

Giza

Memphis

Saqqâra

Dashûr

Springs of Moses
(Uyûn Mûsa)

S I N A I

The step pyramid of King Zoser (Djoser, 2630–2611 BC) at Saqqâra was the first true pyramid to be built in Egypt.

Lake Moeris

Faiyum

Hawara
(Hauwâret el Maqta)

Western Desert

desert trading route

Herakleopolis

Gulf of Aqaba

Mount Sinai
(Gebel Mûsa)

Strait of Tiran

Egypt's involvement in Canaan was continual throughout the Biblical period. There are indications that Egypt's rulers even adopted some Canaanite beliefs. This sculpture of Ramesses II as a child shows the future pharaoh sheltering under the care of the Canaanite god Hurun, the Falcon.

Bahr Yusuf

Nile

Eastern Desert

Faiyum

Strait of Gûbâl

El Ashmûnein

El Armana

RED SEA

main concentration of minerals that added wealth to the kingdoms of Egypt

border of Kingdoms of Upper and Lower Egypt, 2134–2040 BC

desert trading route

Asyut

Akhmin

Dendera

Koptos

Abydos

Tukh

Valley of the Kings

Karnak (Thebes)

Western Thebes

Luxor

U P P E R   E G Y P T

Hierakonopolis

Edfu

Hierakonopolis was one of the first towns in Egypt, c.3300.

CHAPTER TEN

Egypt and the Hebrews

But the people of Israel were fruitful and increased
greatly; they multiplied, and grew exceedingly strong,
so that the land was filled with them.

Exodus 1:7

The relationship between Egypt and the
Hebrew people is a central theme of the
Old Testament and the Jewish Passover
celebrations. We learn how Abraham and the
Israelites first moved to Canaan—modern day
Israel—and how later generations sought relief
from famine by emigrating to the fertile Nile-
lands. As the Hebrew population flourished in
Egypt, so it became enslaved by successive
pharaohs fearing rebellion.

Scholars who accept the essential historical
accuracy of this account place the events
somewhere between the 20th–15th centuries BC.
Later stories of how God inflicted the ten
plagues on Egypt and how Moses led his people
back to freedom across the Red Sea (the
Exodus) are usually dated to c.13th century BC.

Yet from a historical point of view there are
serious problems in verifying Egypt's Biblical
record. For one thing the Bible makes no
mention of dateable events or the names of
individual pharaohs. There are also arguments
about Bronze Age dating systems and the
chronology of Egyptian royal dynasties (some of
which overlapped). The following pages
therefore confine themselves to archaeological
snapshots of Egypt in the time of the Patriarchs
(i.e. Abraham to Moses).

Based on the *Aegyptiaca*, written by the third-
century priest Manetho, the pharaohs are listed
under some 30 separate dynasties. By general
consensus these extend from the pre- and early
dynastic periods (5000–2625 BC), through the
Old Kingdom (2625–2130), the Middle
Kingdom (1980–1801) and the New Kingdom
(1539–1075). The gaps in-between, and
following the end of the New Kingdom, are filled
by the First, Second, and Third Intermediate
periods and, finally, the Late period (664–332).
After this the Hellenistic period, centered on the
port of Alexandria, takes Egypt up to 30 BC and
the final conquest by Rome.

The Patriarchs' era is linked to a long period
of political and religious change in Egypt. The
age of the pyramid-builders was coming to an
end as successive rulers, aghast at the activities
of tomb robbers, looked for more secure burial
arrangements in mortuary complexes. An
economic crisis probably influenced this change
and the pyramids of the Fifth Dynasty
(2450–2321) were built with noticeably smaller,
hastily cut blocks of cheap local limestone. The
last decades of the third millennium BC saw
Egypt torn apart by factional and regional
infighting and it wasn't until Pharaoh
Amenemhet I (r.c.1980–1951 BC) that peace
and unity was fully restored.

During the Second Intermediate period
(1801–1540 BC) the pharaohs were challenged
by the Hyksos, a new threat from western Asia.
Many historians believe this was the age in
which Joseph—he of the coveted many-colored
coat—emerged as a powerful official; a Hebrew
favored by his Egypto-Hyksos masters. Hyksos
armies were finally seen off by Ahmose I in the
mid-16th century BC, beginning the 18th
dynasty and the start of the New Kingdom. It
was this dynasty that began siting its tombs in
the Valley of the Kings near Thebes, arguably
Egypt's most valuable archaeological site.

The outstanding tomb excavated here is that
of King Tutankhamun, a monarch who reigned
for less than a decade and who died in about
1323 BC. The priceless artifacts recovered are
particularly interesting to biblical archaeologists
because they illustrate the wealth, power, and
lifestyle of an Egyptian king at roughly the time
Moses is supposed to have been born (c.1300
BC). If the date is correct, Moses would have
been a prince of the royal court under Ramesses
I (r.1295–1294), Seti I (r.1294–1279) or,
perhaps most likely, Ramesses II,
(r.1279–1213).

30. Giza: Symbol of Power

So they ruthlessly made the people of Israel work as slaves and made their lives bitter with hard service, in mortar and brick, and in all kinds of work in the field. In all their work they ruthlessly made them work as slaves.

Exodus 1:13–14

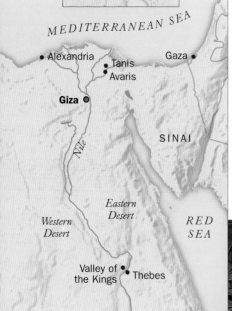

These verses are often cited as evidence that Hebrew slaves were used as forced labor on Egyptian building projects. While slaves *may* have been used there is no clear archaeological evidence to show the practice was widespread. Stone reliefs depicting pyramid building sites rarely carry images of soldiers, even though they would surely have been needed to enforce order.

However, *Exodus* (written many centuries after the events it describes) was certainly right about the hard graft demanded of laborers. Although food rations were distributed three times daily, workers were allowed only one day off in ten. Fatalities must have been an occupational hazard given that two and a half ton blocks of limestone were being manhandled 450 feet into the air using only ropes and sleds.

There are many theories about pyramid construction, from the ingenious to the downright eccentric. One of the more reasoned suggests the use of adjoining or encircling ramps upon which slabs were man-hauled on sleds. A stone relief from the tomb of the Middle Kingdom official Djehutihotep shows this technique being performed on the flat with a colossal statue pulled on a wooden sled by 172 men. The use of a water and lime lubricant on the sled runners would have reduced resistance by some 90%.

It seems likely that peasants labored on state building projects both as an alternative to grain taxes (which many could not afford) and to win favor with their pharaoh, a ruler revered as a living god. Egyptians were obsessed with their prospects in the afterlife, and the annual Nile floods gave farmworkers the chance to impress by pitching in at their ruler's chosen pyramid site. The work must have been directed by highly skilled professional specialists—astronomers, surveyors, architects, and master builders—to achieve such outstanding precision.

Precision builders

Proof of the Egyptians' sophisticated mathematical knowledge comes from the Rhind Papyrus, held by the British Museum. This

Right: Many reliefs and wall paintings have been uncovered depicting the toil of ordinary Egyptian laborers. No doubt there was need for an overseer (the large figure), but it is not clear that this picture shows slaves; they may have been paid.

document, which dates to the mid-second millennium BC, poses various geometrical problems in the manner of an exam paper. One reads: "A pyramid is 93 cubits and ⅓ high. What is the angle if the height of its face is 140 cubits?" Analysis of the Rhind data shows that surveyors understood and practiced the theorum of Pythagoras some 2,000 years before the man himself enunciated it.

The most famous Egyptian pyramids are at Giza, the point where the Nile delta begins. Here stands the Great Pyramid of Khufu (sometimes called Cheops) which rises to 480 feet from a base width of 755 feet. By any standards this was an awesome construction project and in his *Histories* Herodotos claims it took ten years just to prepare the site. There was a canal link to the Nile and docks to handle stone from the great quarries of Tura, on the other side of the river. Herodotos's suggestion that 100,000 people worked on Khufu's pyramid is probably exaggerated, although the famed accuracy of the surveyors is not. In attempting to achieve parallel sides they fell short of perfection

The Biblical notion that the great pharaonic monuments of ancient Egypt were built by the cruelly forced labor of thousands of slaves—largely Hebrew—has been overturned by many recent excavations of towns constructed in the vicinity of the major sites (*see following page*). At Giza, there is a huge cemetery close by the pyramids for the workers and their families. Beyond lies the archaeological site of an area often called the "workers' village." The name belies the size of the vast community that thrived some 4,500 years ago on the Giza Plateau. It may have housed as many as 20,000 people.

by a margin of precisely one inch!

Alongside Khufu's pyramid stand the slightly smaller red-granite pyramid of King Khaefre and the less-ambitious mud-brick tomb of Menkaure. Each was surrounded by mortuary complexes where relatives and important officials could be entombed close to their pharaoh. The religious significance of the pyramid was rooted in worship of the sun god Ra who, according to invocations found on the internal walls, would strengthen his beams on the death of a pharaoh allowing the royal spirit to climb to immortality. The sides of the pyramid were used to begin the ascent from earth.

Below: This aerial photograph shows the Giza Plateau and the pyramids of Khufu, Khaefre, and Menkaure. To the right lie the tombs of the construction workers. The Nile lies to the left, while in the foreground a modern hotel dominates the approach to the Giza Plateau.

31. Valley of the Kings

Now there arose a new king over Egypt, who did not know Joseph. And he said to his people, "Behold, the people of Israel are too many and too mighty for us. Come , let us deal shrewdly with them, lest they multiply...
Exodus 1:8-10

Arguably the greatest archaeological discovery of all time, the tomb of the boy pharaoh Tutankhamun, is tangible proof of Egypt's superpower status during the Pentateuch period. Located in 1921 by the British Egyptologist Howard Carter, the tomb is a rock-cut chamber of such opulence that the treasures found within are still being analyzed by scholars today. It is a time capsule of the pharaohs' extraordinary wealth and influence; a status they jealously guarded against perceived threats from foreigners such as the Israelites.

The tomb lies in the Valley of the Kings, a dried-up riverbed on the west bank of the Nile opposite the capital of Thebes (today's Luxor). The site was chosen by Tuthmosis I and from his death in 1482 BC until the early first millennium BC about 70 royal tombs were located here in tunnels honeycombing beneath the pyramid-shaped mountain. The workforce required to create these monuments was far less than required for undertakings such as at Giza. The laborers and experts were housed in the village of Meir el-Medina (Monastery of the City), close by the western bank of the Nile. We believe its ancient name was *Set Maal*, the Place of Truth.

In its heyday, the village was comprised of over a hundred homes housing stone-masons, carpenters, sculptors, artists, and colorists. Scribes kept records of progress, as well as details such as shipments received, worker absences, and payments. During each succeeding reign the numbers at Meir el-Medina altered, depending on the schemes of the pharaohs, but the general number was split into two *iswt*, or gangs, each under the supervision of an overseer.

Clearly, this was a permanent professional (even hereditary) workforce, but Egypt also used conscripts for extra labor, and this is where the Israelites would have come in, albeit in far greater preponderance in the Nile Delta region than in the south at Thebes. But interestingly, it is in Thebes that the Israelites are first mentioned.

Israel enters history

Tutankhamun died in about 1323 BC, but for all the archaeological treasures he left us, it is a less celebrated king—Merneptah—who has really fueled the debate on the origins of Israel. Merneptah (r.1224–1204), who succeeded Ramesses II, was buried in a mortuary temple in the Valley of the Kings, excavated by Flinders Petrie in 1896. It included a basalt monument extolling the success of his military campaign against the Libyans and other rival rulers. This Merneptah Stela is significant for one overriding reason. It carries the

Left: The aAncient mud-brick walls of Meir el-Medina, village of the workforce for the Valley of the Kings, stand near Western Thebes in the desert west of the Nile at Luxor. Archaeologists have unearthed a mass of finds invaluable to the understanding of the time when Moses walked the banks of the Nile. The tools pictured here, **facing below**, belonged to the foreman Kha, who died during the reign of Amenhotep III (r.1390–52). The relief **below** is from Meir el-Medina and depicts offerings made to Ramesses II by the villagers.

first known reference to "Israel."

The wording reads:

The princes are prostrate, saying: "Mercy"
Not one raises his head among the Nine Bows
Desolation is for Tehenu
Hatti is pacified
Plundered is the Canaan with every evil
Carried off is Ashqelon
Seized upon is Gezer
Yeno'am is made as that which
    does not exist
Israel is laid waste, his seed is not
Hurru is become a widow for
    Egypt
All lands together they are
    pacified…

The controversial nature of this epitaph is that it appears to undermine a popular theory among scholars that the Israelites gradually emerged in Canaan in the mid-12th century BC. The Bible suggests otherwise, indicating a clear Israelite "conquest" at least two centuries earlier. If Israel was indeed a political entity by Merneptah's time this lends weight to the traditional Biblical account.

However, the debate continues to rage. Some experts suggest the Israel of the stela could refer to the Valley of Iezreel or Jezreel (a major east-west route across Canaan). Others say the name is descriptive—the "wearers of the side lock"— and refers to Libyans. Some insist it was simply a geographical territory. Yet the fact remains that Israel was considered important enough to mention alongside the established city-states and kingdoms of the day.

32. Alexandria

There the centurion found a ship of Alexandria sailing for Italy and he put us on board.

Acts 27:6

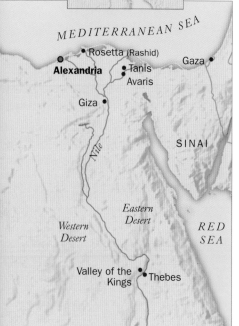

Facing above: Fort Qait Bey, the only Mamluk fort to survive British bombardment in 1888, sits on the site of the ancient Pharos lighthouse.

Facing below: The three layers of three different Egyptian scripts can be clearly seen on the Rosetta Stone, which is now in the British Museum.

The rise of Alexandria as the ancient world's greatest seaport reflected the drive and vision of its founder, the Macedonian general Alexander the Great. Until he arrived in 332 BC en route to conquering the known world the site was an unremarkable village outpost of the eastern Nile delta. Within just a few years it was the new capital of Egypt. The Greeks expanded it into a city some four miles across, its streets laid out symmetrically with stylish colonnades along the main routes.

Perhaps the best-known structures were the Heptastadium, a mile-long breakwater built to provide a harbor, and the Pharos, a 440-foot tall lighthouse which was one of the Seven Wonders of the ancient world. Other great public buildings included the Serapeion (a temple of the Egyptian deity Serapis), the Soma (the mausoleum of Alexander and Egypt's succeeding Ptolemaic dynasty), and the Poseidonion (temple of the sea god Poseidon).

Alexandria's pre-eminence as a Greek commercial, scientific, and literary center was down to good timing. By 327 BC, Alexander's armies had seen off all potential aggressors—utterly destroying the Persian Empire in the process—while the emergence of Rome as a world power was still two centuries away. This brief period of political stability allowed Alexandria to flourish as a cosmopolitan city of learning and a cultural melting pot. By the early third century BC, its Mouseion (Library) held half a million volumes and its population of 300,000 Egyptians, Greeks, and Jews lived together in relative harmony.

The Israelites had of course long succumbed (to Assyria and Babylonia) as a meaningful force. The Jewish religion however was in its formative years and gradually became influenced by Greek thinking and philosophy (*see Olympic Games, pages 172–173*). It was in Alexandria that the Greek translation of the New Testament, known as the Septuagint, was compiled in the first century AD.

By then the city was part of the Roman Empire. The story of how it was annexed by Augustus in 30 BC is intertwined with one of history's greatest love stories; the affair between Queen Cleopatra, last of the Ptolemies, and Julius Caesar's general Mark Antony.

Relics preserved

The destruction of Alexandria by a tidal wave in AD 335 left much of the Old City and royal quarter permanently underwater. The dividend for today's archaeologists is that this preserved statues, jewelry, ceramics, and ancient stone inscriptions, some of which are being recovered from the silt of the city's modern harbor. Perhaps the most exciting find is a complete ship from the first century BC—possibly used by Cleopatra herself on voyages up the Nile. Located in the former royal harbor, it apparently sank after a collision.

The greatest archaeological legacy of Ptolemaic Egypt comes, however, not from Alexandria but the small coastal town of Rosetta further east. It was here that a French officer serving with Napoleon's army in 1799 was overseeing repairs to a fort when he came across a large fragment of black basalt bearing ancient inscriptions. The slab was sent to Cairo for further investigation and seized by the British the following year when they overran Egypt.

The importance of the Rosetta Stone is that it carries a pronouncement in three languages from the 13-year-old King Ptolemy V. At the time (196 BC) the Ptolemaic dynasty was entering a turbulent period in which Egypt's secretive priestly sect was hungry for more power. The stone sets out a treaty of co-operation between king and priests in hieroglyphs (the priestly language), demotic Egyptian (used in everyday matters), and Greek (language of the Ptolemaic administration). To modern archaeologists and linguists this meant

that, for the first time, scholars could use known scripts to translate the long-forgotten language of the hieroglyphs.

Even so, it took the brilliant French linguist Jean-Francois Champollion (d.1832) almost two decades to crack the code. All our knowledge of ancient Egypt—and therefore much of our understanding of Biblical history—stems from his obsessive dedication.

Linguists threaten the stone

The hieroglyphics of the Theban priesthood went out of use soon after the end of the fourth century AD, and soon no one knew how to read them. The realization in the early years of the 19th century that the Rosetta Stone was a key to unlocking the secrets of the ancient Egyptian language led to its near destruction as enthusiasts took hundreds of impressions using damaging inks and damp paper pressed onto the surface. Only in 1999 was the stone finally cleaned and preserved.

33. Cities of Ramesses

> Therefore they set taskmasters over them to afflict them with heavy burdens. And they built for Pharaoh store cities, Pithom and Raamses.
>
> *Exodus 1:11*

The classic Cecil B. De Mille film *The Ten Commandments* shows Yul Brynner as Pharaoh Ramesses II pursuing Moses and his people as they leave Egypt. The above verse offers support for this scenario, since the king commissioned ambitious building projects in the city of Pi-Ramesse (the biblical Raamses) near Avaris (Tell el-Daba) on the eastern Nile delta. Whether or not he was actually the pharaoh of the Exodus is arguable, although his reputation certainly fits the bill.

It is only in the last few years that the archaeological treasures of Pi-Ramesse have begun to emerge. As capital during Ramesses' long reign (r.c.1279–1213 BC) it boasted a magnificent golden palace which, according to the German Egyptologist Edgar Pusch, gives credence to old tales about gold dust lying on the city streets. Pusch excavated the palace during 1998 and recovered a fabulous collection of gold statues, rare ceramics, and intricate bronze work. "There is hardly one cubic centimeter in the palace that does not have some gold," he observed. "When you walk across the floor you stir up tiny flakes of gold dust."

Ramesses' use of Pi-Ramesse as a royal seat showed his political savvy. By shifting the state's powerbase away from its traditional capital Thebes, far to the south, he curtailed the influence and prestige of the Theban priests. At the same time he emphasized his own status, building temples at Luxor and Karnak, the Ramesseum (his funerary complex at Thebes), sanctuaries at Abydos and

Memphis, and the superb rock-cut temples at Abu Simbel. For good measure he also claimed credit for structures built by his predecessors.

Personality cult

Ramesses II carefully promoted his image, and his alleged heroism and leadership in battle. Yet he was not a particularly successful general. Although he campaigned against the Hittites, he eventually resolved the conflict diplomatically by agreeing a treaty and marrying a Hittite princess. His son Merneptah notched more clear-cut victories, defeating the Aegean Sea Peoples and possibly a fledgling Israel (*see pages 134–5)*) during widespread conflict across the Middle East. However, the end of the 13th century BC would mark Egypt's last years as a great imperial power.

Of Ramesses II's character we have only fleeting glimpses. Analysis of his mummy and contemporary portraits tell us that he was 5 feet 7 inches tall, had red hair (unusual among Egyptians), and in old age suffered from arthritis,

Right: The silver coffin of Psusennes I (r.959–45 BC) comes from the most elaborate of tombs at Tanis. Pharaohs of the 21st Dynasty were eager to prove their power and their glory over the traditional royal center at Thebes, which led to some massive construction programs.

Left: The beaten gold mummy mask of Shoshenq I (r.945–924 BC), founder of the 22nd Dynasty, was discovered in his sarcophagus, which lay in the entrance chamber of the tomb of Psusennes I at Tanis. Shoshenq (thought to be the Biblical Sishak, invader if Israel) would have been entombed in some style, benefitting from his plundering of Israel (*see pages 38–39*).

arteriosclerosis, and rotten teeth. These features bring to mind Shelley's poem *Ozymandias*, in which the pharaoh is portrayed with a frown, a wrinkled lip, and a sneer of cold command.

Despite his ego and obsessive ambition, Ramesses seems to have had great affection for his principal wives, most notably Nefertari whose tomb is the highlight of the Valley of the Queens mortuary complex. Nine pharaohs of the 20th dynasty took Ramesses' name and the families of his 100 or so children considered it an honor to claim his bloodline.

The end of the Ramesside period in the mid-12th century BC marked the decline of the New Kingdom and a resurgence in the power of the priesthood at its traditional heartland, Thebes. By 1069 BC, however, a new dynasty—the 21st—had established itself at Tanis, some 12 miles downriver from Pi-Ramesse. To embellish their court the Tanitic kings wasted no time in plundering Ramesses' former capital, removing statues, obelisks, and even entire temples.

Because Tanis was mentioned in the Bible as the city of Zoan it was quickly flagged up by archaeologists. In the 1930s the French Egyptologist Pierre Montet revealed its true importance when he discovered an underground royal cemetery rivaling even the grandeur of Tutankhamun. Of these tombs the most extravagant is that of Psusennes I but the complex also includes the graves of Amenemope (r.993–84 BC) Shoshenq II (r.c.890 BC), and Shoshenq III (825–773 BC).

Below: Arab workers stand among the scattered ruins of Tanis during excavations in the mid-1960s.

CHAPTER ELEVEN

Iraq Gazetteer

God called the dry land Earth, and the waters that were gathered together he called Seas. And God saw that it was good.

Genesis 1:10

If the stories of the Old Testament belong to any geographical place it is surely in the fertile valleys of the Euphrates and Tigris, the heartland of which was once known as Mesopotamia. This land, now mostly Iraqi territory, witnessed the birth of civilization through early farming settlements, the first cities, the invention of writing, and a rich artistic culture. Just about every square mile figured in history at some point.

When archaeologists first began looking for evidence to back up Biblical accounts, Mesopotamia was the obvious place to turn. Between the mid-19th and early 20th centuries some truly spectacular finds were made by Paul Emile Botta at Nineveh, Austen Henry Layard at Nimrud, Sir Leonard Woolley at Ur, and Robert Koldewey at Babylon, all of whom made crucial contributions to our understanding of Biblical history.

The result is a giant of a story that reminds us of the fleeting nature of power. The Akkadians, Babylonians, Assyrians, Persians, and Greeks each established seemingly invincible empires in the region only to see their might crumble in the face of that unforgiving enemy—time. Rulers learned the hard way that although it is possible to take control of a region, it is impossible to keep it in perpetuity.

This chapter looks at the great fortresses of Assyria and Babylonia, the elaborate propaganda of their leaders, and the cruelty and ruthlessness they deployed in oppressing vassal peoples such as the Israelites. But we also go back much further, to the very dawn of agriculture, when the first hunter-gatherer tribes began settling in Mesopotamia. Were these people the inspiration for the story of Adam and Eve? Controversially, some biblical scholars believe that they were... and that the Garden of Eden lies in a fertile plain in the north of Iran.

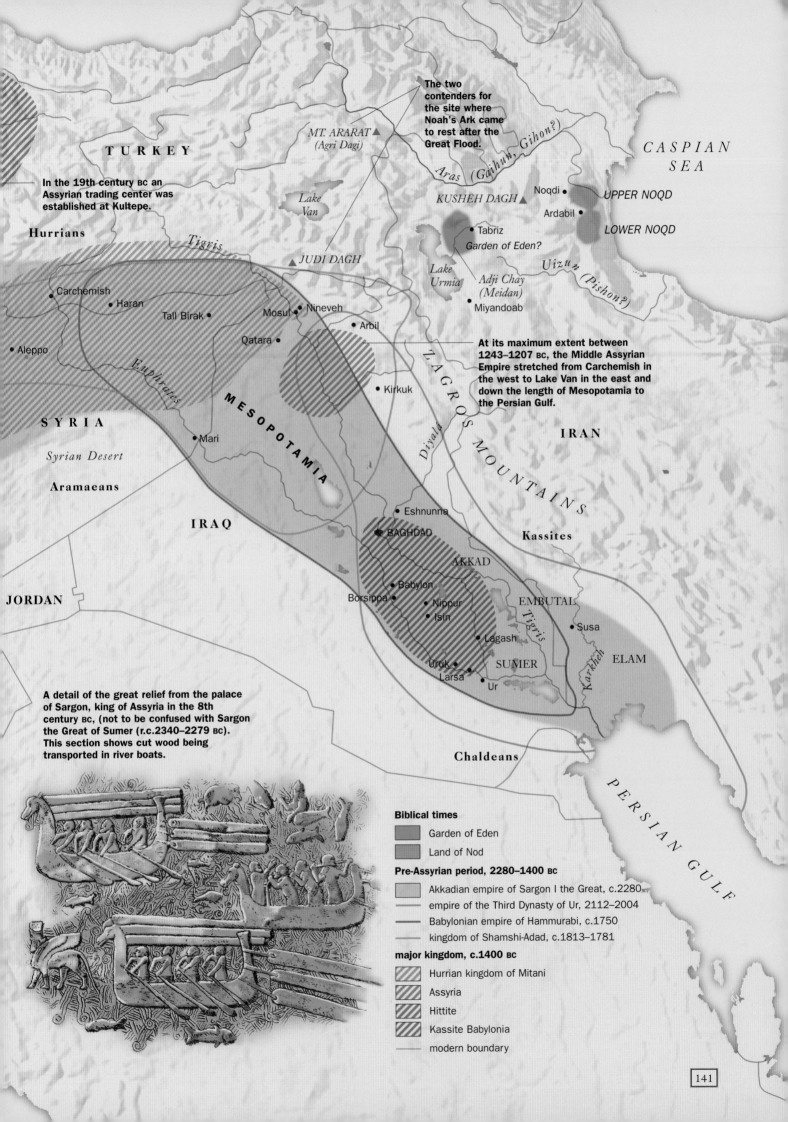

TURKEY

MT. ARARAT ▲
(Agri Dagi)

The two contenders for the site where Noah's Ark came to rest after the Great Flood.

Aras (Gaihun, Gihon?)

CASPIAN SEA

In the 19th century BC an Assyrian trading center was established at Kultepe.

Lake Van

Hurrians

KUSHEH DAGH ▲

Noqdi •

UPPER NOQD

• Ardabil

LOWER NOQD

Tigris

▲ *JUDI DAGH*

Lake Urmia

• Tabriz

Garden of Eden?

Uizun (Pishon?)

• Carchemish
• Haran
Tall Birak •
Mosul • • Nineveh

Adji Chay (Meidan)
• Miyandoab

• Aleppo
Qatara •
▨ • Arbil

At its maximum extent between 1243–1207 BC, the Middle Assyrian Empire stretched from Carchemish in the west to Lake Van in the east and down the length of Mesopotamia to the Persian Gulf.

• Kirkuk

SYRIA

Euphrates

M E S O P O T A M I A

Diyala

Z A G R O S   M O U N T A I N S

IRAN

Syrian Desert

• Mari

Aramaeans

IRAQ

• Eshnunna
▨ • BAGHDAD

Kassites

JORDAN

AKKAD

• Babylon
Borsippa •
• Nippur
• Isin

EMBUTAL
• Susa

Tigris

• Lagash

SUMER

Karkheh

ELAM

Uruk •
Larsa •
• Ur

A detail of the great relief from the palace of Sargon, king of Assyria in the 8th century BC, (not to be confused with Sargon the Great of Sumer (r.c.2340–2279 BC). This section shows cut wood being transported in river boats.

Chaldeans

P E R S I A N   G U L F

Biblical times

▨ Garden of Eden

▨ Land of Nod

Pre-Assyrian period, 2280–1400 BC

▨ Akkadian empire of Sargon I the Great, c.2280

— empire of the Third Dynasty of Ur, 2112–2004

— Babylonian empire of Hammurabi, c.1750

— kingdom of Shamshi-Adad, c.1813–1781

major kingdom, c.1400 BC

▨ Hurrian kingdom of Mitani

▨ Assyria

▨ Hittite

▨ Kassite Babylonia

— modern boundary

34. Babylon

The broad wall of Babylon shall be leveled to the ground, and her high gates shall be burned with fire, the peoples labor for nothing…
Jeremiah 51:58

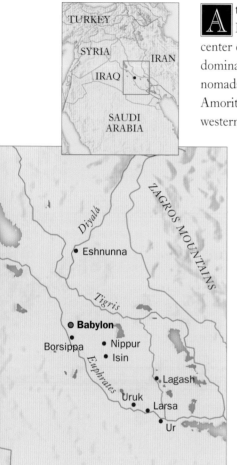

A t the start of the 20th century BC, Babylon was an unremarkable town at the center of an unstable political map. Centuries of domination by Ur were over but Semitic nomads called the Amurru, the biblical Amorites, were fast arriving from Arabia's western deserts to fill the power vacuum. They captured Babylon along with key settlements such as Isin, Larsa, and Eshnunna. By 1894 BC the city was a small independent state.

When King Hammurabi came to power c.1760 BC, he turned his kingdom into an empire stretching from the Habur region of Syria to the Persian Gulf. He proved an outstanding administrator and his Code of Hammurabi, the earliest set of laws yet discovered, is one of history's most important documents. The seven-foot-high inscribed stone was found by French archaeologists at Susa, Iraq, in 1901. Hammurabi is also credited with elevating the Babylonian god Marduk to the head of the state's pagan religion.

This Old Babylonian empire ended abruptly in 1595 BC when invading Hittite tribes destroyed the city. For the next 900 years a succession of ambitious dynasties—Kassites, Elamites, Chaldeans, and various transitory rulers such as the kings of Isin—all had a period governing Babylon until Assyria seized the initiative in the late eighth century BC.

In 625 BC, the Chaldean king Nabopolassar took control of the city, which then flourished independently as the Neo-Babylonian empire. Under his son Nebuchadnezzar II (r.604–562 BC) Babylon became the largest city in the world, covering up to 2,500 acres. Having seen off his Assyrian and Egyptian enemies, Nebuchadnezzar systematically broke up the

Right: The earliest set of coded laws yet discovered are inscribed on the face of this this seven-foot-high stele at the order of King Hammurabi, during the 1780s BC. The king is seen seated on a throne at the top conferring with a learned scribe.

southern Jewish kingdom of Judah, exiling many of its people in Babylonia.

Hanging Gardens

For millennia afterward Babylon was mostly identified with the Hanging Gardens, supposedly built by Nebuchadnezzar. The gardens did not actually hang but grew on terraces and roofs around the king's palace, apparently to please a Median wife who missed her homeland in northern Iran. They were deservedly named as one of the Seven Wonders of the World, yet the archaeology of Babylon goes much further than a famous garden.

In 1899, excavations by the German archaeologist Robert Koldewey established that Nebuchadnezzar's Babylon was not one but two cities. The outer districts were encircled by a triple wall so thick that according to the Greek historian Herodotos it was possible to turn a four-horse chariot around on top. Within this boundary, on the western side, was the king's palace—a citadel within a fortress. Divided by the Euphrates, it included a ceremonial avenue now known as the Processional Way, which opened onto plazas housing the Temple of Marduk and the city's ziggurat of Etemenanki. Some scholars think the story about the Tower of Babel (*also see panel, page 61*) originated with the collapse of the ziggurat, which was later restored by Nabopolassar and Nebuchadnezzar II.

The avenue ran south through the royal quarter from the fabulous Ishtar Gate, where decorative dragons and bulls were set amid glazed, colored bricks. Koldewey also discovered underground vaulted chambers containing wells and asphalt waterproofing—foundations,

he believed, of the Hanging Gardens. Nebuchadnezzar had access to additional apartments and his treasured collection of Mesopotamian antiques, housed in a fortified palace extension outside the citadel.

Despite its military might and carefully-honed reputation for invincibility, Nebuchadnezzar's empire was brought down by a "destroying wind" (as the prophet Jeremiah puts it) just 23 years after his death. In 539 BC the Persian armies of Cyrus the Great captured the city; a reminder—as if Mesopotamia needed it—of the transitory nature of power

Below: The reconstructed Ishtar Gate of Babylon, with reliefs of bulls and dragons, hints at the splendor of Nebuchadnezzar's city. An important Babylonian deity, Ishtar was goddess of the earth and fertility.

35. The Garden of Eden

And the Lord God planted a garden in Eden, in the east, and there he put the man whom he had formed.

Genesis 2:8

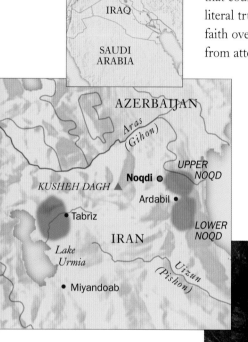

The search for the Garden of Eden is taking place beyond the edge of archaeological convention. It is difficult to imagine any evidence that could prove its existence, and to accept the literal truth of *Genesis* is clearly a triumph of faith over logic. Yet this has not stopped scholars from attempting to tackle the problem. Even the most skeptical can at least accept the notion of a place called Eden which earned a reputation as paradise through its beauty and fertility (*paradise* is derived from the old Persian word for a peaceful garden).

The name is probably connected with Edinn, the Sumerian name for the Plain of Babylon, but the geographical and visual descriptions given in the Bible suggest a site around Tabriz, northern Iran, where the modern borders of Iran, Iraq, and Turkey come together. *Genesis* speaks of Eden encompassing four rivers—the Pishon, the Gihon, the Hiddekel (Hebrew for Tigris), and the Euphrates. There is no debate about the last two; their names remain in use today, but the Pishon and the Gihon do not appear on any 21st-century map.

Creationists explain this by pointing out that the Great Flood (in which all but the tips of mountains was supposedly covered) would have altered the landscape and watercourses. A more plausible explanation is that the rivers now exist under different names, and on this theme the ideas of an obscure British academic who died in the 1990s are intriguing.

Reginald Walker published his findings in the wonderfully named *Still Trowelling* newsletter of the Ancient and Medieval History Book Club in

Right: Is this a satellite photograph of the Garden of Eden? The paler region to the top right (northeast) of Lake Urmia in northern Iran is, according to new thinking, the place revealed in the Bible. A paradise before sin has always exercised artists' imaginations, but *Eden*, the left panel from *The Garden of Earthly Delights*, by Hieronymus Bosch, already hints at the pleasure (and pain) that eating from the Tree of Knowledge will bring.

1986. He pointed out that before the eighth century AD rise of Islam in the region, the Aras was known as the Gaihun (or Gihon in Hebrew). It transpires that Victorian Biblical dictionaries even referred to it as the Gihon-Aras. As for Pishon, Walker argued that this was simply a corrupted name for the Uizun. The "U" sound in Hebrew is pronounced as a "P" and the "z" becomes a "sh."

Scrutinizing the geography

For good measure Walker points out that the modern-day village of Noqdi could be a throwback to the Biblical Land of Nod, where Cain was exiled following the murder of Abel. The "i" in Noqdi actually means "of" and local maps refer to two distinct districts—Upper and Lower Noqd. Assuming the linguistic detective work is right, Noqdi fits snugly into the theory. Just as the Bible says, it lies east of Eden.

The British archaeologist and author David Rohl believes Walker is essentially right. He has highlighted new evidence that locates Eden between two mountain spurs on the Plain of Miyandoab, northern Iran. *Genesis* talks of a fifth river which waters Eden, and Rohl suggests this is the Adji Chay, formerly known as the Meidan, which runs through the landscape. Curiously, *meidan* is the Persian word for walled court or enclosed garden.

There are other coincidences. The mountains around Tabriz are of red clay, while the name Adam means red earth in Hebrew. The Bible tells how the Gihon wanders "all through the land of Cush," and, sure enough, toward the eastern side of Rohl's Eden we find Kusheh Dagh—the Mountain of Kush—rising above the Gihon. And the sheer weight of today's annual fruit and vegetable harvest in the region bears witness to the immense fertility of the land. To an early farmer, it must truly have been paradise.

Perhaps here lies the key to unlocking the Eden mystery. Is it possible that as the Neolithic revolution began to unfold in the late eighth millennium BC, tribes of Near Eastern hunter-gatherers began to settle and experiment with farming. Was "Adam" the name given to a great leader, a man who perhaps married the daughter of a neighboring tribe (Eve) to found a dynasty? Certainly variations of this explanation linger on in Mesopotamian folklore—if not in hard archaeological fact.

Assyrian Art

Hear the word of the great king, the king of Assyria!
Thus says the king: "Do not let Hezekiah deceive you,
for he shall not be able to deliver you out of my hand.

2 Kings 18:28-29

Below: Assyrians often employed foreigners as artists. This ivory panel shows a lioness devouring an Ethiopian in a lotus thicket, carved in the Phoenician style; late 8th century BC, from Nimrud.

T he rebellion of Judah's King Hezekiah in 701 BC resulted in one of the ancient world's bloodiest sieges. Archaeological clues to the Assyrian attack on the Judahite city of Lachish is considered on pages 80–81, but we may also have detailed eyewitness evidence recorded by a war artist. Many scholars believe that a wall relief measuring 60 by 9 feet found at Nineveh is a "talking picture" of this great battle (*see also the picture on page 39*).

Whether or not this is true, the Lachish relief is among the finest surviving examples of Assyrian artistic expression. It was discovered in 1847 during excavations by the British army officer Austen Henry Layard at Sennacherib's palace. Later it was removed from its setting in an interior chamber and shipped to the British Museum in London where it remains on show.

Carved from gypsum alabaster the relief is said to show a heavily-fortified Lachish repelling a ferocious Assyrian assault on the walls. The attackers have built a siege ramp upon which they advance armored battering rams. The desperate defenders respond by hurling flaming torches, trying to set the war engines ablaze. Countering this we see Assyrian soldiers pouring water on the fire, their exposure covered by companies of archers targeting the battlements.

Parading the spoils of war

From here the scene moves to Sennacherib's victory celebration. Judahite captives are marched from the gate but some of the dead are hoisted on spears and paraded publicly. Looting is rampant, with even the sacred vessels of religious ritual taken away as booty. Throughout it all Sennacherib is pictured on a throne beside his royal tent, his face impassive. Underneath an inscription reads: "Sennacherib, king of all, king of Assyria, sitting on his throne while the spoil from the city of Lachish passed before him."

The above interpretation seems unequivocal. And yet debate over the relief is a good example of the way scholarly spats permeate Biblical archaeology. One camp has no doubt that this is indeed the Lachish siege, with the topography of the city, the vegetation, and even the clothes of the occupants faithfully recorded. Some even

Left: Detail from Assyrian relief of the siege of Lachish, c.681 BC. Sennacherib's battering rams led the main assault against the Judahite city. Defeated inhabitants are shown leaving the city, passing captured Jewish soldiers who have been stripped naked and impaled on stakes. When Lachish fell, King Hezekiah of Judah sued for peace and sent tribute to the order of "30 talents of gold, 800 talents of silver, precious stones, antimony, large cuts of red stone, couches with ivory, chairs with ivory, elephant hides, ebony wood, box wood... all kinds of valuable treasurers, his daughters, concubines, male and female musicians." The gleeful detail comes from the Assyrian records.

claim to have identified the spot where the artist stood to make sketches. However other experts insist the picture is simply imperial propaganda and that its detail is generic to other Assyrian battle reliefs of the time.

There is greater consensus on the art itself. For one thing the detail gives us a good idea of eighth-century BC architecture, the design of chariots, weapons, and armor, the prevailing landscape, and the costumes of the day. It can be seen how styles and techniques developed, particularly in the use of perspective. The ninth-century BC reliefs at Nimrud, for instance, make no distinction between the relative size of soldiers and buildings. The idea of depth is conveyed by showing figures in groups, one above the other. By the time of the Lachish relief, early seventh-century BC artists were experimenting with three-dimensional scenes and soldiers were sometimes pictured overlapping each other in battle.

The Assyrian kings' love of art extended far beyond images of war. Arguably the finest animal studies anywhere in the ancient world are the dying lion and lioness pictured in a hunting wall relief at Ashurbanipal's palace in Nineveh (c.668 BC). Another relief from the same period shows the reclining king feasting with his queen in the royal gardens. A harpist and servants wielding flywhisks complete the hedonistic theme.

Given their power, wealth, and influence it is unsurprising that the kings of Assyria sought out the best imported work. At Nimrud two ivory plaques were recovered from a well in the northwest palace, probably hurled down there for safe-keeping when Babylonian-backed forces sacked the city c.612 BC. These stunning pieces were part-gilded and inlaid with lapis lazuli and red cornelian. They were either Phoenician imports or made by Phoenician master-craftsmen in the Assyrian court.

Assyrian Kings

Behold, you have heard what the kings of Assyria have done to all lands, devoting them to destruction And shall you be delivered?

2 Kings 19:11

Above: A sculpture of King Ashurnasirpal II depicts him as a steadfast military commander; his sadistic streak found plenty of outlet in the cruel tortures he devised for his captured enemies.

Of all the Israelites' many persecutors, Assyria was arguably the most enthusiastic. Old Testament writers regard its occupation of Hebrew territory as divine retribution against a disobedient people. Yet the Bible does not portray God as siding with the invaders. On the contrary, it claims he destroyed them.

The Assyrian Empire emerged in the second millennium BC around the upper Tigris in northern Mesopotamia. Until then its rulers had existed in the shadow of the more powerful Sumer and Akkad empires, but an increasingly chaotic political map with few defensible borders created a power vacuum. By the turn of the 18th century BC Shamshi-Adad I had seized control of a vast region stretching from the Zagros Mountains to the Mediterranean.

The problem for the Assyrians was that their aggression and ambition was matched by that of Babylonia. Over the next 1200 years or so these two great rivals fought habitually—like heavyweight boxers unable to land a knockout blow. Their task was complicated by outside powers seeking expansion. At various times the Kassites, Hurrians, and an un-named Indo-European people infiltrated Mesopotamia and, by 1500 BC, Assyria had become dependent on the Mitanni kingdom. This arrangement lasted until the Hittites arrived early in the 14th century BC, yet within 200 years the Hittites themselves were replaced by the Sea Peoples, an assortment of invading cultures. The lesson for would-be rulers was clear. The price of power was unending war.

One Assyrian king, Tiglath-pileser I, embraced this concept from the start of his reign in 1115 BC. Faced with two particularly irksome enemies on his western borders—the Mushki and the Aramaeans (Syrians)—he launched raids for tribute and booty, gearing up to full-blown campaigns of ethnic cleansing. The Assyrian armies soon thrived on their reputation for ruthlessness and cruelty. They were the scourge of the Middle East.

Tyrannical rule

Under Ashurnasirpal II, who became king in 883 BC, this state terrorism reached its apex. Ashurnasirpal was a gifted commander and military strategist who gloried in devising sadistic and unusual forms of execution for his enemies. Inscriptions found at his palace in Nimrud (Calah) tell with blood-curdling frankness how he took revenge on rebels from the city of Suru and their leader Ahiababa, "the son of a nobody."

I built a pillar over against his city gate and I flayed all the chief men who had revolted and I covered the pillar with their skins: some I walled

continued to be ruled by David's heirs. Neither was large enough to stand alone and they survived through delicate diplomacy, seeking either Assyrian or Aramaean support depending on the balance of power. Israel in particular courted the Assyrians, and the Black Obelisk monument of King Shalmaneser III (r.859–824 BC), now in the British Museum, shows Israel's King Jehu kissing Shalmaneser's feet.

For Israel this relationship proved ill-fated. When in the eighth century BC it rebelled, the Assyrians sacked the Israeli capital Samaria and deported its population (the so-called "Ten Lost Tribes"). Sargon II (r.721–705 BC) continued the repression and attention switched to Judah when its king, Hezekiah, withheld tribute. Sargon's successor Sennacherib responded with an invasion and Hezekiah's surrender is outlined in *2 Kings: 18-19*—an account that tallies with Assyrian sources. However there is no supporting evidence for a later Assyrian attack in which the Bible claims the invaders were annihilated by an angel (*2 Kings 19:35*).

up within the pillar, some I impaled upon the pillar on stakes, and others I bound to stakes around about the pillar.

Around this time the Hebrews had fragmented into two states. In the north was Israel, which broke away from King David's dynasty in c.930 BC. Judah, in the south,

36. Nineveh, Nimrud, Khorsabad

Then the word of the Lord came to Jonah the second time saying, "Arise, go to Nineveh, that great city, and call out against it the message that I tell you."

Jonah 3:1–2

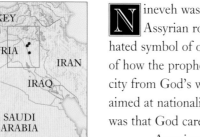

Nineveh was traditionally the seat of Assyrian royalty and, to the Israelites, a hated symbol of oppression. The Biblical story of how the prophet Jonah unwillingly saves the city from God's wrath is thought to have been aimed at nationalists within Israel. The message was that God cared for all—even the despised Assyrians.

The prosperity of Nineveh was rooted in its strategic position on the fertile east bank of the Tigris, close to the foothills of the Kurdish mountains. This gave access to both north-south and east-west trade routes and ensured the king could respond quickly to trouble in outposts of his empire. At the height of its fortunes, Nineveh's walls had a circumference of some eight miles which, according to *Jonah*, housed a population of 125,000.

Archaeological investigation of the city began in 1842 when a French consul, Paul Emile Botta, launched an ambitious dig. Disappointed by the early results, he switched to Khorsabad, eventually locating the palace of Sargon II. Botta was followed in 1845 by a British army officer, Austen Henry Layard, whose work at Nimrud (known as Calah in the Bible) unearthed the palaces of Ashurnasirpal II (r.884–859 BC), Shalmaneser III (r.858–824), and Esarhaddon (r.680–669). Layard later moved to nearby Nineveh, succeeding where Botta failed. He located the palaces of Sennacherib (r.704–681) and Ashurbanipal (r.668–627), completing a decade of outstanding discoveries in Mesopotamia.

Machismo and scholarship

Nineveh's golden years came during the reign of these last two kings. Under Sennacherib, it was remodeled to include wide streets and squares set amid lush parks and flower gardens. The king's evocatively named Palace Without A Rival was linked to a mains water supply through a system of aqueducts and canals. Formidable defenses protected the entire city, its stout outer walls controlled by defensive forts and cunningly designed gateways.

Like similar palaces at Khorsabad and Nimrud, the Nineveh royal residences were built around large courtyards. These served as

Right: Khorsabad is a village that stands on the site of ancient Dur-Sharrukin (Fort Sargon). Built shortly after Sargon II came to the Assyrian throne in 721 BC, to be his capital, the city was largely abandoned by his son Sennacherib, who moved the capital back to Nineveh on his accession in 705.

the king's private quarters but were also a venue for ceremonial functions and state business. Visiting foreign dignitaries were left in no doubt of their host's valor, power, and general infallibility. Throughout the palace, reliefs carved from gypsum alabaster depicted his greatest deeds on the battlefield and in hunting parties; while more reflective scenes showed him worshiping the gods.

The importance of image, status, and propaganda was not lost on the Assyrians. Visitors passing through the gates of Nineveh or Khorsabad would look up at fearsome sculptures—guardian demons, lions with human heads, and giant bulls. This mythological theme was continued inside the palace where statues of winged bulls up to 12 feet high were placed beside the main doorways. The aim was to present the king as a divine being, a custodian of cosmic order whose word was the gift of life or death.

Behind this machismo the Assyrian state concealed a more reflective, scholarly, and bureaucratic face. Rulers such as Sennacherib and Ashurbanipal collected great libraries of cuneiform clay and stone tablets setting out the region's cultural traditions, including Mesopotamian accounts of the Great Flood. There were also more mundane records showing accounts of the royal household and the treasury. The cuneiform script was Akkadian, a language used by the Assyrians and Babylonians and later adapted for communication across the ancient world. Some of the Nineveh tablets were translated by a self-taught British expert, George Smith, who visited the city on a commission from the British *Daily Telegraph* newspaper in the 1870s.

Assyria's downfall lay in its territorial expansion. The empire became unwieldy, and deportation of troublemakers caused regional skill shortages, leading to discontent and rebellion. In 612 BC, Nineveh was sacked by the Babylonian king Nabopolassar and it was his son, Nebuchadnezzar II, who finally defeated an Egypto-Assyrian alliance in 605.

Above: Massive sculptures of winged bulls with the king's face abounded in the royal palaces of Assyria. There are fine examples to be seen in the British Museum, the Louvre (above), and Chicago, among other museums. These, and other oversize sculptures and wall reliefs were all part of Assyrian royal propaganda, designed to overawe visiting foreign dignitaries and vassal princes, and impress on them the might of the empire.

CHAPTER TWELVE

Turkey and the Near East, c.270 BC

Byzantium

SEA OF MARMARA

Kyzikos

Troy

Sakarya

A N A T O L I A   T U R

Simay

Mytilene

LESBOS

Lydia

Gediz

Sardis

Smyrna

Kolophon

Ephesus

CHIOS

Meander

Colossae (Honaz)

Laodicea (Denizli)

Antioch

Psidia

Halys

Caesarea (Kayseri)

Iconimum (Konya)

Heraclea (Eregli)

TAURUS MOUNTAINS

Seyhan

Ceyhan

Maras

Cilician Gates

Samos

Miletos

AEGEAN SEA

Halikarnassos (Bodrum)

Kos

Aksu

Attalia (Antalya)

Perga

Göksu

Tarsus

Pompeiopolis (Mersin)

Alexandretta (İskenderun)

Syrian Gates

Rhodes

Xanthus

Alanya

Cilicia

Silifke

Seleucia

Antioch (Antakya)

Aleppo (Halab)

Antioch (Antiocheia ad Cragum)

Carpathos

Ugarit

LEVANT

Hamath (Hamah)

CRETE

Margat

Homs (Hims)

Tortosa (Tartus)

M E D I T E R R A N E A N   S E A

Famagusta

CYPRUS

Tripoli (Tarabulus)

Orontes

Byblos (Jubayl)

LEBANON

Baalbek

Berytus (Beirut)

Leontes

Turkey Gazetteer

Sidon (Sayda)

Damascus (Dimashq)

Tyre (Sur)

For I bear him witness, that he has worked hard for you and for those in Laodicea, and in Hierapolis.

Colossians 4:13

Acre (Akko)

Haifa (Hefa)

Tiberias (Teverya)

Sea of Galilee

ISRAEL

Megiddo

Caesarea

JORDAN

WEST BANK

Jordan

Jaffa (Tel Aviv-Yafo)

Jericho (Ariha)

Rabbah, Philadelphia (Amman)

M odern Turkey embraces an area laden with significance for the Christian churches. It was here, under the guidance of St. Paul, that new congregations were established and ultimately thrived. Indeed, within what are now Turkish territories the term "Christian" came into common usage.

Ashdod

Jerusalem

Bethlehem (Bayt Lahm)

Dead Sea

MT. NEBO

Gaza

BLACK SEA

RUSSIA

GEORGIA

• Trezibond
(Trabzon)

Kura

ARMENIA

AZERBAIJAN

MT. AREGATS ▲

Lake Sevdna

K E Y

Karasu

Aras

MT. ARARAT ▲

• Tabriz

Ardabil •

Peri

Lake Van

Aras

Tigris

Lake Urmia

Uizam

JUDI DAGH

Great Zab

• Edessa
(Urfa)

• Mardin

Carchemish   • Haran
Barak)

• Khorsabad (Dur Sharrukin)

Mosul   • Nineveh
(Al Mawsil)

• Arbil

Z A G R O S

IRAN

• Nimrud
(Calah)

Euphrates

Khabur

Little Zab

• Kirkuk

M O U N T A I N S

Ecbatana •
(Hamadan)

M E S O P O T A M I A

Wadi ath Tharthar

I R A Q

Tigris

• Palmyra
(Tadmor)

Mari •

Lake Tharthar

Diyala

S Y R I A

Baghdad •

Turkey only emerged as an independent nation in the 20th century. The region was in the sphere first of the Anatolians, then the Assyrians, Greeks, Romans, Islamic Arabs, and then the Seljuk Turks until the advent of the Ottoman Empire.

When St. Paul and his fellow missionaries were traveling far and wide to spread the word they remained at all times within the boundaries of the Roman Empire. However, St. Paul's thrust into western Turkey was immortalized by the New Testament epistles that bear the name of his destinations.

There is the epistle to the Ephesians and one to the Colossians. (The city of Colossae—Honaz today—lay on the main road to Ephesus). There is firm evidence that Christian communities existed at Laodicea and Hierapolis. Laodicea, with its large Jewish community, rapidly adopted Christianity and was one of the seven churches of Asia spoken of in *The Revelation to John*. It has been deserted for centuries. Hierapolis is, like Laodicea, marked by Roman ruins but is best known for its natural hot springs. It was here that the Apostle Philip was martyred in AD 80.

The Hellenistic world, c.270 BC

 Seleucid kingdom

 Ptolemaic kingdom

37. Antioch

So Barnabas went to Tarsus to look for Saul:, and when he had found him, he brought him to Antioch. For a whole year they met with the church and taught a great many people. And in Antioch the disciples were first called Christians.

Acts 11:25, 26

There is little to mark out modern Antioch (Antakya) from any other place in the region. Evidence of its previous architectural triumphs is scant and is overshadowed by the modern town with its industrial factories. Yet this unpromising spot was pivotal in the history of Christianity.

It was here that Saul (Paul) recruited Gentiles (non-Jews) into the new Church and that the term Christianity was first coined. This flagged up a forthcoming schism between Jews and the newly identified Christians who until that point had been sitting rather uncomfortably under the same umbrella. Jesus was a Jew, of course, as were all his immediate followers. Paul decided to preach to non-Jews after he got a poor reception from Jews in Athens. To counter reluctance among those non-Jews who did not wish to be circumcized for the faith he declared that the ancient tradition need no longer apply. This was radical and he had a task to persuade his brother preacher Peter that it was the way forward. But because he was successful, so was Christianity.

Antioch was founded in 300 BC by Seleukos I Nicator, one of Alexander the Great's generals, who named the settlement for his father. As the center of the Seleukid kingdom it was embellished with fine buildings and earned a reputation for its sports and its statuary. It became a busy junction at the western end of the Silk Road, bringing prosperity and, by all accounts, decadence. Control was wrested from the Greeks by the Romans in 64 BC.

Instantly appreciating its potential, the Romans made it the capital of their Syrian province. By the time of Jesus, Antioch was ranked the third

Right: Remains of the Roman baths at the "other" Antioch. In Roman times, Antioch-in-Psidia was an important center. It continued in prominence well into the late Byzantine period, eclipsing the more famous Antioch of the Holy Lands.

largest city in the Roman Empire, after Rome and Alexandria, and was adorned with magnificent temples, theaters, baths, and aqueducts.

It was to here that the followers of Jesus fled when the backlash began against them in Jerusalem. A few shared their beliefs with the resident Greeks and found a willing audience, so early Christian churches were established in and around Antioch to cater for the converts.

Battleground of faiths

With churches founded by the Apostles, Antioch assumed a leading role in the emerging hierarchy of the Church. Bishops in Antioch had much weight in defining Church policy. So the invasion by Persians and then Muslims was a cause for Christian dismay. When the crusaders stormed through the region, Antioch was considered as important to reclaim for Christianity as Jerusalem. It became a Christian principality and survived as a European outpost for nearly two centuries.

Trade remained key to the city's success, and for expediency Christians and Muslims bought and sold from one another, the Christians benefiting from superior Islamic craftsmanship in the process.

When the Mamluks stormed to victory in the city in 1268, buildings old and new were razed to the ground. Antioch was reduced to village status and was ruled by the Ottoman Empire from 1517. Following the First World War, the French administered the town along with Syria, and finally it was incorporated within Turkish borders in 1939.

Fire and flood have done much to destroy the former glories of Antioch although excavations between 1932–39 revealed some intriguing mosaics. The famous Antioch is not to be confused with another city of the same name, Antiocheia-in Psidia, in the region of Psidia, also visited by Paul and Barnabus and likewise within the boundaries of modern Turkey (close to the modern town of Yalvac). The preachers were in fact thrown out of this other Antioch, although Paul returned there some years afterward to encourage Christianity.

Above: In mid-October 1097, soldiers of the First Crusade arrived outside the walls of Antioch. To the crusaders, Antioch was almost as important as Jerusalem. A bitter siege lasted months, and when the city finally fell, the crusaders became in turn besieged. Despite its crucial role in history and to the crusades, in less than 200 years Antioch would be razed by the Mamluks and reduced to little more than a village.

38. Tarsus

Paul replied, "I am a Jew from Tarsus in Cilicia,
a citizen of no obscure city I beg you,
permit me to speak to the people.

Acts 21:39

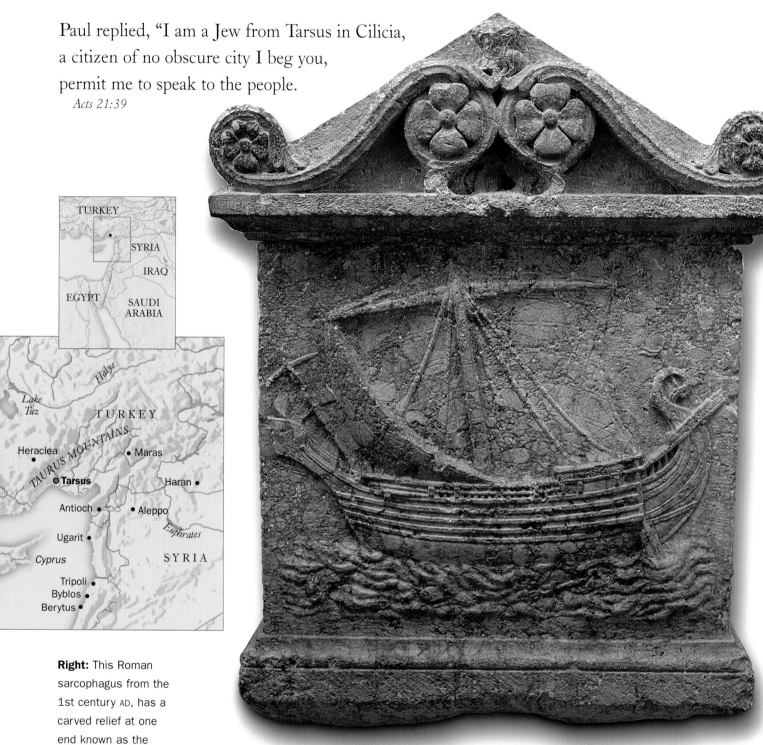

Right: This Roman sarcophagus from the 1st century AD, has a carved relief at one end known as the "Boat of Tarsus." It depicts a merchant ship that harks back to more ancient days of Phoenician trading.

Early settlers rightly picked Tarsus as a place brimming with natural attributes, sheltered by snow-capped mountains, served by a natural harbor, and surrounded by rich plains. It seems that the process of domesticating animals and working the land got underway early in Tarsus. By the second millennium BC, it had evolved into the Kingdom of Kizzuwadna.

Its ancient history is sketchy although Assyrian records tell us the place was rebuilt by Sennacherib in about 690 BC. The Greeks later ruled the region. But it is apparent that trade backed by an agricultural heritage helped to keep Tarsus wealthy. The only access to the major pass through the Taurus Mountains was from Tarsus, through what is known as the Cilician Gates. This is the daunting route used by Cyrus the Great, Alexander the Great, the crusaders, and numerous camel caravans. Its harbor gave it excellent seaborne links to the Levant. So the city, tucked inside the eastern rim of the Mediterranean, was something of a pearl.

In 67 BC, Tarsus became part of the Roman province of Cilicia, and developed into a university city that specialized in the study of Greek philosophy. The respected philosopher Athenodoros lived and taught in Tarsus, and his pupils included the young Augustus, future emperor of Rome. Given the typically broad Roman view regarding religion, Tarsus was something of a crossroads of cultures.

City of influence

Tarsus's main claim to fame is as the birthplace of St. Paul. He was a Jew and a Roman citizen, rabidly anti-Christian until he underwent a profound experience on the road to Damascus. That he proudly mentioned his birthplace implies he was from a wealthy, well-regarded family.

Later, several saints were martyred in Tarsus, including St. Pelagia and St. Boniface. The fact that some Roman emperors are buried here, among them Tacitus (r.275–6, not to be confused with the Tacitus who wrote histories of the early emperors) and Julian Apostate

(r.361–3), reflects its former glory.

Romantics might also recall it as the place where Cleopatra, Queen of Egypt, first met Mark Antony in 41 BC. She had been summoned by Antony for assisting his recently defeated enemies. The historian Plutarch describes the arrival of the queen in Tarsus, describing in detail this exotic femme fatale: "She came sailing up the Cydnus on a galley whose stern was golden; the sails were purple, and the oars silver. These, in their motion, kept tune to the music of flutes and pipes and harps. The queen, in a dress and character of Aphrodite, lay on a couch of gold brocade, as though in a picture, while about her were pretty boys… like cupids who fanned her." Paul's immediate family may have been among those intoxicated by the perfumes that wafted from the ship.

The sea has retreated about 12 miles from Tarsus now, leaving it high and dry. The Roman monuments are buried some 16 feet below today's ground level, except for one temple platform and a stray Byzantine arch. Some distance away the old city walls are visible, like so many broken teeth. But the linen and tent-making industry that distinguishes Tarsus today was prominent in Paul's time.

Below: By the 3rd century, Tarsus had enjoyed the prosperity of a major Roman city for over 200 years, and many of the merchant-class afforded splendid decoration for their houses. This mosaic from Tarsus shows Orpheus playing his harp to attentive animals.

39. Ephesus

And it happened that while Apollos was at Corinth, Paul passed through the inland country and came to Ephesus. There he found some disciples.

Acts 19:1

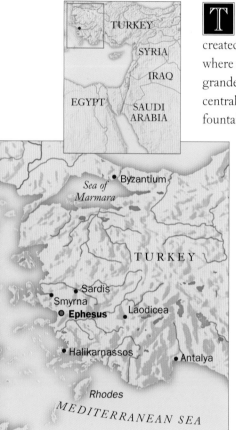

To one ancient traveler Ephesus represented "the most beautiful work ever created by humankind." Even today it is a site where ancient ruins vie one next to the other in grandeur. There is a magnificent theater, a central road lined with stately columns, fountains, temples, and baths. Its Roman remains are surpassed in scale and beauty only in Rome itself.

However, its architectural and archaeological legacy is not restricted to the Roman days but extends further back, into Greek times. This is the home of the Temple of Artemis; a gigantic complex devoted to the Greek goddess Artemis (or Diana, as she was known in Roman times), and one of the Seven Wonders of the ancient world.

Artemis was introduced to the Ephesians in about the eighth century BC by Ionian migrants who were responsible for fortifying the settlement. The Mother Goddess always loomed large in Ephesus, which is said to have been founded by Amazonian warriors. Before the arrival of Artemis the cult worship was for Cybele, a Syrian equivalent.

Conspicuous in their devotion to Artemis, the people of Ephesus constructed the largest building in ancient Greece, the first made entirely from marble. It was decorated with bronze statues and featured no fewer than 127 columns. The legendary wealth of King Croesus (r.c.560–546 BC) initially paid the bills. It was destroyed on several occasions, by fire and by plundering Goths, but on each occasion lovingly restored by the faithful. Only when the region had become predominantly Christian did the edifices of the temple become a towering embarrassment. In AD 401, St. John Chrystostom took matters into his own hands and tore down this monument to polytheism.

Center of pagan worship

Today visitors to the site of the Temple just outside Ephesus have little before them to stimulate the imagination. There remains a single column (re-erected) and the foundations of the mammoth building, measuring 430 by 260 feet. No one knows precisely what it looked like, but by using detailed descriptions made of the temple when it was still standing, archaeologists have been able to produce artists' impressions of its appearance.

In its glory days pilgrims flocked here to worship Artemis or, later, Diana. She was as important a figure then as Jesus or Mohammed is now, so St. Paul was in the heart of enemy territory when he preached here on his missions around Europe and Asia Minor.

His words, which rang out around the

Right: Wherever Romans went, their engineers and architects left behind a wealth of stunning buildings. But it is often overlooked that Romans were among the first to create modern sanitary arrangements, even in far-flung outposts of the empire, as these public toilets in Ephesus prove.

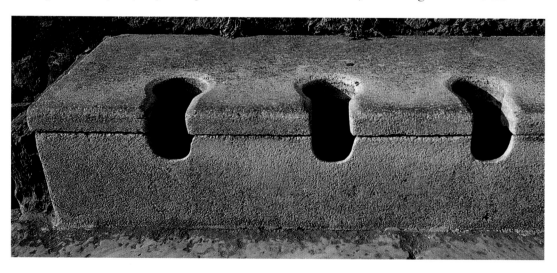

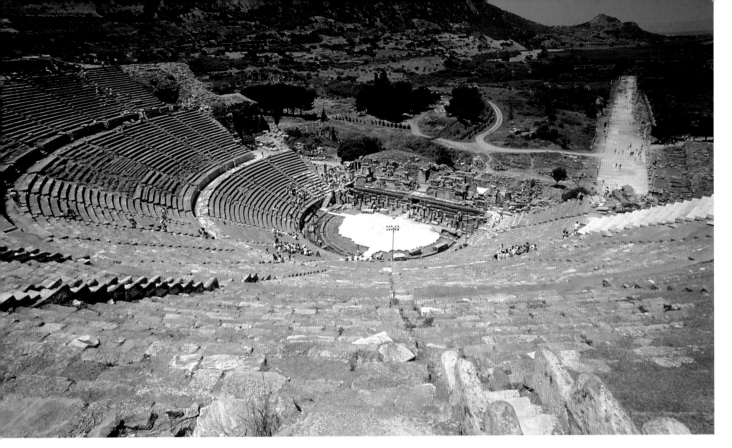

spectacular Roman theater, were poorly received by an incredulous and hostile crowd. The most scornful of his opponents were the silversmiths who earned their living by forging models of goddess and the temple. They realized that if Paul's new religion was adopted they would be tossed out of work. With the chant of "Great is Diana of the Ephesians" drowning his message, Paul left Ephesus and subsequently commented several times on the enmity he received there.

According to the Bible, Jesus directed his mother Mary to look after John following the crucifixion. If she heeded his words then she would have spent her last days in Ephesus for it was from here that John came. A basilica-style building devoted to the Virgin Mary was erected in the second century and consequently modified and expanded in subsequent centuries. On a nearby hilltop there is a church dating from the sixth century in honor of St. John, allegedly built on his house and tomb.

Despite the best efforts of ancient engineers, the harbor at Ephesus eventually silted up, eliminating its potential for trade. With the fall of the Romans, raids by Goths and Arabs, and the arrival of the plague, Ephesus could no longer sustain its population and it was abandoned.

Above: In the massive Roman amphitheater at Ephesus, Paul preached to a hostile audience, who viewed Christianity as a threat to their livelihoods as manufacturers of the best-selling Artemis statuettes. Little now remains of the massive Temple of Artemis, **left**.

40. Mount Ararat and Noah's Ark

And of every living thing of all flesh, you shall bring two of every sort into the Ark, to keep them alive with you.

Genesis 6:19

The story of Noah's Ark is not exclusive to the Bible. Similar folk legends about a Great Flood have existed among the world's ancient civilizations for thousands of years, perhaps inspired by a sudden and catastrophic rise in sea levels at the end of the last Ice Age. Greek mythology has Deukalion building an ark, the Indians have Manu, father of humanity, being guided by a fish to save "the seed of all things," while the Chinese remember Yu as a hero responsible for controlling flood water. The Maya of Central America and the Australian aborigines have similar stories.

In Mesopotamia, the heart of Old Testament country, the Epic of Gilgamesh is another flood tale that has survived several millennia. Traced back to Sumerian and Babylonian sources, it tells how the great god Enlil sends a rainstorm to destroy humankind. One man, Utnapishtim, survives in a cube-shaped boat that he builds and stocks with the creatures of the world. Given that the region's two great rivers—the Tigris and the Euphrates—once flooded on a regular basis, it is easy to see how this would be a popular story among local people.

When written history began, various stories were recorded, each claiming to identify the spot where the Ark grounded. The Bible speaks only of "the mountains of Ararat" (as opposed to Mount Ararat itself) and according to Jewish and early Christian scribes this puts Noah's landfall somewhere in the Land of Kardu (an ancient name for Kurdistan) in the Zagros Mountains. Berossus, the third-century BC Babylonian priest and historian, tells how inhabitants of the area would remove chunks of bitumen from the ship to use as talismans. The great Assyrian king Sennacherib apparently went even further during his conquest of Kurdistan, chopping off a plank to take home and worship.

Berossus is one of several sources which narrow the Ark's location down to Mount Judi Dagh, near the Iraq-Turkey border. We know Sennacherib visited this mountain because he had reliefs of himself carved at its foot. Both the Koran and the tenth-century AD historian Ibn Haukal mention the site, and a fifth-century AD Christian sect called the Nestorians built a number of monasteries there, one of which was named Cloister of the Ark. Mount Aregats, in eastern Turkey, was first suggested as the "Mountain of the Descent" in Marco Polo's time and is still the current favorite among many Christian explorers.

Right: A shepherd tends his flock in the shadow of Mount Ararat, on the eastern border of Turkey. Once the favorite site for the grounding of Noah's ark, Mount Ararat still beguiles with its mysteries—as recently as 1997, the CIA thought they had detected the ark under a sheet of ice.

Archaeological evidence?

If the Ark truly existed in its biblical proportions (300 x 50 x 30 cubits or 500 x 80 x 50 feet) it would probably have left a trace somewhere—even if only as a "shadow" in soil strata. In November 1997 ark-ologists believed the breakthrough had come when the CIA released pictures taken by a U2 spy plane flying over Mount Ararat. Analysts puzzled over the Ararat Anomaly, an elliptical shape concealed beneath the ice. Academics spoke breezily of "the remains of a ship… a manmade structure under the ice."

The excitement did not last. A retired CIA photo analyst, Dino Brugioni, was quoted in the *Washington Times* as saying: "If you didn't have the biblical dimensions in cubits you could pick up those pictures and say they looked like a ship. But when you measure it up it doesn't come out right. At no time did we say we saw an ark."

The Ark may elude us but evidence of cataclysmic flooding in the ancient Near East grows stronger. In September 2000, the marine archaeologist Robert Ballard discovered the remains of buildings in 311 feet of water, some 12 miles off the Turkish Black Sea coast. The same expedition located an ancient shoreline at a depth of 550 feet—evidence that an area half the size of Britain disappeared under the Black Sea some 7,500 years ago as the earth's ice caps receded and sea levels gradually rose.

Great Flood stories

The Noah of the Bible is not the only ancient figure associated with the flood, Noah has three other identities: the Sumerian Ziusudra, Old Babylonian Atrahasis, and the Akkadian Utnapishtim who, likeNoah, sent out a dove and a raven to find dry land. The British archaeologist/author David Rohl (*also referred to on page 145*), after exhaustive examination of evidence, has dated the Great Flood of the Bible to about 3100 BC. He identified no less than 150 flood myths worldwide, but was most taken with that of the Mesoamerican Maya. These exceptional record-keepers had fixed the date for their great deluge at 3113 BC.

CHAPTER THIRTEEN

Greece Gazetteer

And now will I show you the truth.
Behold, three kings shall arise in
Persia, and the fourth shall be far
richer than all of them. And when
he has become strong through his
riches, he shall sti rup against the
kingdom of Greece.

Daniel 11 : 2

Before the emergence of the Romans as the
defining civilization of Asia and Europe,
there came the inspirational Greeks. Theater,
philosophy, and democracy were all born and
thrived in the city-states that together formed
Greece. Draco gave the Athenians their first
written law in c.630 BC. Math and astronomy
were hotly debated subjects too, as was the role
of the gods. Greece was working hard to refine
its culture at a time when barbarians
proliferated. Other peoples, empires, or kings
did not goad them into the intellectual
challenge, the advances came from within.

Greece notched up its cultural successes at
the same time as the Babylonians reigned
supreme. Their mutual enemy was Persia,
although there were many disputes between the
Greeks and Babylonians too. Greece forged an
impressive military tradition out of necessity.
And from that tradition emerged Alexander the
Great, who strode around the Middle East and
Asia to forge a huge empire.

It is perhaps easy to view Greek social and
political achievements through rose-tinted lenses.
For with democracy came corruption, and
military triumphs brought about bankruptcy.
Nevertheless, the Greeks were more successful
across a range of fields—political, military,
artistic, and cultural—than any civilization
before. Sophisticated and influential, Greece was
a natural venue for the Apostles to visit. Such
was the relevance of the culture at the time, the
language of the early Christians was Greek.

Roman provinces in Greece
at the time of St. Paul

Macedonia

Epirus

Achaea

Thracia and
Moesia Superior

BLACK SEA

THRACIA

Philippi

Neapolis

Abdera

Elon

Stageiros

Stratonikaia

Thasos

Thasos

Samothrace

Imbros

Lemnos

Agios

Byzantium

Chalcedon

SEA OF MARMARA

Marmara

Kyzikos

Sestos

Abydos

Hellespont, Dardanelles

Sigeion

Ilium
(Troy)

Tenedos

Antandros

Polymedion

Assos

In 133 BC, the king of Pergamon willed his kingdom to Rome, which became the first Roman province in the Middle East. The Romans named it Asia.

Skiathos

Pelagos

Peristera

Skopelos

Northern Sporades

Skros

Euboea

Chalkis

Eretrea

EUBOEA

Marathon

Attica

Athens

amis

gina

ydra

Andros

AEGEAN SEA

Ienos

Tzia

Cythnos

Skyros

Serifos

Cyclades

Naxos

Paros

Sifnos

Adiparos

Paros

Naxos

Melos

Folegandros

Sikinos

Ios

Amorgos

Thera
(Santorini)

Anafi

SEA OF CRETE

Eresos

Mytilene

Lesbos

Pergamon
(Bergama)

Sardis

ASIA

Psara

Chios

Chios

Klazomenai

Teos

Kolophon

Ephesus

IONIA

Samos

Laodicea

Fournoi

Ikaria

Miletos

Mykonos

Khora

Patmos

Leros

Halikarnassos
(Bodrum)

Kalymnos

Kos

Kos

Nisyros

Astiplaia

Sporades

Symi

Tilos

Ialysos

Rhodos
(Rhodes)

Chalki

Lindos

Rhodes

163

41. Patmos, the Prison Island

I, John, your brother and partner in the tribulation and the kingdom and the patient endurance that are in Jesus, was on the island called Patmos on account of the word of God and the testimony of Jesus.

Revelation 1:9

Remote and unyielding, the island of Patmos appeared through Roman eyes to be the ideal prison island for banishing exiles. Abandoned on this small landfall in the Dodecanese island group without access to communication, the discontented grumblings of troublemakers would surely be silenced.

So it was here that John, Jesus' companion, is said to have been dispatched by the Romans, who were concerned at his persistent prophecies regarding God and Jesus Christ. It is said that he received divine communicationn in a cave on this volcanic island and wrote the *The Revelation to John*, which later proved so significant for Adventist spurs of Christianity.

Some of the story at least is rooted in fact. The author of *Revelation* certainly lived and wrote on Patmos. But was it John, an early follower, described as the disciple "who Jesus loved best"?

Certainly John, son of Zebedee and younger brother of James, was one of Jesus' apostles and went on to be a pillar of the early Christian church. After the death of Jesus he is strongly linked to Ephesus (*see pages 158–159*), some 65 miles across the sea from Patmos.

He was accepted as the author of the *Gospel according to John*, although there is nothing to confirm this fact in the New Testament. But there remains doubt over whether he authored the *Revelation*, the last book in the Christian Bible, named for the Latin word *revelatio*, meaning an unveiling of the truth.

As early as the third century, learned Bible students questioned whether the same person wrote the *Gospel according to John* and *Revelation*. There were glaring differences in style, language, and thought processes and it seemed likely that there were two Johns figuring

Right: "St. John in Patmos Dictating the Apocalypse," a medieval icon panel, depicts the imprisoned saint with his scribe. In most paintings of the subject, John is shown actually writing himself. In fact, this image is probably nearer to the truth.

prominently in the young Christian church at a similar time. It now seems likely that there was a "Johannine circle," supporters of John the Apostle, writing in Ephesus between AD 80 and 90 and producing work in his name. The practice of pseudepigraphical writing—or ghost writing as it is better known today—was relatively common in the ancient world. Signing off work in another's name was one way to pay tribute to that person.

Enigma remains

John was then, and still is, a popular name. It is of limited assistance to know that there were once two revered tombs attributed to John dating from similar eras at Ephesus. The second-century bishop called Papias identifies John the Seer as a writer of Scriptures. He was a Jewish Christian and a prophet who lived in seclusion on Patmos. Almost certainly the writer on Patmos was put there during the reign of the Emperor Domitian (AD 81–96), who repressed Christian activity.

Patmos bears all the hallmarks of being subject to a catastrophic volcanic eruption in prehistoric times, which left half of the original island submerged. Today it measures just ten by six miles with a coastline some 37 miles long. Local worship in John's time was for the Greek goddess Artemis.

Later in the first millennium it apparently became deserted, probably because of Saracen raids. But in 1088, the Byzantine emperor Alexius I Comnenus paid due heed to its Biblical associations by granting the island to an abbot, Christodoulos Letrinos, who set about building a monastery dedicated to St. John at Khora, the elevated main town on Patmos.

Fittingly, it became famous for its library, which comprised an enviable collection of illuminated manuscripts, patriarchal seals, and books. There are also Byzantine icons, sacred vessels, and ninth-century embroideries now housed there. Today there is a college of theology near the grotto that John is said to have inhabited, while the cave itself is contained within a white block building that also houses numerous chapels. Pilgrims who flock there can still see a carved cross on the wall, said to have been created by the author of *Revelation*.

Above: The rocky nature of the tiny island of Patmos made it an ideal site for a Roman prison. Now the town of Khora is dominated by the monastery of St. John, its most famous prisoner.

42. Thessalonika

But when the Jews from Thessalonika learned that the word of God was proclaimed by Paul at Berea also, they came there too…stirring up the people.
Acts 17:13

A mixed reception greeted Paul when he reached Thessalonika (Thessaloniki, Salonica). On one hand he found willing ears to receive his message as he preached for three Sundays in the synagogue. But his words sparked fury in sections of the Jewish community who then incited thugs and hooligans to run him out of town. His brief time there might have been lost in obscurity but for the fact that he later penned two letters to the church he established and left behind. Both became books of the New Testament.

Rising from the Aegean Sea, the settlement was once called Therma, for its warm springs to the south and east. Cassander (Kassandros), son of Antipater, Alexander the Great's regent in Greece, made it a city after 315 BC, and named it for Alexander's sister, Thessaloniki. Cassander became effective king of Greece in 319, and Thessalonika prospered for the connection. Then in 148 BC it became the Roman headquarters for their operations in the region, and was called the "Mother of Macedonia" in contemporary accounts. With the Romans came an even larger measure of prosperity, particularly after the construction of the *Via Egnatia*, which included Thessalonika on its route.

It is difficult to say just how Thessalonika looked to Paul's well-traveled eye. In its ascendancy, the city had overtaken Athens in terms of importance. It had been made a free city after 42 BC as a reward for supporting Antony and Octavius in their domestic strife. There were an estimated 65,000 people living within the city walls, a significant number being Jewish.

Paul traveled along the *Via Egnatia* from Philippi, passing through Amphipolis and Apollonia, two cities that have vanished from the modern map. There was an agora where Paul doubtless trod, under excavation today. The Gate of Axous built by the victorious Octavius was surely viewed by Paul but is not in evidence now. The most remarkable sites still in existence include the Galerius Arch, built in AD 303, together with city walls from the fourth century, and Byzantine churches built after the fifth century. These survived a massive fire in 1917, which destroyed much of the city. Afterward, buildings were erected on the ashes of the old.

A bloody history

Today a monastery has been built on the site of a house in the old city where Paul is reputed to have knelt and prayed. There is a chapel behind the hospital where Paul is said to have spent his last night in the city, avoiding a hostile crowd. The tears he shed on that occasion allegedly sparked a stream of holy water. Paul went onward to Berea, some 40 miles southwest of Thessalonika, where his enemies once again

Right: Thessalonika came to rival Constantinople (Byzantium before the 4th century AD) in opulence and culture. Among the splendors of the Byzantine period is the church of Santa Sophia, with its magnificent mosaics.

Left: The 4th-century city walls still stand, despite continued assaults by Romans, crusaders, and Ottoman Turks. This is the Djinghirli Tower, much older than the imposing 15th-century White Tower, which is one of Thessalonika's tourist attractions.

sought him out.

Afterward, Thessalonika endured a roller-coaster ride between prosperity and horror. The massacre of 7,000 residents—killed in punishment by Theodosius the Great (r.379–95), emperor of the Eastern Roman Empire, following an attempted uprising—is a stain on its history. On July 31, 904 Leo of Tripoli bridged the defenses and sacked the city, shipping off a great number of Thessalonians into slavery. In the summer of 1185, Guillaume d'Hauterive, king of Sicily, marched victoriously through the city streets, condemning rebels to death as he went. When the Ottoman Empire moved in during 1430, the Greeks once again faced barbarous retribution. In addition there were many other blood-spattered episodes that occurred during those centuries.

When Ferdinand and Isabella expelled Jews from Spain at the close of the 15th century, many moved to Thessalonika, where the Sephardic Jewish community assimilated well and thrived despite the Muslim domination that lasted nearly 500 years. Thessalonika was even known as a Jewish City. However, German expansion into Greece during the Second World War left Jews at the mercy of Hitler's Final Solution, and the majority died in extermination camps.

43. Corinth

Paul, an apostle of Christ Jesus by the will of God, and Timothy our brother, to the church of God that is at Corinth, with all the saints who are in the whole of Achaia.

2 Corinthians 1:1

When it came to strategic positions, Corinth (Korinthos) was almost unbeatable. Occupied at least as early as 2000 BC and possibly long before, Corinth by classical times possessed a stunning harbor and was backed by the amber Akrokorinthos, a sheer rocky citadel. Conquered by the Dorians before 1000 BC, Corinth capitalized on its position at the crossroads of busy trade routes, and became a colonial power and prime trading port in the eighth and seventh centuries BC.

With the emergence of Athens as a trading and seafaring city, there began a rivalry that spilled over into outright war during a series of skirmishes and one devastating conflict. Corinthians joined with Sparta in the Peloponnesian War (431–404 BC) and finally triumphed against Athens. However, political expediency forced it to back the former foe in a fight against Sparta in the Corinthian War (395–86 BC). But dreams of glorious independence came to an end with Philip II of Macedon occupying the Akrokorinthos in 338 BC before his untimely death at the hand of an assassin. His son, Alexander the Great, barely cast a glance in Corinth's direction before sweeping eastward.

Nevertheless, Corinth did not survive unscathed for long. She hitched herself to the wrong wagon during the battles to keep mighty Rome at bay, consequently being destroyed in 146 BC by the Roman general Lucius Mummius. Once again its glorious geography came to the rescue. Julius Caesar appreciated its natural virtues and reestablished Corinth as a colony that quickly became an administrative capital. Archaeological remains from this era include a market place, small theater, public baths, pottery factories, and villas. Much of the Roman construction obliterated the Greek buildings that had occupied the site previously.

However, the oldest building in Corinth is the South Stoa, once the longest building in Greece, and constructed in the sixth century BC. There is also a large temple devoted to Apollo dating from the same era. The remains of a fortress built and destroyed on numerous occasions since the Byzantine period, stand on top of the Akrokorinthos. Once, the fortress surveyed the ports that were the lifeblood of Corinth.

Its eastern harbor, at Lechaeum, bristled with the masts of Egyptian, Phoenician, and other trading vessels, while across the narrow neck of

land lay the harbor of Cenchreae. A road connected the two, used for transporting ships between the Gulf of Corinth and the Aegean.

Nero's ill-fated canal

Since 1893 a canal has dissected the isthmus, measuring just under four miles but shortening the journey from the Adriatic to Athens by more than 200. A waterway had been dreamed of since antiquity, not least by the poor souls compelled to drag ships from one side to the other. Many attempts were made to cut a canal, but all failed, giving rise to a superstition that the earth spouted blood whenever the project was undertaken.

Nero was among those who tried and failed. It is said he heralded the start of the canal scheme in AD 66 by singing an ode to Neptune and Aphrodite while strumming a lyre, then he cut the first sod with a golden spade. His workforce consisted of 6,000 young Jews captured on the shores of Lake Galilee during the Jewish rebellion. For no convincing reason, the trench was abandoned.

During about 18 months spent in Corinth, St. Paul worked as a tent or sail maker, established a church, and authored some of the letters that now feature in the New Testament. Significantly, in his time "Corinthian" was a by-word for vice, greed, and evil behavior, which gave him fertile ground in which to preach. Later he was compelled to pen powerful missives to the Corinthian church after it had become elitist, factionalized, and succumbed to idolatry.

Above: The temple of Apollo frames the Akrokorinthos. Seven of the Doric columns remain, some supporting the architrave of the temple, which was erected in the 6th century BC. One of Corinth's major exports was currants; the word is derived from "Corauntz," the way the city's name was once pronounced.

44. Athens, City of Gods

Now while Paul was waiting for them at Athens, his spirit was provoked within him as he saw that the city was full of idols.

Acts 17:16

Think of Athens (Athinai) and for most people images of the Parthenon, the huge temple perched on top of the city's Acropolis, immediately spring to mind. The Acropolis is a natural hill fortress, looming some 500 feet above Athens, and the term—derived from the Greek words *akros* meaning highest and *polis* meaning city—has come to embrace this spot and everything on it.

Occupied from Neolithic times (c.5000 BC), the Acropolis was long used for defensive and religious purposes. Following a Persian invasion in 480 BC and a 30-year period of recovery, the statesman Perikles directed the building of the Parthenon to reinvigorate the city's sacred life. Noted for his integrity in Athens, the city-state's allies in the Delian League thought differently of him— the funds for his civic works came from the League's joint treasury on the island of Delos, which Athens appropriated for its "safe-keeping."

It was awesomely proportioned, built from marble out of a quarry at Mount Pentelikon and measuring some 228 feet by about 100 feet. Supported by eight columns on each end and 17 on each side, the Parthenon had two sections and contained a 39-foot gold and ivory statue of the goddess Athene, to whom the temple was devoted, and also a 480-foot long frieze of the Panathenaic Procession.

For centuries it stood unsullied as a triumph of geometry, and might have remained so had it not been for the 17th-century conflict between occupying Turks, who stored gunpowder inside it, and the Venetians. In 1687 cannon from the Venetian fleet scored a direct hit, igniting the gunpowder, blowing off the roof, and killing 300 Turks. Despite this, the building remained standing. So striking is the sight of the Parthenon even today that it has been adopted as the symbol of UNESCO.

Multitude of religions

But when St. Paul visited the Parthenon it was in its prime, although Athens was suffering from a diminished profile on the world stage.

Paul could be forgiven for thinking that Athens basked in idolatry given the great number of festivals and celebrations carried out in honor of one god or another. As the importance of Athens receded, it enhanced its reputation by organizing an uncommon number of sporting and pseudo-religious events. Apollonia of Tyana (c.AD 3–c.97), a philosopher and renowned miracle worker, remarked that in Athens "altars are set up in honor even of unknown gods."

Paul addressed the crowds at the hill of Areopagus, west of the Acropolis, dedicated to Ares, the Greek god of war. The hill boasted temples sworn to numerous deities but Paul was undaunted and drove home the Christian message. Dionysus, a senator in the crowd, was converted and was thereafter known as St. Denis of Areopagite.

The Athenians did not know what to make of Paul: "Some of the Epicurean and Stoic philosophers also conversed with him and some said, 'What does this babbler wish to say?' Others said, 'He seems to be a preacher

Right: A small figurine representing the goddess Athene, dating from the 5th to 4th centuries BC, is only one of thousands made by Athenian artisans of the city's patron deity. Although the most significant of the Greek pantheon to Athenians, St. Paul encountered many other gods and minor deities in Athens.

of foreign divinities'—because he was preaching Jesus and the resurrection." (*Acts 17:18*)

His words would have been discussed by people gathered in the agora, the marketplace and ceremonial center that stands in a hollow between the Acropolis and the Areogpagus. Dating from the sixth century BC, it was frequently modified, not least by the Romans.

Here, in the fifth century BC, politicians debated the advantages of the infant democracy, and the place wafted with civility. Criminals were not allowed to enter. To ensure that no one would wander in without permission, the agora possessed prominent stones on its outskirts inscribed: "I am the boundary of the agora."

Above: Perikles' great civic building, among many he supervised, is undoubtedly the Parthenon on the Acropolis, which housed a giant statue of Athene.

45. Olympia, Spirit of the Body

Being then God's offspring, we ought not to think that the divine being is like gold or silver or stone, an image formed by the art and imagination of man

Acts 17:29

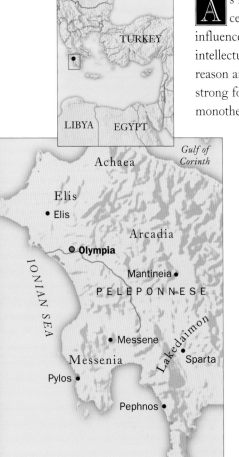

As rulers of the known world in the fourth century BC, the Greeks exerted massive influence on culture and politics. Their intellectuals were leaders in philosophy and reason and their pantheon of gods reflected a strong focus on religion. The idea of a monotheistic religion was risible to most Greeks, as the apostle St. Paul later found when he tried preaching to them of the one true God. He encountered resistance in all the Greek cities, but his message would have been received with even more hostility in Olympia.

The spirit of the ancient Olympics was very much at odds with Jewish and Christian thinking. For one thing it was a pagan religious festival held in honor of Zeus, king of the Greek gods. The site of the games at Olympia was devoted to Zeus and included a 42-foot-high gold and ivory statue of the god, one of the Seven Wonders of the ancient world, by the sculptor Pheidias, chief architect of the Parthenon in Athens.

The festival was open to all athletes of the Greek city-states and their numerous overseas colonies. They would travel from as far away as Egypt, Spain, Italy, Libya, the Ukraine, and Turkey during a month-long international truce. The athletes were treated as celebrities, their muscular bodies symbolizing the beauty and vitality of youth which so obsessed ancient Greeks.

Those who returned home as winners could look forward to a life of ease subsidized by the state, their sporting feats idealized by poets. Losers were simply ridiculed for besmirching the image of the city. With this in mind athletes

Right: The original statue of Discobolus by the Greek artist Mryon, sculpted in c.440 BC, was later lost, but the ancient Roman copy survives to leave us with an impression of the ideal of athletic youth in Greek eyes.

prayed to the gods for assistance and presented offerings of thanks—usually animals or cakes—when it seemed those prayers had been answered.

The Olympian event became the most celebrated of four ancient athletic contests, ahead of the Isthmian, Pythian, and Nemean games. It was probably founded well before 776 BC (when winners' names were first recorded), but a complete list of sporting champions between then and AD 217 was later put together by Eusebius of Caesarea. Only males could compete, and female spectators weren't admitted because the athletes performed naked. Given the Greek record on sexual mores this seems curiously prudish, although the rule's purpose was to ensure that

combination of both) held in a nearby stadium. The boxers initially used gloves of wound, soft leather strips but these were later replaced with lead-weighted animal hide. The *pancration* was not a sport for the faint-hearted; contests were never halted until one or other fighter publicly accepted defeat, which would be an intensely shameful experience.

Other disciplines included horseracing (riders supplied their own horse), the *pentathlon* (sprinting, wrestling, javelin, discus, and long-jump), and a debilitating finale in which athletes ran in armor. Discuses were bronze and oval-shaped, while javelins were thrown using a slingshot technique in which a strap wound

everyone's attentions were focused only on sport. One known exception to the rule was the priestess of Demeter—presumably because of her ability to rise above carnal instincts.

Sport taken seriously

During the first 300 years of their history the Games took place on a single day. By 472 BC, however, the program had expanded to five days, the first of which was solely devoted to the sacrificial worship of Zeus (not entirely different from today's opening ceremonies). The running race was the main discipline, with fighting arts such as boxing, wrestling, and the *pancration* (a

around the shaft was pulled down sharply at the point of release. This gave greater distance and accuracy.

When Rome replaced Greece as Mediterranean superpower the cultural influence of the Games faded. By the time of the later emperors acts of pagan worship were anathema to Rome, and in AD 391 Theodosius I banned such gatherings outright. The Dark Ages saw the end of major international sporting contests and it was not until the 19th century AD that Europeans began reviving the Olympic ideal.

Above: This detail from a relief sculpture shows wrestlers from the early Classical period, c.510 BC. Sporting events featuring naked youths abounded in Athens at the time of St. Paul's visit. His Roman citizenship would not have overcome his Jewish dislike of public nudity.

CHAPTER FOURTEEN
Italy

Now after these events Paul resolved in Spirit to pass through Macedonia and Achaia and go to Jerusalem, sayong, "After I have been there, I must also see Rome."

Acts 19:21

At first Italy seems an odd contender for a slot in a book about the Holy Lands. Prophets were not born there, nor were any battles fought for or against the Israelites. The roots of its importance lie in the era when the Roman Empire encompassed the entire Mediterranean fringe and all roads led to Rome. At this point, crucially when Christianity was rapidly developing and spreading, the religious spotlight shifted away from Palestine and toward Europe.

"There has never been anything more remarkable in the whole world," said Pliny the Elder of Rome and its empire. He was speaking in the first century AD, before succumbing to the toxic fumes of Mount Vesuvius during its explosive eruption of AD 79. At this time in European history it was possible to travel between Britain and Egypt, or from the Straits of Gibraltar to the Caspian Sea, without ever leaving the Roman Empire. For the Romans the empire was supreme, and they considered that outside their realm lay only barbarian lands.

There were aspects of Roman civilization that offended the Israelites, for example, its pantheon of gods, the sexual excesses, and political corruption. For this reason Rome was known in the Bible as "Babylon." In the *Revelation* Rome is depicted as a prostitute drunk with the blood of God's chosen people. Yet still St. Peter and St. Paul were drawn there.

Christianity was fresh and radical, and it was exported quite naturally to the hub of the empire from the outpost where it first emerged. In the process Rome became the center of Christendom, a status which, for many, it still holds today.

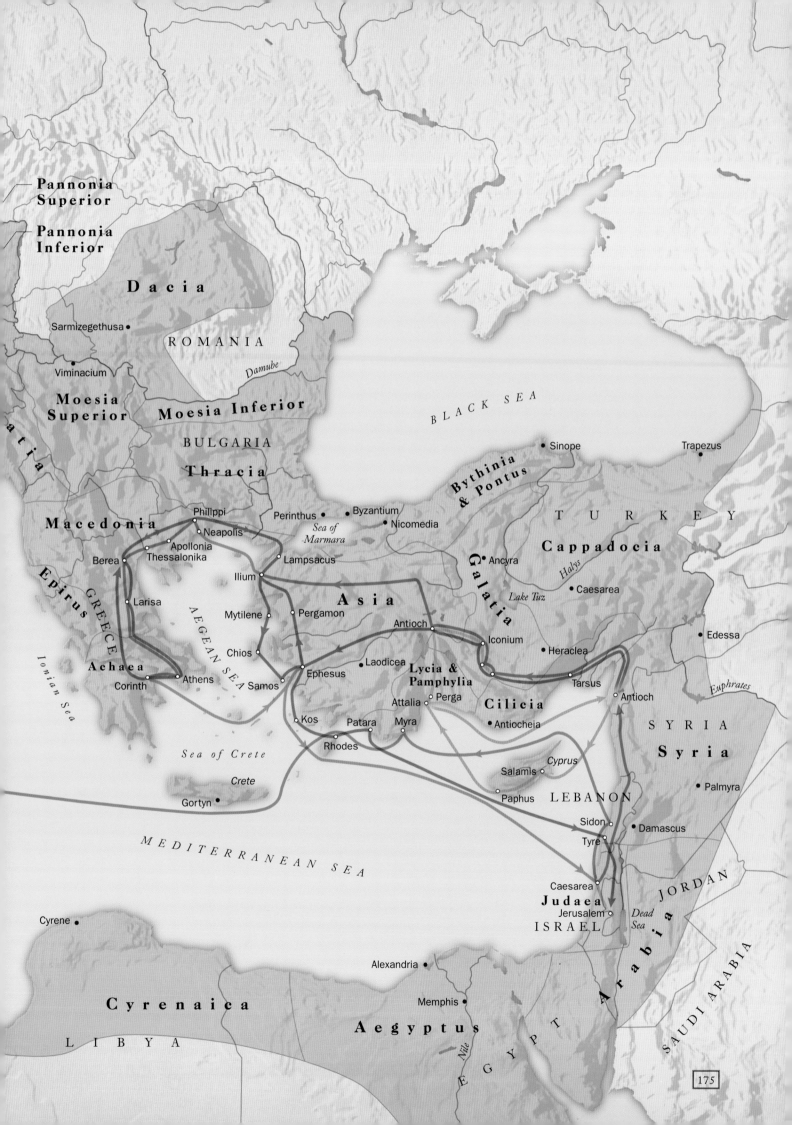

Dacia

Sarmizegethusa

ROMANIA

Danube

Viminacium

Moesia
Superior

Moesia Inferior

BULGARIA

Thracia

BLACK SEA

Sinope

Trapezus

Macedonia

Phillippi

Neapolis

Apollonia

Thessalonika

Berea

Perinthus

Byzantium

Nicomedia

*Sea of
Marmara*

Bythinia
& Pontus

Lampsacus

Ilium

TURKEY

Cappadocia

Ancyra

Halys

Caesarea

Galatia

Lake Tuz

Epirus

GREECE

Larisa

Mytilene

Pergamon

Asia

Antioch

AEGEAN SEA

Chios

Iconium

Heraclea

Edessa

Achaea

Ephesus

Laodicea

Athens

Samos

Lycia &
Pamphylia

Tarsus

Antioch

*Ionian
Sea*

Corinth

Attalia

Perga

Cilicia

SYRIA

Euphrates

Kos

Patara

Myra

Antiocheia

Syria

Rhodes

Cyprus

Palmyra

Sea of Crete

Salamis

LEBANON

Crete

Paphus

Gortyn

Sidon

Damascus

Tyre

MEDITERRANEAN SEA

Caesarea

JORDAN

Judaea

*Dead
Sea*

Jerusalem

Cyrene

ISRAEL

Arabia

SAUDI ARABIA

Alexandria

Cyrenaica

Memphis

Nile

LIBYA

Aegyptus

EGYPT

Rome in St. Peter's Time

And he found a Jew named Aquila, a native of Pontus, recently come from Italy with his wife Priscilla, because Claudius had commanded the Jews to leave Rome. And went to see them…

Acts 18:2

Below: This romantic image of Imperial Rome painted in 1838 exaggerates the vertical scale for effect, but gives an impression of the grandeur St. Peter faced when he visited the new "Babylon."

Rome was considered the capital of the world in Jesus' time. Had Jesus lived a full lifespan, he would almost certainly have gone there to preach, for acceptance of his doctrine in this cosmopolitan metropolis would surely have been his ultimate goal.

As events unfolded, Peter went instead and he found a small but vibrant Jewish community. It is thought that up to 50,000 Jews lived in Rome in the first century AD. Most inhabited the lower social orders, indicating that they were probably brought into the city as slaves. There were at least ten synagogues in existence when Peter arrived as well as catacombs for secret prayer meetings. It is likely that Christianity, as a sect of Judaism, had also reached the city before Peter arrived.

The dates for Peter's time in Rome are uncertain but it was unlikely to have been during the reign of Claudius (r.AD 41–54). In AD 49, following civil unrest, the emperor expelled all Jews from Rome. Later, the historian Suetonius (c.AD 60–c.140) wrote that the exile was ordered because of "disturbance at the instigation of Chrestus." This suggests that Christianity spread to Rome at a very early date indeed, less than two decades after Jesus' death. Jews were permitted to return after the death of Claudius.

Another historian, Tacitus (c.AD 55–c.120), explained that Jews were disliked for living separately in their own community. "Among themselves there prevails a persistent combination and ready liberality, but toward all others an intense hatred. They never eat, they never sleep with strangers. Those who go over to them they instruct in contempt of the gods, in disowning of one's fatherland, the despising of one's parents, children, brothers and sisters." Of course, those "who went over to them" sought something deeper than the prevailing polytheism.

Hotbed of paganism

Judaism was not, of course, the majority religion of Rome. Rather surprisingly, that title went to Mithraism, a faith imported from Iran lauding the power of the god Mithra and involving bull sacrifice. There was also emperor worship and sun worship alongside a number of imported cults from the Roman colonies.

As he walked the streets of the city, what would Peter have seen? He might have traveled there along the Via Appia, running arrow-straight from Rome to Brundisium (Brindisi). Perhaps he cast his eyes in wonder on an Egyptian obelisk dedicated to Ramesses II that was already more than 1,000 years old when the victorious Augustus transported it to Rome.

The focus of Roman life was the Forum, a market and meeting place. It was flanked by temples including the fifth-century BC Temple of Castor and Pollux, and by administrative buildings like the Basilica Julia. The architectural splendors fashioned at the behest of Augustus (63 BC–AD 14) were new. The emperor recorded: "I built: the Curia and the Chalcidicum which adjoins it, the Temple of Apollo on the Palatine and its colonnades, the Temple of Divus Julius, the Lupercal…" The list rambles on to include no fewer than 17 major works, of which 12 were temples.

However, the Coliseum had yet to be built. It was not opened until AD 80, when Titus (r.79–81) celebrated with a 100-day festival of bloodsports, costing the lives of 5,000 animals.

Some Christians would later be murdered here although the majority lost their lives in the imperial circuses.

Amid Rome's sometimes violent paganism Peter lived, worked, and died. The New Testament is sketchy about his time in Rome but the future pope, Clement of Rome, writing just before the end of the first century, and Ignatius of Antioch, writing in the early years of the second century, concur that he was there. Tradition has it that he was crucified by Nero, Peter requesting that his cross be inverted because he felt unworthy of the same death as Jesus.

According to Irenaeus of Lyons, writing in about 180, the bishopric of Rome was entrusted to St. Linus, a companion of St. Paul on his missions. It is impossible to say what he achieved in the dozen or so years he held office. It is said he died a martyr and was buried near St. Peter but this may merely be a legend. Nevertheless, Rome was firmly on the Christian map, and would one day be at the center of it.

Above: It was said that Peter wished to be crucified upside down, since he considered himself unworthy of the same death as Jesus. It gave Renaissance artists a dramatic image. This painting is by the Italian artist Ventura Salimbeni (1568–1613).

Fire and Martyrs

Then a mighty angel took up a stone like a great millstone and cast it into the sea, saying, "So will Babylon the great city be thrown down with violence and will be found no more…"

Revelation 18:21

Below: The bust of Nero, an emperor who started well and ended badly. Because of his persecution of Christians, Nero became the first "Antichrist."

W hile the Romans were generally relaxed about religion and rites, that did not prevent outbursts of persecution against the minorities. Before the Christians became a force to be reckoned with, the Jews were first in line for oppression. But Nero (r.AD 54–68), the flamboyant emperor of Rome at the time of the Great Fire, chose to make the Christians scapegoats for the city's disaster. Although Christianity was still regarded as a cult of Judaism, he could distinguish the differences and made capital from them.

Nero was the stepson of Claudius, and thanks to his mother Agrippina's paranoid plotting and poisoning, he came to the throne just prior to his 17th birthday. For a while he was a just and amenable ruler, guided by his tutors rather than his ambitious mother (whom he eventually had put to death in AD 59). He encouraged honesty among senators, avoided using the death penalty, and sought to reduce taxes. At the urging of Josephus (*see also pages 72–3, 79, 86, 117*), he issued aid to hard-pressed Jews.

However, he became fanatically fond of poetry, music, and theater, the latter still believed to be somewhat scandalous. He also had a reputation for sexual indulgence. By the time of the Great Fire his popularity had plummeted. Many thought he started the blaze; other reports place him 35 miles away in his country villa at the time the first flames ignited.

According to Tacitus: "[The fire] began in the Circus, where it adjoins the Palatine and Caelian hills. Breaking out in shops selling flammable goods, and fanned by the wind, the conflagration instantly grew and swept the whole length of the Circus. There were no walled mansions or temples, or any other obstructions, which could arrest it. First, the fire swept violently over the level spaces. Then it climbed the hills—but returned to ravage the lower ground again."

Tacitus, who did not know how the fire began but acknowledged a rumor that it was the work of the emperor, revealed: "Of Rome's fourteen districts only four remained intact. Three were leveled to the ground. The other seven were reduced to a few scorched and mangled ruins."

Nero may have been innocent of starting the fire, but he still greeted the news with unseemly glee, taking up his lyre and singing about the fall of Troy. Further, he took advantage of the destruction by instituting a plan for a new palace called the Golden House and a giant statue of himself—the Colossus, that later gave its name to the Flavian Theater, or Colisseum.

Martyrdom makes converts

To deflect criticism, Nero began a program of persecution so brutal that he became an Antichrist figure for subsequent generations of Christians. His victims were fed to wild dogs, crucified, and even covered in pitch to be set alight as human torches. Nero may have been the first Roman emperor to victimize Christians but he certainly was not the last. Non-Christians quickly took alarm at the activities of the faithful for, to the ill-informed, the Eucharist was cannibalism and the communal meal was confused with sexual orgies. Christianity was a heretical cult to the Jews and a baffling mystery to the Romans. Consequently, marginalization and persecution continued.

In 106, Pliny the Younger freely told the emperor Trajan about the torture he had inflicted upon a slave girl. It was done, he insisted, because Christians were obstinate and because their secret ceremonies encouraged superstition.

The most notorious of the emperors were Decius (201–51) and Diocletian (245–316), who were both advocates of Roman religion. However, the barbarous treatment meted out to Christians failed to dent the growing popularity of the religion. Indeed, onlookers—even guards—were so impressed with the dignity and forbearance with which many Christian martyrs met death that they became converts.

St. Peter's Basilica

To all those in Rome who are beloved of God and called to be saints: Grace to you and peace from God our Father and the Lord Jesus Christ.

Romans 1:7

Jesus urged his disciples to "preach the gospel to the whole of creation." Simon, known as Peter, the fisherman turned Apostle, took his duties as the first evangelist very seriously. Peter was devoted to Jesus, although he is perhaps best remembered for denying any knowledge of him at the time of the crucifixion. Nevertheless, Jesus never lost his belief in Peter. According to the gospels, it was Peter he named as "the rock" on which the Church was to be built, and he was further entrusted with "the keys of the Kingdom of Heaven." He was undoubtedly the chief of the Apostles.

As the earthbound voice of the Messiah, life was far from easy for Peter or indeed any of the other disciples. A clampdown on Christians began immediately following Christ's death, supported by the Jews and, to a lesser extent, the Roman authorities. Stephen, one of seven men recruited by the disciples to help establish the early Church, was an early victim. A talented preacher and a miracle worker, he was arrested for speaking out against Jewish Law. His passionate defense inspired only wrath among his accusers and in a fury they seized him and stoned him to death. Among those who witnessed the terrible event was the Pharisee Saul, who would later convert to Christianity on the road to Damascus.

So the dangers of being a missionary were starkly apparent. Nevertheless, Peter and John went to Samaria to baptize converts, on the first stage of a journey that would take them across the Holy Land and beyond.

Peter illustrated his healing powers when he raised a woman from the dead in Jaffa. In Caesarea he converted the family of a Roman centurion called Cornelius. This was significant because Jews like Peter would usually have nothing to do with Gentiles, or non-Jews, in accordance with the laws given by God through Moses. Peter had a vision in which he learned that Gentiles were no longer "unclean" in the eyes of God. It was another example of the

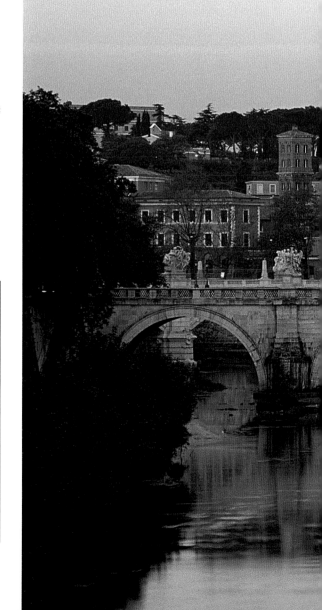

A work of generations

The foundation stone of the new St. Peter's basilica was laid on April 11, 1506 by the elderly Pope Julius II, who had appointed Bramante to be his architect. Work went slowly. Julius died in 1513, and the new pope, Leo X, made Raphael chief architect after Bramante's death in 1514. Lack of funds still held up work and Raphael never completed the project. Five or six other architects served at one time or another before the aging Michelangelo was put in charge. His greatest addition was the huge dome. He replaced Bramante's original, rounder structure with the tall, baroque dome we know today. By the time he died in 1564, only the shell was complete. The cathedral was finished in 1626, although Carlo Maderna later added the facade.

radical nature of Christianity at the time.

Returning to Jerusalem, Peter implored fellow believers to preach to Gentiles as well as Jewish people, thus instantly broadening the scope of the mission. Ultimately Peter was arrested and jailed, but an angel appeared one night to release him from his fetters. The furious Herod Agrippa I had the guards—who had slept throughout—executed.

After this incident the movements of Peter are shrouded in mystery. No one knows precisely which routes he took through the region, although it is generally accepted that he traveled in the east. Indications are that he was instrumental in promoting the fledgling Christian community in Antioch along with Paul, Timothy, and Barnabas.

Foundation of the Church

However, there is a body of evidence that shows Peter worked in Rome for some time. His *First Epistle*, which comprises part of the New Testament, was written from there, urging others to stand firm in the face of persecution. Peter was arrested in Rome and eventually martyred, probably in AD 60, although the details surrounding his death remain a mystery. As early as AD 95, Clement of Rome wrote to the Corinthians of how Peter "in consequence of unjust zeal, suffered not one or two but numerous miseries… (and) has entered the merited place of glory." Peter's apparent martyrdom marked Rome forever as a city at the heart of Christendom.

He surely could not have foreseen the splendor that would one day adorn his tomb. Constantine (r.305–37) commissioned a mighty basilica over what was just a humble shrine. The building had become dilapidated over a thousand years later when Pope Julius II gave the go-ahead for a new basilica in 1506. It took 120 years to complete under 13 chief architects. The main structure is 613 feet long and stands 67 feet higher than St. Paul's in London, and 148 feet higher than the dome of the United States Capitol.

The interior of St. Peter's is lavish, with astonishing baroque sculptures, paintings, and mosaics. Ironically this is all done in the name of a man who never wore anything other than roughly woven materials, and who followed Jesus' habit of living frugally.

CHAPTER FIFTEEN

The Holy Lands Today

In ancient times the Holy Lands endured one miserable military episode after another. But that came to an end with the expansion of the Ottoman Empire into the region, which for 400 years provided cohesion and stability. Muslims living in Palestine were kept under the political control of the Ottoman sultans while Jews were scattered across the world, with apparently no prospect of return.

A plea to return to Jerusalem formed part of the daily prayers of Jews worldwide. But it was uttered simply as a plea, with little hope of success. Many Jews had more pressing and immediate problems to contend with, including regular waves of antisemitism which ebbed and flowed, especially in Europe. One such wave engulfed the continent in the latter half of the 19th century. It was evident in Russia, where there were pogroms directed against Jews, and in France, where a Jewish army officer, Dreyfus, was falsely accused of espionage, provoking a surge of anti-Jewish sentiment.

Antisemitism was rife too in the Austrian Empire where Theodor Herzl, a journalist and

Egypt's siezure of the Suez Canal from France and Britain in 1956 led to an abortive joint expedition to regain control. As a pro-Western ally, Israel seized the opportunity to attack Egyptian Sinai.

Arab-Israeli tensions and conflicts, 1948–83

Palestinians in the Gaza Strip and West Bank were promised autonomy under the Camp David Treaty of 1979.

In October 1973, Egypt attacked across the Suez Canal without warning on the Jewish Day of Atonement. In the resuting three-week "Yom Kippur War," Israel decisively defeated Egyptian forces in the Battle of Chinese Farm, the largest tank battle ever fought, and held off Syrian assaults against the Golan Heights.

GOLAN HEIGHTS captured, 1967; incorporated into Israel in 1981

Beirut

Sidon

Damasc

Tyre

Acre

Haifa

Janin

Al Mafr

W E S T

Nablus

B A N K

Tel Aviv-Yaffo

Ram Allah

Amman

Jerusalem
Bethlehem

Hebron

Gaza

GAZA STRIP

Beersheba

I S R A E L

Dumyat
(Damietta)

Bûr Sa'îd
(Port Said)

El Mansura

El 'Arîsh

Inchas

Români

Deversoir

Gebel Libni

Ismlâ'ilîya

Abu Suweir

Bîr Gifgâfa

Bîr Hasana

Fâyid

Gidi Pass

Bîr el Thamâda

Cairo

El Kûbri

E G Y P T
United Arab Republic
(with Syria), 1958–61

El Suweiz
(Suez)

Mitla Pass

El Kuntilla

Sudr

El Thamad

S I N A I
to Israel 1967, returned
to Egypt by treaty, 1982

Eilat

Aqaba

Beni Suef

Territories held in 1956

	Israel
	Egypt
	Jordan
	Syria

Abu Zenima

S A U D I

A R A B I A

Abu Rudeis

El Minya

Israeli Suez Crisis campaign, 1956

Israeli gains 1967

Dahab

When Egypt closed the Strait of Tiran to Israeli shipping in 1967, it sparked a pre-emptive strike by Israel, which became the Six-Day War.

○ Arab airfield destroyed by Israel, 1973

Egyptian re-conquests, Israeli temporary gain, 1973

Syrian occupation limit, 1976–83

Israeli occupation limit, 1983

GULF OF SUEZ

GULF OF AQABA

Strait of Tiran

Strait of Gûbâl

Sharm el Sheik

JORDAN

playwright, lived. The strength of feeling against Jews convinced him it was no longer feasible for Jewish people to assimilate. Now was the time for organized emigration to a newly defined Jewish state. The most obvious place for such a state was Palestine, although Argentina, Africa, and Sinai were also suggested.

Early Zionists

Herzl became a figurehead for Zionism, the political movement pursuing a Jewish homeland. At the end of August 1897 he hosted a Congress in Basel, Switzerland, outlining his aspirations: "We want to lay the foundation stone," he declared, "for the house which will become the refuge of the Jewish nation. Zionism is the return to Judaism even before the return to the land of Israel." A Zionist Organization, with Herzl at its head, was founded with the

it." His foresight was, frankly, astonishing. At the time of his death in 1904 the creation of Israel was less than a half century away.

The Basel Congress had a precedent in the form of a group of Russian Jews who had been pursuing the same aim independently of Herzl for some time. Antisemitism in Russia had been acute since the assassination of Czar Alexander II in 1881 by a gang of anarchists, some of whom had Jewish names. Those leaving Russia, joined by Jews from other eastern European regions, headed for America, Canada, Argentina—and to Palestine. Once in the Holy Land they sought to make a living off the land. Many moved on again, disheartened by the difficulties involved. Others with more resilience formed the first Jewish presence in the Holy Land for centuries, at a colony called Richon Le-Zion, south of Jaffa.

Before his death, Herzl received an early

Below: "The Germans destroyed our families and homes—don't you destroy our hopes." Jewish refugees crowd the deck of the *Theodor Herzl* cargo vessel as they arrive in Palestine, April 24, 1947. Two British sailors watch from a tender; early British attempts to prevent landings were overwhelmed by the sheer mass of returning Jews.

declared aim of winning a Jewish state. Later, he wrote: "If I had to sum up the Basel Congress in one word—which I shall not do openly—it would be this: At Basel I founded the Jewish state. If I were to say this today, I would be greeted by universal laughter. In five years, perhaps, and certainly in 50, everyone will see

warning about life in Islamic Palestine from Yusuf Diya al-Khalidi, a moderate former mayor of Jerusalem: "By what right do the Jews demand [Palestine] for themselves?" he questioned. Predicting an explosive response to the proposal of a Jewish homeland in Palestine he appealed: "For the sake of God, leave Palestine in peace."

meir

Al-Khalidi's words were prophetic. As early as 1907, the small number of Jews carving a niche for themselves in Palestine were compelled to form self-defense groups to counter Arab hostility.

WWI and Balfour

Problems in the Middle East were quickly overshadowed by the onset of the First World War. The Ottoman Empire sided with Germany and finished the conflict on the losing side, stripped of its land. Before the end of the war, Arthur Balfour had already issued a momentous and hopelessly naïve declaration through Baron Rothschild regarding a Jewish homeland: "His Majesty's Government view with favor the establishment in Palestine of a national home for the Jewish people, and will use their best endeavors to facilitate the achievement of this object, it being clearly understood that nothing shall be done which may prejudice the civil and religious rights of non-Jewish communities in Palestine, or the right and political status enjoyed by Jews in any other country." His words made

nonsense of Britain's existing pledges to Arabs. Nevertheless, Britain was given an international mandate to rule in Palestine and Mesopotamia, while France was given a mandate over land occupied today by Syria and Lebanon.

Arrayed before the Europeans were Arabs dreaming of a united Islamic state and Jews seeking a homeland. Clearly, it would be impossible to satisfy both groups' aims, no matter how intense the diplomacy. Britain appeased the Hashemite prince Abdullah by creating a new territory known as Transjordan and placing it under his governance.

Even without the hoped-for homeland, Jewish immigration to Palestine continued. British authorities, faced with increasing Arab unrest, tried to limit the numbers entering. Jewish people formed the Haganah to defend their communities. When the Arab Revolt, inspired by British rule and Jewish expansionism, broke out in 1936, British troops fought alongside the Haganah to restore peace. The response to the Arab uprising was brutal because the British authorities finally recognized that they had a dilemma of the most intractable sort.

The creation of Israel

With the Second World War on the horizon, the British government tried to conciliate the Arabs by giving them effective power of veto over Jewish immigration—this during the years of Hitler's viciously antisemitic regime in Germany. New proposals were drawn up for partition of Palestine. Although the Jewish side grudgingly accepted them, the Arabs were outraged. Britain continued to walk a tightrope between the two communities, to serve her own ends during the war.

At the end of the war, Jewish extremists attacked British interests and personnel in Palestine. In February 1947, unable to find a way forward, Britain asked for United Nations assistance. With scenes from the Holocaust fresh in the memory, diplomats decided that Palestine should be divided into a Jewish state comprising 55 percent of the land, the rest being an independent Arab state. There would be international trusteeship of Jerusalem and Bethlehem. Arabs were violent with rage. However, the Haganah soon established Jewish rights and, as the British pulled out in 1948,

an independent state called Israel was declared. Immediately Israel faced a barrage from Arab states intent on reclaiming Palestine. Fighting for her existence, Israel fielded Jews from the Holy Land and abroad to fend off the threat and even seized more land than the United Nations agreement permitted. Hostilities had ended by 1949, with Israel the victor. The map, so recently drawn up by the United Nations, was redrawn to accommodate the situation on the ground.

The West Bank now came into being in an agreement between Israel and the Kingdom of Jordan, also newly created in the aftermath of the Second World War, and was put under Jordanian control. A problem from the outset, few countries supported Jordan's King Abdullah in his bid for the territory. It virtually doubled his realm's population at a stroke. Other Arab nations wanted a new Arab state—and the West Bank didn't measure up. Israel wanted to consolidate its perpetually threatened position in the region and needed the West Bank to do so. Israel and Jordan were also to share Jerusalem.

The Six-Day War

Nevertheless, the agreement brought a measure of peace to Israel, although Abdullah paid the price for his ambitions when he was shot dead by a Palestinian assassin in 1951. Arab refugees flooded out of Israeli territory by the thousand to camp in neighboring Arab lands amid fears for their safety. There were cross-border skirmishes on an almost daily basis. These were contained until 1967 when brinkmanship boiled over into outright war. Israel struck first, demolishing the Egyptian air force on the first day of what became known as the Six-Day War.

The West Bank fell to Israel on day three and the Golan Heights were snatched from Syria on day five. Israel was now in control of more land than ever before. The response of the Arab world was to issue a declaration insisting there would be no peace with Israel, no negotiations with Israel, and no recognition of Israel.

Now Palestinian terrorist activity began with a vengeance, on a worldwide basis. Armed Palestinians were seen as enemies even by some Arab governments, who feared their destabilizing influence. In September 1970 King Hussein of Jordan ordered that Palestinian power in his country be crushed, and Palestinians were forced to regroup in Lebanon.

Left: By June 10, 1967, when fighting in the Six-Day War was halted, Israel had won territory four times the area it had held in 1949, with an Arab population of over 1.5 million. This territory included all the Sinai, taken from Egypt. In 1973, newly elected President of Egypt Anwar Sadat launched a surprise attack across the Suez. The Yom Kippur War, as it became known, lasted only three weeks, by which time the vast array of Egyptian tanks lay wrecked in the sands of Sinai.

A surprise attack launched by Egypt and Syria against Israel in 1973 was finally beaten off. There was international concern that Israel would resort to nuclear strikes if she were defeated, as she nearly was. Both sides retired wounded from the assault. Now the United

The next flashpoint came in 1982 with the civil war in Lebanon (between Christians and Muslims), which ended up involving the Palestine Liberation Organization, Syrian combat forces, and the Israeli army and air force. The Israelis succeeded in ousting the PLO leader

States sent Henry Kissinger to enter the fray, pulling off what seemed to be an impossible feat—a negotiated peace between Israel and Egypt. However, despite early promise, the deal failed to institute far-reaching changes, although Israel did at last withdraw from Sinai in accordance with the agreement.

Yasser Arafat from Beirut, forcing him into exile. However, the Lebanon venture was stained by the activities of Christian Phalangists who went into two Palestinian refugee camps and carried out a systematic slaughter of its occupants. Israeli troops were apparently at the gates of the camps and even provided illumination so the killing could continue after dark. Israeli public opinion was appalled, and reluctantly a commission of inquiry was established. It singled out defense minister Ariel Sharon for special criticism, and he was duly stripped of his title.

Palestinian anguish and anger once again

erupted in 1987 when Arabs in the Israeli-occupied Gaza strip staged an uprising known as the Intifada, or "shaking off." The aggression generally involved Palestinian stone throwers aiming at Israeli soldiers, who responded by shooting and beating their unarmed assailants. During the Intifada, Arafat tried to achieve a Palestinian state via diplomacy, a course he had made little use of to this point. He recognized Israel, renounced terrorism, and agreed to talks. But his credibility was badly damaged in the Gulf War of 1990 when he supported Saddam Hussein of Iraq against America and a coalition of Arab nations, who consequently ceased funding his cause.

The Oslo Accord and beyond

There was hope and then desolation with the 1993 Oslo Accord agreed by both Israel and the Palestinians, which was intended to pave the way for the establishment of a Palestinian state. Extremists on both sides launched campaigns of violence. They included the first suicide car bombing by a Palestinian militant, in 1994, and the assassination of Israeli premier Yitzak Rabin by a radical Jew in 1995. The Palestinian Authority came into being, to govern the West Bank and Gaza. But Israel quickly became disillusioned with the antics of the Islamic hard-liners and Arafat's seeming inability to bring them under control. Palestinians meanwhile witnessed encroachments by Israeli settlers on land they had believed would be theirs under the agreement.

There was a further peace agreement held at Camp David and presided over by U.S. President Bill Clinton in 2000. Israel offered to return tracts of land occupied since 1967 and also offered Palestinian sovereignty over the Dome of the Rock (the site of the revered Jewish temple—*see pages 50–51*). However, Arafat believed Israel would still be in occupation of land rightfully belonging to the Palestinians. Furious Israelis marched on the Dome of the Rock, causing another Intifada, and ending any notions of Palestinian authority in Jerusalem for the immediate future.

The story since then has been of Palestinian suicide bombings followed by Israeli reprisals. Israel maintains that Palestinians have no serious interest in the peaceful co-existence, as witnessed by the constant harassment of Israel. In response Palestinians maintain that Israel should return the land occupied by force in 1967 without seeking further concessions on those borders.

The history is so complex, the distrust so tangible, the hatred so intense, and the wounds so deep that the prospects for peace at the start of the 21st century seem as remote as they have ever been.

Left: Young Arab boys in 1970 stand with rifle and fixed bayonet during war exercises at a guerilla training camp on the outskirts of Amman, capital of Jordan. The camp was sited close to a refugee center housing over 65,000 Palestinians who had fled from the West Bank in the aftermath of the Six-Day War. Only days after this photograph was taken, Jordanian military authorities took severe action against the Palestinians and eventually drove them out, to regroup in Lebanon.

Conclusion

In recent decades archaeological discoveries have frequently caused experts to question the historical authenticity of much of the Bible. Many scholars regard the entire Old Testament as essentially legend rather than fact, and claim events in *Genesis*, *Exodus*, *Samuel*, *Kings*, and *Chronicles* are simply incompatible with present archaeological understanding. Certainly, few archaeologists see any sign of a Hebrew sojourn in Egypt or evidence of mass destruction in the cities of the Promised Land during the Israelite "conquest."

They may, of course, be right. The difficulty with the argument is that it assumes almost everything in the Bible is unreliable and that scholarly interpretations of archaeological data and non-Biblical sources are essentially sound. Yet archaeology is far from an exact science. How is it really possible to say *anything* meaningful about the past based on mere fragments obtained in the present?

There is also an increasing body of opinion that suggests our understanding of Bronze and Iron Age chronology in the Near East is perhaps questionable and at worst seriously flawed. If we cannot reliably fix dates to known events then much of the evidence we interpret becomes unreliable too.

Chronology

BC

(BC dates are approximate)

3300 Rise of Sumerian city states.

2360–2180 Akkadian Empire, created by Sargon, flourishes.

1900 Suggested date for earthquake that destroyed Sodom and Gomorrah.

1800 Abraham arrives in Canaan.

1760 Era of King Hammurabi, the law giver, begins in Babylon.

1700 Two hundred years of Hyksos rule begins in northern Egypt.

1300 Moses leads Exodus of Jews out of Egypt toward Promised Land.

1200 Philistines arrive on coastal plain of Canaan.

1115 Tiglath-pileser I comes to power in Assyria.

1020 Saul named first king of Israel.

1000–961 Era of King David.

961–922 Era of King Solomon.

922 Divided monarchy establishes Israel and Judah.

835 Victory of King Hazael of Syria over kingdom of Israel.

814 Carthage founded by Phoenicians on North African coast.

776 First Olympic Games.

753 Rome founded.

721 Assyrians capture Samaria and end the kingdom of Israel.

597 Babylonians capture Jerusalem and end kingdom of Judah.

587 Babylonians destroy the Temple.

538 Jews return to Jerusalem.

515 Second Temple consecrated.

450 Perikles orders the building of the Parthenon.

431–404 Peloponnesian War leads to the defeat of Athens.

332 Alexander the Great sweeps through Palestine.

276 Seleukids and Ptolemies battle for control of Syria and Phoenicia.

167 Maccabean rebellion begins.

134 John Hyrcanus II becomes High Priest.

64 Collapse of Seleukid Empire.

63 Jerusalem falls to the Romans and the Hasmonean dynasty ends.

But this is an overly pessimistic view. The fact is that biblical archaeology over the last 150 years has increased the pool of knowledge exponentially to the point where we have an excellent idea of how ancient societies lived—their laws, conflicts, and lifestyles. Archaeology cannot prove the Bible right or wrong but it can give extraordinary insights into the cultural past that has shaped today's world.

In the 1970s, a new range of multi-disciplinary techniques involving aspects of geology, botany, biochemistry, and zoology were adapted for archaeologists—vastly increasing the quality and nature of data obtained. Scientists began to collate data and look at the wider influences of cultures rather than simply focus on single sites.

Use of new technologies is now accelerating this trend. A unified method of recording computer data will be a major step forward, and improved aerial photography, geophysical surveying (such as magnetometry, electrical resistivity, and ground radar) and radiocarbon dating will further extend the archaeologist's armory. Advances in marine archaeology should be especially rewarding, as is already evident from work at Alexandria and submerged villages in the Black Sea.

All this may be seen as a conflict between faith and fact, yet, as we have seen, there are indeed many points on which archaeology and religion agree. It is entirely possible to accept that there may be historical discrepancies in Biblical texts without viewing such discrepancies as weakening one's faith.

27 BC–AD 14 Octavian reigns as Caesar Augustus.

26 BC Pontius Pilate becomes governor of Judaea.

c7 BC–AD 29 Life of Jesus.

AD

AD 14–37 Reign of Tiberias.

34 Conversion of Saul on the road to Damascus.

37–41 Reign of Caligula.

41–54 Reign of Claudius.

54–68 Reign of Nero.

60 Possible date for martyrdom of St. Peter.

64 Fire of Rome.

66–73 First Jewish Revolt against Roman rule. Destruction of the Second Temple.

132–135 Second Jewish Revolt, followed by Jewish diaspora.

312 Constantine experiences Christian revelation and goes on to install Christianity throughout Roman Empire.

527 Byzantine Empire founded under Justinian in Constantinople.

632 Death of Mohammed.

692 Dome of the Rock completed in Jerusalem.

1095 Pope Urban II calls for a crusade to recapture the Holy Land from Muslims.

1099 Jerusalem taken by crusaders.

1146 Call for the Second Crusade.

1169 Saladin comes to power.

1187 Saladin captures Jerusalem.

1401 Palestine invaded by Tamerlane.

1626 Completion of St. Peter's Basilica in Rome.

1897 Congress of Basel organized by Theodor Herzl.

1918 Palestine under British control.

1922 Opening of Tutankhamun's tomb by Howard Carter.

1936 Arab Revolt in Palestine.

1947 Discovery of Dead Sea Scrolls.

1948 Israel declared an independent state.

1967 Six-Day War ends with Israel as victor. West Bank, Sinai, and Golan Heights occupied.

Glossary

Ark of the Covenant: Ornate wooden chest said to contain tablets bearing the Ten Commandments, a symbol of the divine guidance of the Jews, which went missing about five centuries before Jesus' birth.

Astarte: Mesopotamian mother goddess, also known as Ishtar, identified with the planet Venus.

'Ayn: Hebrew/Aramaic for a spring of water.

Ayyubids: Dynasty begun by Saladin in Egypt (AD 1137–93).

Baal: Phoenician god of rain and fertility who became chief cult in Canaan; also Hebrew for "lord."

Bayt, Bet: Hebrew/Aramaic for a house.

Be'er: Hebrew/Aramaic for a well.

Biq'at: Hebrew/Aramaic for a plain, valley.

Byzantine Empire: Eastern portion of Roman Empire, which survived its western counterpart by many centuries. It was Christian rather than pagan, and over time became characterized by Greek culture rather than Latin.

Canaan: Land roughly equating with today's Israel and Syria, named for a son of Ham.

Colonnade: Series of columns usually supporting a roof or arches.

Diaspora: Dispersal of Jewish population at the time of the Exile and afterward.

Essenes: Pious sect which retired to the Dead Sea area to await the coming of the Messiah. Its members may have been the authors of the Dead Sea Scrolls.

Exodus: The leaving of Egypt by the Israelites under Moses.

Fertile Crescent: The region that supports agriculture and which stretches in a crescent shape from the eastern Mediterranean coast across to the Persian Gulf, now incorporating Israel, Lebanon, Syria, and Iraq.

Gebel, Jabal, Jebel: Hebrew/Aramaic for mountain(s).

Haganah: Jewish underground militia, forerunner of the Israeli army.

Hammat: Ancient site, ruin.

Hashemite: A descendent of the Prophet Mohammed; monarchy of modern Jordan.

Hellenization: Exposure to Greek culture after Alexander the Great.

Holy Grail: Chalice used by Christ at the Last Supper, widely believed to possess supernatural powers.

Intifada: Term for Palestinian uprising in Gaza in 1987, now used for all mass movements against oppression; literally "shaking off."

Kafr, Kefar: Hebrew/Aramaic for a village.

Khirb-at: Hebrew/Aramaic for an ancient site or a ruin.

King's Way, Highway: Ancient trading route between Egypt and Mesopotamia that crosses Sinai before turning north through modern Jordan to Damascus, east of Dead Sea.

Madaba map: A mosaic discovered in Syria bearing the oldest map of the Holy Land.

Mamluks: Army of slave soldiers first formed in Egypt by Saladin, which later constituted ruling Muslim dynasties. Massacred in 1811.

Mazzebah: Standing stone.

Me'arot: Hebrew/Aramaic for a cave.

Mesopotamia: Literally translated it means "the land between the rivers," and refers to territory bordered by the Euphrates and the Tigris, the home of the Sumerian, Babylonian, and Assyrian civilizations.

Mohammed: (c.570–632) Founder of Islam.

Mount Carmel: Part of a mountain range near Mediterranean port of Haifa, where the prophet Elijah challenged the prophets of Baal to a contest. (*1 Kings 18:19-46*)

Murex: Carnivorous marine snail, from which Phoenicians made purple dye.

Nahal: Wadi (dried-up river bed).

Nahr: River, stream, wadi.

Nestorian: Branch of Christianity that believes Christ had two natures, one human, one divine.

Ostraca, ostraka: Pottery fragments used for inscribing information; used by ancient Greeks to record names in a casting a ballot or vote (*ostrakon*, singular).

Palestine: Historic area of Middle East along eastern Mediterranean coast.

Pantheon: Collection of deities.

Passover: Jewish holy thanksgiving for God sparing the first-born males of Hebrew households in ancient Egypt before the Exodus.

Patriarchs: Literally translated to "head of family," it is used in the Old Testament to describe those considered the fathers of monotheism.

Pax Romana: Period of stability in Roman Empire beginning after 31 BC.

Pentateuch: The first five books of the Old Testament; from Greek *penta* (five) *teuchos* (books).

Pentecost: Fiftieth day after Passover.

Ptolemaic Dynasty: Ruling dynasty founded by former general Ptolemy I Soter (c.366–283 BC) in Egypt following the death of Alexander the Great.

Qal'at: Hebrew/Aramaic for a fort.

Qasr: Hebrew/Aramaic for a castle, fort.

Qiryat: Hebrew/Aramaic for a settlement.

Rambam: Short name for Moses Mamonides (1138–1204), a revered Jewish philosopher and teacher who became physician to Saladin.

Seleucid: Greek dynasty founded by Alexander the Great's general Seleucus (c.358–281 BC), which controlled then lost an Asian empire.

Sha'ar: Hebrew/Aramaic for a gate.

Stele: Carved or inscribed upright rectangular stone, used as a gravestone or a marker.

Talmud: Compilation of rabbinic traditions and a detailed discussion about Jewish life and law.

Tartars: Turkic-speaking people from Russia.

Tel, Tall: Hill or mound created by centuries of over-building.

Torah: (Usually) a parchment scroll containing the whole body of Jewish religious literature, including Pentateuch, Scripture, Talmud, etc.

Via Maris: Roman name for the ancient road along the Palestinian coast that links Egypt with Mesopotamia via Damascus.

YHWH or Yahweh: Mysterious initials and word used by Hebrews to describe God, whose real name could not be revealed by Hebrews.

Index